PRAISE FOR

'FXT COM...

"Mind expanding, beautifully written.
..., a book that gets to the core of complex adaptive systems,
revealing new ways to 'see' the world and to lead".

John Seely Brown, Chief Scientist, Xerox PARC

"They are a pair of very heavy hitters indeed, and this well-
written and carefully constructed book reflects their depth of
knowledge and intellectual rigour.

It's a challenging and rewarding read for anyone seriously
interested in dealing effectively in a rapidly changing world."

Alex Benady, Amazon

"Michael Lissack and Johan Roos give us the wise advice that
we must find our own way of doing things, making the complex simple. Read this book carefully and you will learn how
to navigate through complexity towards common sense."

Rafael Suso, Managing Director,
Federation for Enterprise Knowledge Development – E·K·D

A "must read" for managers, which understands that we live in a
changing world.

Jan Nilsson, Chairman, SwitchCore, Sweden

SIMPLY—COMPLEX.COM INC.

E-MANAGER'S WELCOMING TOOLKIT

Please read before reporting to work

Position: E-Manager

Qualifications: Mastering of terabytes of information, understanding of hundreds of targeted customer demographic clusters, fluency in the latest protocols for asp/crm transmissions in a fail-safe remote site network environment, photographic recall of every Dilbert cartoon, and an unwillingness to express the frustrations and stresses associated with all the above.

Job requirements: Managing an e-team in an e-way with minimum e-ffort and maximum e-ffect.

Rewards: A chance to stay e-mployed in the e-conomy.

Risks: E-verywhere.

THE NEXT COMMON SENSE

THE e-MANAGER'S GUIDE TO MASTERING COMPLEXITY

MICHAEL LISSACK AND
JOHAN ROOS

NICHOLAS BREALEY
PUBLISHING

LONDON

This paperback edition first published by
Nicholas Brealey Publishing in 2000

36 John Street
London
WC1N 2AT, UK
Tel: +44 (0)20 7430 0224
Fax: +44 (0)20 7404 8311

1163 E. Ogden Avenue, Suite 705-229
Naperville
IL 60563-8535, USA
Tel: (888) BREALEY
Fax: (630) 428 3442

http://www.nbrealey-books.com

First published in hardback by
Nicholas Brealey Publishing in 1999

ISBN 1-85788-235-0

British Library Cataloguing in Publication Data
A catalogue record for this book is available from the
British Library.

Printed in Finland by WS Bookwell.

⋮ CONTENTS

Foreword by Thomas Petzinger, Jr   ix

Evolution: Managers → E-Managers   xiii

1 MASTERING COMPLEXITY THROUGH COHERENCE   **1**

The arrows, not the boxes   2

Making sense with coherence   5

Complexity science is about simplicity   10

Guiding coherent action   14

Practicing the next common sense   16

2 USE SIMPLE GUIDING PRINCIPLES   **24**

Six bad rules   26

Guiding principles that work   28

Why simple rules?   29

Great words – what do they mean?   31

Simple rules lead to meaning only through interaction   35

Interaction happens in context   37

Guidelines for using simple guiding principles   38

3 RESPECT MENTAL MODELS: YOURS AND OTHERS'   **40**

Simple rules guide mental models   43

Mental models are toolsets   45

Actions depend on interpretations   47

Exploring the context and setting the stage   50

Detecting creativity and obstructionism in a mental model   55

Creative mental modeling   58

Guidelines for respecting mental models   61

4 USE LANDSCAPE IMAGES   **64**
Why landscapes?   67
Gaps and bridges   70
Using landscape images   74
Landscape images can create coherence   77
Guidelines for using landscape images   81

5 COMBINE AND RECOMBINE   **84**
Building blocks are integral to how we think   86
Context is the most important building block   90
Seeing is the first step   94
Functionality is an important component   97
Coherence has building blocks too   99
Guidelines for combining and recombining   101

**6 RECOGNIZE YOUR MULTIPLE ROLES,
DON'T HIDE FROM THEM**   **104**
Success through multiplicity   108
Holon not synthesis   110
Failure in artificial unity   114
Why Richard Branson doesn't knit, or using multiple
roles as building blocks   116
Separate out the foreground   118
Guidelines for recognizing your multiple roles   120

7 CREATE CANYONS, NOT CANALS   **122**
Following the least action principle   124
Create canyons   128
Depth comes from values   130
Width provides opportunity   133
Dams are obstacles (not, as your CFO would tell you,
a revenue source)   136
Side canals only confuse   138
Guidelines for creating canyons   138

8 TELL STORIES   **142**
   Sense making   145
   We learn by doing   146
   Stories are verbal simulations   147
   Stories reinforce images   149
   Not icons, not symbols, not commands: stories   151
   Guidelines for telling stories   153

9 SEND OUT SCOUTING PARTIES   **156**
   Where to go – Part 1: Within the canyon   158
   Where to go – Part 2: And beyond   160 ⚯
   What to look for   163
   Bring back stories   165
   Discuss them   166
   Guidelines for sending out scouting parties   167

10 POST AND ATTEND TO ROAD SIGNS   **170**
   Taking and giving credit   173
   Managing signs   175
   Conflated purposes and meanings   177
   Dealing with the issues   179
   Resolving the tension? No. Striking a balance? Yes.   181
   Guidelines for posting road signs   183

11 USE ALIGNED WORDS TO FUEL COHERENCE   **186**
   The right words at the right time   190
   Words shape thinking and actions   192
   Coherence can be fueled by aligned words   196
   Which words to pick   199
   Guidelines for aligning words   201

12 THE FIVE STEPS   **204**
   Step 1: Identify yourself and your goals   208
   Step 2: Use the right language   213

Step 3: Create the right context   216
Step 4: Turn people loose and then get out of the way   223
Step 5: Use communication that works   226
Applying coherence in an e-world   227

Index   237

FOREWORD

Take a good look around the next time you're in the bookstore. (Maybe you're standing in one right now.) Thousands of cookbooks. A wall of travel guides. Shelf after shelf on addiction and recovery. You're surrounded by titles promising to simplify the complex, whether in cooking, carousing, or coping with the stress of modern life. Step right up for easy answers.

Now, put all these books together and quadruple them. That's how many business books you may see. And like all those other instruction manuals and how-to guides, the business books promise to solve your most complex problems with easy, step-by-step solutions.

Michael Lissack and Johan Roos stand apart with *The Next Common Sense*. They make no attempt to solve your particular problem; how could they, when they haven't met you? They offer no recipes for success in your industry; why would they dare, when you know your industry a hundred times better than they ever could?

Not much of a business book, you say? If you're looking for pat solutions and easy answers, I strongly urge you to turn elsewhere – perhaps to the recovery section, for aid in curing your addiction to insipid business books. Instead, *The Next Common Sense* is about the universal rather than the particular. It is about being human as much as about being in business. It reveals how nature organizes itself while exposing the conceit of our attempting to organize ourselves much differently. It discusses the leading of one's self as much as the leading of others.

As managers increasingly recognize, the command-and-control model of organization is untenable in this era of dizzying change and ghastly complexity. Yet even as we demand more flexibility and creativity of our organizations, the need has never been greater for unity, identity, and direction – "coherence," as these authors call it. How shall the leaders and members of organizations cohere in such times as these? Perhaps through "the next common sense," a concept, as the authors explain it, that calls on us to use fresh eyes and simple tools to interpret and shape a complex world.

As the greatest scientists have acknowledged, what we see depends where and how we look. Said the physicist Walter Heisenberg: "What we observe is not nature itself, but nature exposed to our methods of questioning." Said Einstein: "Our theories determine what we measure." Metaphors and mental models are the tools we use to shape our realities. As the science historian Thomas Kuhn said, "You don't see something until you have the right metaphor to let you perceive it."

This is where *The Next Common Sense* most clearly stands out: as an exploration of the power of metaphor in organization life, indeed as the foundation for the next common sense itself.

Lissack and Roos are deeply taken with landscapes as metaphors in organizations and economic life; a strange idea, you might think, until you consider that humans succeeded as a species through their skill at navigating the vicissitudes of savannas, foothills, and wetlands. Deeply held values, they suggest, can be thought of as canyons, which permit an infinite variety of action within an unbreakable boundary. In another valuable landscape metaphor, the authors present the notion of backgrounds and foregrounds as venues within which to organize our multiple roles as humans, an original and insightful concept.

Lissack and Roos also counsel us to think about thinking in terms of a child's building blocks; a simplistic notion, you might say, until you realize that the most fundamental cognitive skill in humans – perhaps the only one we bring into the world – is the ability to perceive contrasts and to assemble them into simple structures. Our judgment and intelligence grow in accordance with our skill at recognizing patterns from among the myriad structures we've observed and assembled. If you are dismissive of the simplicity of the building block analogy, bear in mind the words of the mathematician and historian Jacob Bronowsky, who once commented that "every act of imagination is the discovery of likenesses between two things which were thought unlike." One makes such discoveries only by picking things up and seeing how they fit together.

I've spent more than 20 years, the better part of my life, as a business journalist. I make my living telling stories. Thus I especially enjoyed the authors' extended treatment of storytelling as a metaphorical tool. Stories, like landscapes and building blocks, are ways of looking at the world that help define us as human. Human evolution, after all, had run its course long before we had web pages, moveable type, and even cuneiform writing as media of communications, leaving us with stories for making sense of the world and helping others do the same. (In casting modern-day eyes toward this ancient practice, the authors ingeniously discuss stories as verbal simulations. "Long before we had computers to do fancy simulation exercises on," they note, "we had our brains.") The discussion of storytelling provides a welcome antidote to the Powerpoint cult of business, in which issues, ideas, and experiences are reduced to bullet points on an overhead slide. Today's most powerful breakthroughs in performance and coherence come from using technology not to tick off items on a checklist but to enrich our storytelling and to spread it more widely.

Apropos of which, this book adopts storytelling not just as a subject but as a method. The text is filled with anecdotes and accounts of effective managers putting to use the very skills that Lissack and Roos call on the rest of us to develop. We visit Southwest Airlines, IKEA, Tripod, and other exemplars of success. Though there is much discussion of chaos and complexity theory, there is no showy science or gratuitous mathematics. Though a work of philosophy by a pair of professional scholars, there's not a speck of academic pretension.

No, you won't find recipes, roadmaps, or 12 steps to recovery here. But as you read this book you may find yourself asking why you ever thought other authors could provide such all-purpose solutions to the unique vexations of your own organization life. You can find those answers only for yourself, only by searching through your own senses – only through your common sense. And as others join you in the search, together you may find yourselves practicing "the next common sense."

Thomas Petzinger, Jr.
Weekly business columnist and the author of three books,
including The New Pioneers: the Men and Women Who Are
Transforming the Workplace and Marketplace

EVOLUTION:
MANAGERS → E-MANAGERS

Well, maybe. The internet changes e-verything. At least that is what the media tell you. Magazines like *Fast Company*, *Wired*, *Business 2.0*, *The Industry Standard*, *Upside*, and *E-Company* have created a whole new genre out of the saga of getting ahead faster, more interconnectedly, and in an "e" or an "m" way. The "new economy" holds a special place for you. You are an e-manager. Or you want to be. Or your boss says you have to be. Or your friends are. Or your spouse is.

So what's different about being an e-manager, rather than a "manager?"

Nada. We repeat. Zilch. Nothing. Nil. *Ingenting* (Swedish—Johan's native tongue—for "nothing").

The internet has altered the environment in which the manager's job is done, but not the job itself. The real change happened nearly 20 years ago. Once the fax machine and the mobile telephone sped up our ability to connect and be connected, the old linear sense of time was destroyed. We have lived in an interconnected world for 20 years. It is the interconnections that changed the tasks of management and of what it means to be a manager—all interconnections, not just net ones.

In an interconnected world, actions do not just have immediate consequences. What the economists call second- (and even third-) order effects take on new prominence. The effects of one action lead to actions by others that in turn lead to still other actions by perhaps even still others and so on. Little things can snowball into big things. A little boy survives the sinking of a boat and the world seems to believe it is in the midst of a global morality play. An arrogant executive writes emails about "burying" the competition and an entire industry faces redefinition. It is the need to anticipate and deal with such chains of actions, reactions, and sometimes escalating actions that characterizes the "new economy." Interconnections are the key puzzle here, not that mysterious letter *e*.

What matters is being a manager, a good manager, a manager with common sense. We don't mean the common sense of the industrial age, where hierarchy was king and the factory line the model. The world of getting the milk in the bottle without spillage and at minimal cost is still with us, of course. And the old common sense works fine in a world where things are what matters, not how those things relate. Filling the bottle is an "old economy" job. Getting the bottle to Betty Jo's refrigerator five minutes before she seeks a glass of milk—now that's a "new economy" job. The old job can be commoditized and automated. Linear, industrial rules—efficiency and effectiveness—apply, and so does the old common sense so decried by the new age prophets and pundits alike.

The new job is more complex: Where is Betty Jo's refrigerator? When might she seek a glass of milk? Is there already milk in the fridge? Is it fresh? Is it cold? What do we need to know and how can we know it?

When you take millions of Betty Jos and a whole shopping list, the complexity abounds. The vast numbers of such potential connections and interactions are enough to make one's head spin. Trying to service those people and that list over the internet seems more complicated than programming the space shuttle to land on the moon (at least there is only one moon). But, in the western world at least, most Betty Jos on most days can get their milk when they want it. Cities get fed without some master programmer directing the ebb and flow of foodstuffs. The e-business we read about and talk about is still just business: Anticipating the needs of others, finding a way of fulfilling them, and making a bit of money doing it. If New York and London can get fed, you can manage. But it takes a new common sense.

This new common sense is focused on relationships, not things—the arrows not the boxes, the phone lines not the telephones. The communication and its meaning, not the form of the letter or the CAPITALIZATION in the email. As Ericsson puts it, "It's about people, the rest is technology." Its competitor Nokia phrases it as "Connecting people." The connections, the interweavings, the multiplicity of relationships and interrelationships are the business environment of the twenty-first century. The industrial age had its common sense. The connected age has what we call it *The Next Common Sense*.

The Next Common Sense recognizes that the "e" in e-manager describes the environment, not the tasks—despite the hype to the contrary from the magazines listed above. Despite the millions of pounds and dollars spent by consulting firms to convince you that everything is different and you need to hire them to "see the light." Despite the hundreds of books saying "change is good and faster change is better." *The Next Common Sense* knows that adding an "e" (or an "m") does not change the job of management:

- ❖ To hire the people best suited for the tasks at hand and to come.
- ❖ To create an environment that allows both employees and customers to seek and achieve most of their potential.
- ❖ To continuously promote the development of new ideas.
- ❖ To leverage available resources wisely with an eye on both immediate returns and longer-term needs.
- ❖ To forge an organizational identity with which employees, customers, vendors, investors, and neighbors are proud to be associated.
- ❖ To assist the organization in earning a living.
- ❖ To be a part of the world around you—both in the immediate vicinity and the larger one.
- ❖ To act as eyes and ears for others.
- ❖ To give voice.
- ❖ To absorb stress.
- ❖ To live and help others live—productively, if not better.

To do the manager's job well requires you to develop your talent for enabling coherence around you. Notice we said enabling—not creating, not demanding, but enabling. Coherence is about acting in a manner consistent with who you are. Coherence cannot be summoned on the spot. It cannot be created overnight. But when an organization, a company, or a team has coherence, amazing things can happen.

Coherence is respectful of the full identity of the person, group, or team. Members of the group have their own identities separate and apart from their group membership. Thus, while the coherent perspective and actions of a group will overlap, for its individual members they will not be identical.

Coherence builds on itself. It results from people feeling that the actions required of them are consistent with their own sense of purpose and identity and that of the organization of which they are a part. This feeling can only occur when the values and guiding principles embodied by the corporate purposes and expressed identity align with how the person defines and embodies their sense of self. We know coherence when we have acted coherently. It is not for others to judge, others can only ask us questions about it. The coherence comes in the acting. And guiding actions, creating a context for fruitful actions—such is the manager's job.

So what does coherence mean for the e-manager? As the rest of this book will tell you, coherence is the key to finding simplicity in the complex e-world and non-e-world alike. When you act from coherence you do not need to rationalize, justify, elaborate, threaten, pontificate, or filibuster—you just act.

Are we going to tell you the 20 killer apps of the next decade? No. The 15 best ways to ASP your latest customer service offering, the 10 rules for the new economy, or the 5 requirements for successful CRM? No. This e-management book is different. No recipes for web this or mobile that. No hyperbole about network effects and the critical role of biological modeling in your mental schemas. No fancy computer simulations to explain that cooperation is "nice" but that viciousness wins in the end. Instead, we offer you a simple guiding principle—coherence. When the management behaviors stemming from coherence become "just common sense," then as an e-manager you are prepared for the many challenges of the internet age. More importantly, as a manager (e, m, or not) you will be able to treat the complex as simple, and your company's many problems as the opportunities they truly are.

To Thomas Paine, in 1776, common sense was liberty from England. To Samuel Clemens' Mark Twain, common sense was life on a Mississippi riverboat. To the e-managers of the twenty-first century, common sense is coherence and its practice.

To August and Pandora – complex systems whose individual drive for coherence inspired us as we wrote

1

MASTERING COMPLEXITY THROUGH COHERENCE

The old common sense was about dealing with the discrete elements of a **complicated** world. The next common sense is about mastering the **complex** swirl of events and situations around us through coherence. The old world was a complicated agglomeration of many discrete items. The new world is a complex one of interdependencies and interrelationships.

The complex versus complicated distinction can be explained by the roots of the words. In Latin, plic is "fold" and plex is "weave." We fold to hide facets of things and to cram more into a crowded space – this is complicated. We weave to make use of connections and to introduce mutual dependencies – this is complex.

Complicated

A flat tire on a local dairy farmer's truck may inconvenience a few customers, but it will not affect the food markets of a big city. By contrast, closing Chicago's O'Hare Airport because of bad weather causes havoc in the US transportation system for days. The local dairy may

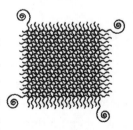

Complex

Complicated – folded or twisted together, combined intricately, combined or associated so as to make intricate or difficult. Difficult to analyze or understand.

Complex – composed of two or more parts, composite, not simple, intricate. A conceptual whole made up of complicated and related parts.

Coherence – an alignment of context, viewpoint, purpose and action that enables further purposive action.

be complicated, but the airline transport system is complex.

In a complex world, it is not enough to understand discrete events such as the dairy truck's flat tire. There are so many discrete items, events and situations that it is foolish to pursue their mastery as the way to "make sense" out of what occurs. Knowing that United Airlines owns 800 airplanes will not tell you where each of them flies and why; neither would a knowledge of the route structure or the cargo demands or passenger loads or any other discrete piece of information.

If you are to master the complex challenges offered by today's business world, your actions need to be coherent. This book offers 10 guiding principles to provide you with the sense of **coherence** you need, as well as five practical steps for putting the principles into action.

Our purpose in writing this book is to help you to be like Alexander the Great. When confronted with the legendary knot of tangled rope tied by King Gordius, Alexander knew what to do. Faced with the traditional challenge, he accepted without hesitation: the complexity of the knot did not phase him. He drew his sword and cut the Gordian knot with a single, dramatic stroke, thereby ensuring that he would rule all of Asia. Many before Alexander had tried and failed, thinking that the knot was complicated and needed to be untied. Only Alexander saw that a simple action would move through the complexity to a higher plane. Untying your own Gordian knots requires nothing more than common sense – the next common sense.

The arrows, not the boxes

Managers go to business school and learn "global" management concepts where the belief is that a small set of "correct ways" can lead a company along a golden road to success. It certainly worked that way for the leading companies of the 1960s and 1970s, up until the merger boom of the 1980s. But the old style of management won't work for the new companies of tomorrow.

Today's management is all about **inter-actions** rather than **entities**, about the effects of relationships between people inside and outside the organization rather than about controlling entities like distinct groups of employees, customers, suppliers. Others may refer to factories, industries, companies, work units, SBUs, or teams. We will refer to all of these "things" as entities.

Interaction – an action, process or influence that occurs among two or more entities.

Entity – a thing, group, team, organization or environment that we treat as a real being, whether in thought or in fact.

Entities, the things, dominated the world most of us knew before the 1990s. Interrelationships, communications and dependencies among such entities dominate the world of today. The focus of management has shifted from things to processes; from entities to interactions.

Contrast the world of the automaker of the early 1980s with the universe of America OnLine (AOL) of today. Automakers operated supply chains that culminated in assembly plants that shipped to one-brand distributors and thence to the general public. Each part of the chain could be severed and operated independently. Indeed, much of the "management revolution" that shook the auto industry in the 1980s and 1990s took the form of outsourcing and reengineering many of the individual pieces of the value chain. Lopez at GM outsourced and outcompeted each supplier along the chain. Saturn was created to reengineer the factory and to change the public's perception of the "crooked" dealer.

Let's assume you are a mid-level manager in an automaker in the mid-1980s. What guiding principles would you use to be successful? Find the lowest cost. Simplify the supply chain. Externalize cost, i.e. outsource. Demand increased productivity from staff. Streamline work practices. Manage delivery times of both product (deliver cars to dealers) and required supplies (make the suppliers hold inventory) so as to maximize quarterly financial performance with an eye on return on assets. Manipulate sales statistics to meet the targets established in the company incentive scheme. You are dealing with entities – the company, the team, the suppliers – and you have rules and regulations about how those entities conduct themselves (e.g. the workday begins at 9 a.m.).

By contrast, Internet service provider AOL operates a complex web of network services, content provision, and memberships that depends not on entities, but on myriad interactions. Members interact with each other and demand content, the provision of which requires network services, and each generates either added demand or frustration when dialing into the network by telephone if a busy signal is reached instead of a connection. Content can be found almost anywhere on the Internet. Network services can be found independently. But the entire concept of membership is dependent on interactions. While entities can be managed in the sense of being controlled, interactions can only, at best, be guided in the sense of shaped and nurtured.

As a mid-level manager of AOL, your mission, under the banner of "Clarity, Communication, and Community," is to increase membership "time." What guiding principles would contribute to your success? Finding the lowest cost may risk making use of less dependable network services, which could lead to member dissatisfaction and exiting. Simplifying the supply chain is great in terms of being timely – get the news in real time – but risky in terms of deliverables – simple content is not targeted content. Externalizing costs may also be a bet on less dependable suppliers of either content or network services or both. Demanding increased productivity from creative staff is an invitation to them to leave, as is a demand that they "streamline" their work practices. Creative types do not usually understand when the boss says "your desk is a mess." AOL tried to manipulate delivery times and sales statistics of product and supplies and Wall Street rebelled. That option is best considered foreclosed. Return on assets is rather nebulous in a company with an infinite price/earnings (P/E) ratio. So much for traditional "best practices."

Return for a moment to this manager's goals – the more membership time sold, the better off both the manager and the company as a whole. How is membership time sold? It isn't. Membership time is consumed. So the manager must get out of the mindset of "sales" with its notions of product and customers and into the imagined mental models of the members, with notions of interesting, fun, informative and communicative. The manager is not a sales manager *per se*, but instead an encourager of increased consumption. But what should be encouraged?

Here is where the switch in mindset or **mental model** matters most. The manager must imagine that he or she is the member. From that perspective, what should be encouraged is what is already appealing. New ideas are great as trials but if there is no demand, away they go. No incentive pricing, no package deals and no coer-

Mental model – an image inside one's head used to help make sense out of any situation.

cive bundling. If the manager can make the member's access easier, the member is likely to increase usage. So simplify the demand chain, not the supply chain. The very use of the word member is important. Members are part of a community, not merely customers to be sold to.

The notion of community is integral to the massive growth of AOL. From the perspective of community, content offerings are determined by community wants and desires, not by corporate demands; network services are provided at a level and a dependability that keep the community happy, not by cost controls; and communication is among the members, not one-way broadcasts from advertisers to a passive audience. The community perspective informs nearly every aspect of the tasks that lead to increased "sales." Only by forming this perspective on the job can the manager be assured of a reasonable chance of success. The "practices" stem from the perspective, not from the accumulated wisdom of "business greats." Those people are not the members, or at least not a large number of members, and it is the members that matter. That is just common sense if your job is to sell membership time.

Making sense with coherence

Finding coherence, enabling coherence, and communicating coherence are the critical tasks of management in the era of the next common sense. We call this **mastering complexity through coherence**. Such mastery is different from merely acting, no matter how powerfully. Power is not mastery. Action alone is not enough. In our interwoven world, something additional is needed: we have to have an understanding at a level separate from the actions. Such an understanding will encompass both purpose and identity.

When purpose and identity are aligned, they create a **context** from which actions can be understood as well as performed. That

Context – that which surrounds, and gives meaning to, a situation or event.

alignment evokes a point of view that we will call the "coherent point of view." Coherence is necessary if actions are to make sense. Those actions then promote further development of the coherent point of view. It is this positive spiral of coherence – a set of interactions that lead to further interactions – that makes possible the where and why of how United flies, the magic of how the city gets fed, and the increasing returns that evidence why just-in-time delivery has meant big revenues for carriers such as Federal Express.

By **purpose** we mean the reason for being or doing: Why am I doing what I am doing? By **identity** we mean an evolving, moving intersection of the inner and outer forces that make each of us who we are, converging in the answer to the question: Who am I? Both purpose and identity are rooted in a set of basic human values ("right versus wrong," "good versus bad") and filtered through a set of guiding principles ("to be honest"). These filters are not grand missions ("to be the leading biotech company in the world") or high ideals ("the bottom line") or instructions ("render unto Caesar"). Instead, they are simple checks and balances that what is expressed as purpose or identity matches the values from which they are drawn.

What coherence can do is enable actions to be grounded in certainty of purpose, identity, context, and further actions. Incoherence and decoherence reveal themselves by uncertainty, shame, or actions which defy sense making. Coherence is only a part of culture – in society or in an organization. Cultures provide context for being coherent or not. An organizational culture which thrives on inducing shame is incoherent. By contrast, an organization whose actions make sense to its members and stakeholders must have found a coherent viewpoint from which to guide such actions. It has coherence. In this book we will be providing examples of such coherence and of its absence.

There are many ways to see coherence:

❖ Coherence as a potent binding force.
❖ Coherence as what makes a company more than the sum of its parts.

❖ Coherence as glue.
❖ Coherence as the directional arrow on a compass.
❖ Coherence as allowing flexibility, sharing, communication, and linkages.
❖ Coherence as a process of change.

While the importance of coherence has not yet become conventional wisdom in managerial contexts, its critical role is well recognized in other fields. In psychology, for example, professional practice is based on the recognition that a unified perspective is needed to make full sense of the world as each of us perceives it. That unified perspective is described by psychologists as "coherence" and those who possess it are "coherent." A sufficient lack of psychological coherence renders one eligible for institutionalized care.

From a biological perspective, entities are distinguished from one another by boundaries, e.g. a cell wall or skin. What is within the boundary is said to "cohere." If an outside observer, or a self-reflective observer in the case of humans, can ascribe purpose to the location of the boundary, the entity is described as "coherent." So, for example, cancers that serve no purpose for their host entity are incoherent with their host, but certain parasites that have a symbiotic relation to their host are considered to be part and parcel of the coherent entity.

Physics lends its own credence to the concept by positing coherence as the opposite force to entropy. If the basic tendency of all systems is to dissipate in the absence of new energy inputs, it requires energy to hold the system together. When the system has an attractive force – gravity for the solar system, psychological coherence for humans – there is less energy required to hold it together than when such forces are absent.

Biology and physics are combined in the study of ecosystems. Here, it is held that coherent organizations (meaning groups of plants or animals that occupy a given space) are nature's most effective means of capturing the added energy of the sun and not allowing it to be merely dissipated away, as the second law of thermodynamics would otherwise suggest. Psychology rejoins the arena when we consider the field of organizational ecology, which holds that human endeavors and groupings can be studied as a series of ecosystems. Coherence is the glue that holds the organized entities (be it an ant colony or a city) together in their ecosystems and renders them more ecologically fit for survival to the next generation. From the organizational ecosystem perspective, coherence is a vital contributor to sustainability.

And, to return to the study of business, in *The Centerless Corporation* Pasternak and Viscio write:

> *Coherence is what holds the firm together. It is the glue that binds the various pieces enabling them to act as one. It includes a broad range of processes. It begins with a shared vision and shared set of values, and expands to include numerous linkages across the company. Firms are tied together with communications, management processes like planning, human resource management, and knowledge management. Coherence also includes the more structured information technology of the firm, the hardwiring of the business through which the various parts communicate.*

When making sense revolves around a point of view held in common by those who need to act, coordinated action can occur without the need for coercive control. The group becomes more effective because it no longer requires significant energy to be expended on such coercion or the threat of it. The freed-up energy can be devoted to useful tasks. At the firm level, the process is similar as it applies not only individual by individual, but also group by group, business unit by business unit.

Coherence is the antidote to uncertainty. In organizations, uncertainty is evidenced by an unwillingness to act. Once the will exists, so too does the certainty. A coherent perspective increases the willingness and reduces the periods of uncertainty.

And coherence is tolerant of that kind of ambiguity described by the scientist and writer Arthur Koestler as "the sudden interlocking of two previously unrelated skills or matrices of thought." Just as the creative fusion of ideas can occur by holding seemingly antithetical ideas in the mind simultaneously, so creative collaboration between people can occur by an effort to retain conflicting cultural and disciplinary viewpoints in the mind without discarding one or allowing either to dominate.

Today's world of confusion, uncertainty, and ambiguity is a large-scale manifestation of too many emergent events, situations, and behaviors happening all at once. The reductive practices of examining individual parts, searching for individual causes, and sorting things out, fail to eliminate much of the uncertainty. In that failure lies the explanation for many if not all of the incoherent actions we each observe (be that rigging the stock market, blocking an ambulance's way, or having an extramarital affair). Uncertainty is accompanied by a perception of diminished control or power – few of us like that perception, in fact it is the source of the emotion we call shame. Shame leads to even greater search for certainty, control, and a firm place to stand (perhaps even explaining why Bill Clinton kept on "seeing" Monica Lewinsky). The vicious cycle of uncertainty, shame, and incoherent actions may seem unbreakable. But complexity science suggests a way out.

Mastering complexity means not letting complexity get the better of you. It means having a coherent viewpoint to guide action *in spite of* the confusion, uncertainty, and ambiguity that are introduced by the swirl of events and interactions going on around you. The mastery we are alluding to is that of the craftsman, not that of the M in MBA. The ability to act coherently in the face of complexity, and to do so on an ongoing basis, is the hallmark of a true master. That ability can only be gained through life experiences, as with the craftsmen of old, and not from months of lectures and a framed diploma.

The social commentator Walter Lippman noted that "mastery means the substitution of conscious intention for unconscious striving." The master is one who carries out purposeful acts. We note that coherence is an alignment of context, viewpoint, purpose, and action that enables further purposive action. Coherence is the key to mastering complexity because it is the enabling force that allows conscious intention to replace inertia, overload, and unconscious flailing about. It is all too easy to let complexity get the better of you. Coherence offers you the alternative of mastery – but the choice is yours.

Complexity science is about simplicity

In a book about mastering **complexity**, it would be only natural to assert that what scientists refer to as "complexity theory" holds the answer to simplifying the vast muddle of our world. We only wish we could do so. At best such an assertion would be misleading and, at worst, might give rise to especially poor business practices with nice labels.

Complexity – a term used to refer to a collection of scientific disciplines, all of which are concerned with finding patterns among collections of behaviors or phenomena.

Complexity theory is a new field, although not yet a distinct one. It involves scientists from such disciplines as biology, mathematics, physics, cognition, computation, philosophy, medicine, psychology, and even human organizations. The field looks at patterns across a multitude of scales in an effort to detect either "laws" of pattern generation or "rules" that explain the patterns observed. Much of the research is heavily mathematical and many of the "conclusions" apply only to very narrowly restricted domains.

Computers have opened up a whole new world of possible observations. Because of the rapidity with which they can do well-defined calculations and simulations, computers have made it possible to explore the consequences of interactions of relatively simple things in a way never before possible. In a variety of different disciplines, this new capability for observations makes possible significant insights into phenomena long believed to be too complex for serious analysis.

Complexity science takes its roots from the concept of emergence – the idea that wholes can be greater than merely the sum of their parts and that by changing scales it is possible to observe "new, emergent" properties of the whole. These "new" properties are the product of the interactions of the parts. Thus, a person is more than just a torso, head and four limbs; a car is more than just wheels, axles, engine and chassis; and an organization is more than just a collection of people thrown together in the same room with a few desks and telephones. When the parts interact (the body parts function together, the wheels turn by action of the engine and carry the chassis along with them; or people start communicating and then acting together), something "greater" emerges.

It is this emergent behavior which complexity science studies. The parts and wholes together are referred to as systems; when they interact and adapt to changes in the environment in which they are located, such systems are referred to as "complex adaptive systems" or CAS. Most companies we know, most families we know, meet this definition of complex adaptive system. Writings abound describing the organization as a CAS and explaining why it is better to view the organization as such. However, these descriptions are not what this book is about.

Complexity science aims beyond description to discover what commonalities may lie behind emergent behavior. It is not sufficient to observe that birds often fly in flocks. That observation leaves too much room for one to assert "and the flock has a leader." Only by the further probing of the complexity scientists do we learn that the front position in the flock rotates among the birds and that the nice, symmetric V-shape of the flock is the result of a few simple interacting rules – not the orders of a leader and the followership of a flock. As with birds, so too with people.

Complexity science allows us to study underlying rules of interactions and interdependencies with the aim of explaining how it is that complex phenomena emerge from handfuls of simple guiding principles. The aims of complexity science fit well with the demands of the struggling manager – explaining complex situations with a few simple rules would be the magic bullet that many CEOs and mid-level managers cry out for. But, and it is an important but, complexity science is not yet at the point of being able to consistently deliver outputs which match its aims. The risk to managers lies in the attraction of a magic bullet which does not yet exist.

The worlds of nature and of humans function as two interrelated but separate domains. Steven Vogel highlights these differences in his *Cat's Paws and Catapults*. He points out that nature:

❖ is usually information constrained
❖ is involved in the continual making of things
❖ is not time constrained

- ❖ allows variation and selection to choose development paths
- ❖ prefers environments that are wet, structures that are flexible, and angles other than right angles
- ❖ uses highly complex composites all the time.

Humans, by contrast:

- ❖ are usually information overloaded
- ❖ make things once and have time constraints
- ❖ use intent to choose development paths
- ❖ prefer environments that are dry, structures that are stable and semi-rigid and right angles
- ❖ make as much use of homogenized, ordered, and simple materials as possible.

Vogel contends that the domains differ in kind, i.e. that they belong to different categories. To assert that scientific observations from nature are likely to find direct application in the domain of humans is unreasonable. Instead, the domains of nature and of humans operate side by side. In the mechanical realm (making things and making them work), nature can provide humans with insights and analogies, but rarely solutions. We would extend Vogel's reasoning to include the realm of management. Ant colonies, genes, bird flocks, and prairie dog towns are not human companies. Complexity science may work well in describing nature – but its role in regard to management is far more limited. You can't take concepts that are true with regard to nature and say that they are literally true with regard to organizations. Just because ants do something doesn't mean that people do the same.

Unlike those who use the science to prescribe a new theory of management, we take a different approach. **It is the method that can be applied to a different sphere, not its lessons.** We examined the mathematics of complexity science to extract a few key points about patterns in complex systems and then asked how knowledge of these points would alter what managers did day to day. By examining how application affects actions, we are using the methods of cognitive science. Our root philosophy was the notion of a system that is capable of self-examination and change – what the late Donald Schon called "reflective practice" and what practitioners of the "learning organization" refer to as double- and triple-loop learning.

This book, and the next common sense it describes, are the outcome of that examination. The observations have been tried out on managers throughout the world as a result of our teaching, research, public speaking, and consulting.

The old common sense was an understanding of cause and effect in the complicated world of discrete events. The next common sense is a description of cause and effect in a world of interweavings. Complexity science tells us that the first step in understanding interweavings is to recognize parts, wholes, foregrounds and backgrounds and, most importantly, to be aware of the stance you take in recognizing these items. This is fundamental to how scientists go about their mathematical tasks and, if complexity science is to have relevance to management, it seems that the same fundamental method should apply. Thus we will not use complexity science to label this or that as complex or as a strange attractor or as a bifurcation point. Instead, we will use its investigative methods to discover the simple guiding principles that form the basis of the next common sense.

Thermo Electron's George Hatsopoulos is a master of interweavings in the corporate world. Thermo Electron does a little of everything, from biomedical instruments such as mammography equipment and artificial hearts to power generation, radiation detection, soil recycling, and even de-inking. Hatsopoulos has grown what began as a single technology company into a multibillion-dollar empire of companies using a strategy he calls "spinouts," where he first encourages his staff to think of innovative new products and then forms companies around them. As a result, Thermo Electron retains a web of talented people and a portion of profits from the new ventures, while its employees satisfy their entrepreneurial urges and enjoy the security a large company has to offer.

Guiding coherent action

Coherence alone will not make for a successful organization. Getting the members of an organization's network to function in a coherent way requires leadership. (Or, to use the complexity science jargon, self-organization will not happen without a nudge.) What do we mean by leadership? In a complicated world, leadership can take the form of command and control over discrete elements. In a complex world, leadership is about guidance, about creating and shaping context in a manner which enables others to do what they should be doing.

Leaders' effectiveness lies in their ability to make activity meaningful for those they lead. They do this not by changing behavior, but by giving others a sense of understanding of what they are doing – a coherent viewpoint. If the leader can put such understanding into words, then the meaning of what the group is doing becomes a social fact. Only with adequate words can the group now communicate about the meaning of their behavior. The best leader is the one who both makes sense of things and puts that sense into language meaningful to large numbers of people. Leadership in this sense is about helping others to be coherent and to act coherently.

Coherence results from people feeling that the actions required of them are consistent with their own sense of purpose and identity and that of the organization of which they are a part. This feeling can only occur when the values and guiding principles embodied by the corporate purposes and expressed identity align with how the person defines and embodies their sense of self.

Consider the example of the credit card agency Visa. Its member financial institutions are fierce competitors. They – not Visa – issue the cards, which means that they are constantly going after each other's customers. On the other hand, the members also have to cooperate with each other: for the system to work, participating merchants must be able to take any Visa card issued by any bank, anywhere. This means that the banks abide by certain standards on issues such as card layout. Even more importantly, they participate in a common clearinghouse operation, the system that reconciles all the accounts and makes sure that merchants are paid for every purchase, that transactions are cleared between banks, and that customers are billed. Running this organization means reconciling a large set of tensions. Keeping the organization from flying apart requires continuous acts of leadership.

So how does Visa do it? Its first leader, Dee Hock, tells the tale:

> *Within 10 years, the infant [credit card] industry was out of control. Operating, credit, and fraud losses were thought to be in the tens of millions of dollars.* Life *magazine ran a cover story depicting banks as Icarus flying to the sun on wings of plastic above a Red Sea labeled losses into which banks were to plunge, wings melted, and drown. In the midst of the mess, Bank of America called a meeting of licensees to discuss operating problems. The meeting disintegrated in acrimonious argument. In desperation, the bank proposed forming a committee, of which I was one, to suggest a solution to one of the critical problems.*

There was no coherent viewpoint or actions. From those committee meetings, Hock's team established a context that was highly decentralized and highly collaborative. Since command and control were not working, authority, initiative, decision making, wealth – everything possible – was pushed out to the periphery of the organization, to the members. But decentralization alone would not resolve the inherent tensions. Visa needs its central functions and so do its member banks. To develop coherence in action and viewpoint, Hock got the organizing team to articulate a few key values around which this decentralized organization could cohere:

❖ Power and function must be distributive to the maximum degree. This meant that no function should be performed by any part of the whole that could reasonably be done by any more peripheral part, and no power vested in any part that might reasonably be exercised by any lesser part.

❖ Governance should be distributive to the maximum degree, meaning that no individual, institution or combinations of either,

particularly management, should be able to dominate delibera-
tions or control decisions.

❖ It must be ideally suited to lead, not follow, change, meaning that
it must create conditions in which people are secure and productive when moving from the known to the unknown, expert at managing the very process of change itself.

From the clear articulation of simple guiding principles organized
around values came a successful organization that still thrives more
than 15 years after Hock's departure.

Coherent action requires a coherent viewpoint. But it is
important to be clear about what should be cohered – values or
actions. The greater the sense of coherence about key values, the
more coordinated actions can be without a need for overt control. By
contrast, the greater the sense of coherence about particular actions,
the more rigid the overall structure and the less able it will be to cope
with new events. Coherence feeds further coherence: it is self-
reinforcing.

Leadership in the era of the next common sense is about helping others to act coherently. How to create a coherent viewpoint, how
to enable it and how to communicate it – these are the basic tenets of
the next common sense.

Practicing the next common sense

In this book we present 10 scenic vistas on the corporate landscape. All have elements that derive from complexity science but,
more importantly, all relate to management. From each vista, you the
reader are encouraged to extract simple guiding principles that make
sense to you. Creating your own coherent point of view will be the
takeaway from reading this book. We hope you enjoy the view!

The 10 scenic vistas are:

1   Use simple guiding principles.
2   Respect mental models, yours and others'.

3   Use landscape metaphors.
4   Combine and recombine.
5   Recognize your multiple roles, don't hide from them.
6   Create canyons, not canals.
7   Tell stories.
8   Send out scouting parties.
9   Post and attend to road signs.
10   Fuel coherence with aligned words.

Use simple guiding principles. Life is complex enough without adding complication to it. The guiding principles that work are those that are aligned around basic values. It works much better to be like Steelcase and say "we help people work efficiently" than to be like Novartis and have a 20-page lesson plan on how. When your employees need a week off to study your operations manual and your mission, you have a problem. If instead, like at Herb Kelleher's Southwest Airlines, they can repeat a simple mantra – "we are family" – the results will flow to the bottom line.

Respect mental models, yours and others', for those mental models hold the key to how the interactions among you get shaped. Every action is interpreted through your mental model and each of your next actions is based on that interpretation. As with you so, too, with the other person. But that person's model may be very different. Not only is that OK, but it matters a lot.

Use landscape metaphors to describe both the environment and processes taking place within it. Humans are genetically programmed to deal with landscapes – the same is not true for 2×2 matrices, board games, accounting statements, and bubble diagrams. Don't make interpretation any harder than it need be. Landscapes have worked fine for thousands of years – go with it.

Combine and recombine and avoid trying to impress yourself or others with holism. The advantage of building blocks is that they come apart and can be put together in new ways. Holistic thinking does not lend itself to new combinations – after all, what would they be new combinations of? The unrelated conglomerate age ended as a flop in the 1960s. Parts and wholes, components and recombinations

Management principles

	Next common sense	**Old common sense**
The world	Complex	Complicated
Management	Guiding interactions	Leading entities
Simple principles	Adopting a global viewpoint, allowing interactions to happen	Dealing with local situations and trying to "sort things out"
Mental models	Recognizing that my model does not need to be yours, and things can still work	Giving lip service to difference, while giving incentives to conformity
Landscape metaphors	Thinking about ecosystems	Thinking about a car race or a football game
Combine and recombine	Asking about how parts can be combined into new and better wholes	Segregating parts to be treated as their own self-sufficient wholes
Multiple roles	Allowing people to be themselves	Insisting that the company come first

Canyons not canals	Guiding viewpoints not controlling actions	Controlling actions in an attempt to control outcomes
Tell stories	Providing meaningful context and allowing employees to draw their own conclusions	Providing bullet lists of conclusions and demanding that employees fill in the necessary details
Scouting parties	Asking what can be learned from the environment and, on finding a good idea, using it	Asserting that we know best and that all good ideas are invented here
Road signs	Recognizing individual contributions and promoting leverage	Staking out territories and allowing individuals to post "no trespassing" signs
Align words	Using words to create meaningful context	Assuming that words all have one global meaning – the boss's meaning

Coherence is Mastering Complexity

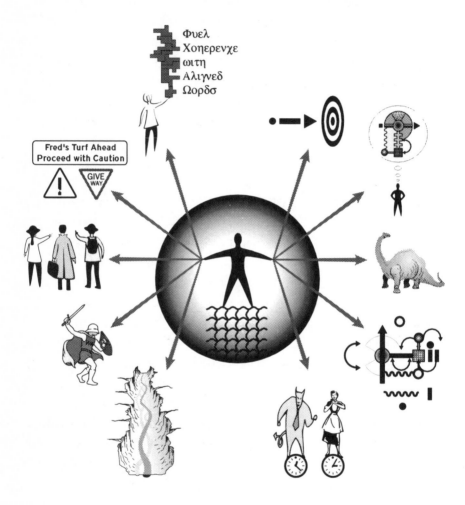

– recognize the first and you are well on your way to finding the second.

Recognize your multiple roles, don't hide from them. In each role, what is called to the foreground will differ, as will the context we label background. To assert otherwise is to risk dropping your 18-month-old at the important client's for daycare and taking the babysitter to a $200 lunch. The babysitter will wonder what is up, you won't get the big contract and your boss will be a mite perturbed. Not only do you have multiple roles, but so does everyone around you. When the roles are aligned, purposeful action happens easily. When they are not ... the babysitter gets the Dom Perignon.

Create canyons, not canals. Rivers need lots of room, yet when bounded by canyon walls they are still free to explore. Not so with a canal. Millions, if not billions, of dollars go into keeping that river right where it is. As with rivers, so too with other flowing processes, like new product development, recruiting, marketing, and customer service. Building a canal for these flows is locking them into a reality that will be outdated before the canal even opens. Imagine if your finance department insisted that everyone had to use those 386 computers until the full end of their 10-year accounting life. Canyons work better – they require more digging but less maintenance.

Tell stories to allow others the benefit of shared experiences. Merely repeating conclusions or instructions will not do the trick. Stories allow others to relate to fact, context and emotion and to bring their own interpretation to what they hear or read. Conclusions and instructions provide no room for the person hearing the conclusion or receiving the instruction. Meaning happens from interaction, not from blind passive reception. Can you imagine a dinner party where your host read a telephone directory to you?

Send out scouting parties to probe the environment. Send them out far and wide with the goal of finding stories to bring back. What Jobs found at Xerox PARC, what Lewis and Clark found on the Columbia, you can also find in your landscape. But you have to look, and with an open mind. A weekly trip to Radio Shack is unlikely to reveal what the latest fashions are from Paris or Milan. Notice that Sears finally figured this out and its clothing sales have improved greatly. How can you ascribe background or foreground to what you cannot see or have never heard about? The biggest risk of personal newspapers on the Internet is that we may only read what we asked for. Wearing dark glasses indoors is only fashionable for those who have written off tomorrow or make Ray-Ban commercials.

Post and attend to road signs. It's hard to find your yard sale without them. Even the otherwise incorrigible London bookstore Foyles has them. Labels tag items to make them easier to find, but they come with a downside. Too much labeling or the wrong kind allows the label to become a fence. To individuals, tags are how they get known for doing things, i.e. credit is assigned. But to the organization that same tag may signal, "This is Fred's domain, back off." Good for Fred in the short run, bad for the organization in the not so short. Balance is essential. A highway of billboards isn't scenic no matter what the scenery is around it.

Fuel coherence with aligned words. Leadership is a journey and coherence your vehicle. Just as your auto won't work with the wrong kind of gas, mixed messages and "do what I say and not what I do" behavior will not a coherent organization make. Vehicles can be towed and people coerced, but these are not coherent actions, just temporary aberrations. Both come with a cost. Language and word choice form a manager's primary tool. Used wisely, sound guidance can grow from the seeds of aligned words. Used poorly and all you get are weeds.

We close this introductory chapter with a story (since it is best to tell stories and not state conclusions). Southwest Airlines embodies coherence by having each of its employees "think and act like an owner." Owners think differently from non-owners because ownership is a state of mind. It's about caring, about becoming fully engaged in the active pursuit of organizational objectives. For example, non-owners are more apt to worry about how their actions are perceived by their superiors. Owners focus on the business results of their actions, regardless of who's watching. Non-owners may be more inclined to protect functional areas, pursue self-interest and approach the business from a parochial point of view. Owners transcend functional boundaries. It doesn't matter where an idea comes from, owners evaluate its merit based on whether it contributes to the ultimate objective of delivering customer value.

Non-owners have a greater tendency to live by the rules, even when the rules run contrary to common sense. Owners bend, stretch and even break rules that don't serve the organization's purpose. If breaking the rules is not an option, owners take the initiative to change them. Owners pay attention to details that others fail to notice. When people have a vested interest in the outcome of a business, they become more cost conscious, industrious, and imaginative. Owners are also different from non-owners in their willingness to take action without being asked; they are rarely spectators. An owner takes the time to follow up with a customer who expresses a concern during a casual meeting. An owner picks up the piece of trash that others have been ignoring for hours. An owner makes the extra phone call to pass on a small but important piece of information that could be helpful to another employee.

Southwest has eliminated inflexible work rules and rigid job descriptions so that its people can assume ownership for getting the job done and getting the planes out on time, regardless of whose "official" responsibility it is. This gives employees the flexibility to help each other when needed. As a result, the whole operation becomes more adaptive. Employees adopt a "whatever it takes" mentality. Southwest mechanics and pilots have the freedom and latitude to help ramp agents load bags. When a flight is running late because of bad weather, it's not uncommon to see pilots helping customers in wheelchairs board the plane, helping the operations agents take boarding passes, or helping the flight attendants clean up the cabin between flights. All of these actions are their way of adapting to the situation and taking ownership for getting customers on board more quickly. They are practicing the next common sense.

Use Simple Guiding Principles

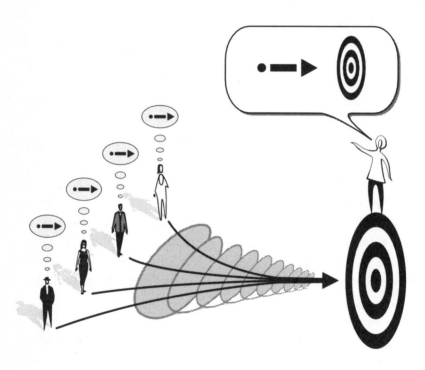

2

USE SIMPLE GUIDING PRINCIPLES

The next common sense is about making simple rules interact to enable a coherent viewpoint to emerge, which will drive coherent actions.

"Only self-confident people can be simple," says Jack Welch. "Think about it. You get some engineer who is nervous and not too sure of himself. He can't explain his design to you in very simple terms, so he complicates it. If you're not simple you can't be fast, and if you're not fast you're dead in a global world. So everything we do [at GE] focuses on building self-confidence in people so they can be simple." Steve Case of AOL agrees when he says, "The essence of AOL is simplicity."

In the traditional "decision making is everything" business model, rules are used as a shortcut. In a complicated world, the trick was to cram more into less and to hide things that were uncomfortable. Rules provided a heuristic device so that thinking was less necessary and more time was available for deciding and acting. The intriguing thing about the old rules of business is that we succeeded in creating vast corporate empires in spite of them. Today's complexities did not happen overnight – weaving relations and dependencies takes time. Yet the old rules and their users carried on, oblivious.

Six bad rules

Let's look first at some of these traditional rules, or as we like to call them, six simple rules that lead to failure.

1. Treat business as if it were a war fought on a battlefield

This rule suggests that managers view business as a series of conflicts between companies in a market, between departments in a company, between groups in an organization, between individuals in a group and (by extension) between customers and vendors. What results? Managers build big empires and "armies" of employees to fight the war. Managers order the "troops" around, while the troops wait around for "marching orders." Customers become territory to be conquered rather than potential partners, and the competition is demonized into the "enemy."

2. View the corporation as a machine

This rule suggests that the corporation is a Rube Goldberg device in which employees are faceless cogs. Nobody is indispensable, and everybody is as replaceable as a spare part. Individual initiative, goals, and desires are completely subsumed by the demands of the corporate machine. What results? Managers create rigid organizations with rigid roles and rigid functions. Managers and workers alike become convinced that change is very difficult, similar to retooling a complicated machine. Managers are encouraged to think of themselves as "controllers" whose job it is to make sure that people follow the rules of the "system." Employees are treated in dehumanizing ways while the corporation centralizes control at the top.

3. Practice management as control

This rule suggests that the real job of the manager is to control employees' behaviors so that they do exactly what management wants them to do. Employees who disagree with a manager or refuse to do something are "insubordinate" and therefore dangerous. What results? Managers create organizations that can't adapt to new conditions because there are conflicting power structures, each of which is trying to "control" the corporation. Management gets involved in a supercharged political atmosphere where productive work becomes difficult. Individual initiative is killed in favor of a "let's wait and see what the boss says" mentality.

4. Treat your employees as children

This rule suggests that employees are too immature and foolish to be assigned real authority, and simply can't be trusted. If not restricted by complicated rules and regulations, they'll steal the company blind. What results? Employees develop a deep and abiding resentment toward management. They refuse to do anything until they're certain that they won't get blamed if something goes wrong. Employees spend more time "covering their butts" than doing productive work. Employees only work when they're being watched, if then.

5. To motivate, use fear

This rule suggests that employees only work because they're afraid of getting fired. Managers must therefore use the fear of getting fired, the fear of ridicule, or the fear of loss of privilege to motivate people. What results? Employees and managers alike become paralyzed, unable to make risky decisions or take courageous action. Work becomes a loathsome experience filled with truckling, ass-kissing, and compulsive corporate politicking.

6. Remember, change is nothing but pain

This rule suggests that managers and employees alike see change as complicated and difficult and something that companies only undergo if they're in desperate shape. What results? Reengineering, restructuring, and downsizing operations fail as people in the organization torpedo the change efforts to avoid the pain of change.

These rules don't allow for autonomy or for a context-dependent reaction to each situation. They do not allow room for interaction. And interaction is what the next common sense is all about.

⋮ Guiding principles that work

For a telling example of what the interaction of simple rules can achieve, consider Southwest Airlines. The airline began service in 1971 with flights to Houston, Dallas, and San Antonio. Southwest has grown to become the fourth largest US airline (in terms of domestic customers carried). It became a major airline in 1989 when it exceeded the billion-dollar revenue mark. What has made Southwest a success? Certainly, its strategy of being the shorthaul, low-fare, high-frequency, point-to-point carrier in its chosen markets has made a difference. But so too do the simple rules which Southwest transmits and expects of its employees: Trust, Interdependence, Genuineness, Empathy, Risk and Success.

Herb Kelleher, the chairman, says:

> We don't have many rules because I think that rules, in a lot of cases, are substitutes for management. Somebody wants a manual to hide behind instead of evaluating something on its merits. I've often advocated inconsistencies of corporate doctrine, and some people are astounded to hear that ... Somebody's got to have the power to say, hey stop, whoa, this person is being ground up in the mills of the gods, and the mills weren't intended to grind this piece of grain. So we're not going to slavishly follow our remorseless rules.

The key to Southwest's policy is that if someone does make a judgment call, management gives them full support, because they consider the person making the decision the expert in that situation. Take the notion of hierarchy. Herb says:

> Avoid hierarchy to achieve productivity. A hierarchical organization breeds the idea that some people are superior to others because of their title and position alone. And I think most of us have known some pretty dumb rich people, and some pretty smart people who weren't rich – some pretty dis-

honest pillars of the church and some pretty honest gamblers.
My only point is that title and position alone signify nothing
about what you really are or what you're really worth.

If there is one word around which Southwest coheres it is family. Family does not tell the airline where to fly next or what to charge, but it guides every employee's day-to-day understanding of what it means to be part of the Southwest team. Treating people right is central to Southwest's philosophy. For this reason, the company is renowned for taking special care to get to know those it employs. Kelleher knows an astonishing percentage of his 12,000 employees' names, and can recount details of past conversations – frequently asking about children, spouses or outside interests.

Southwest values this caring attitude, as this classic quote from Herb illustrates:

We want people who are "other" oriented. We don't want people who like to sit around and study their navel, no matter how pretty and lint free it may be.

Southwest coheres around family. Your firm may cohere around some other key value. The important thing is to have some internalized notion among your team around which they cohere.

Why simple rules?

Where did all this emphasis on simple rules come from? After all, we live in a world that appears complex on the surface. The answer lies in a computer model – a model that one Craig Reynolds built in 1986. Craig wondered how birds and fish are able to travel in large groups and act as one unit. A flock of hundreds of birds can speed up in one direction, then suddenly, in unison, decrease their velocity and turn to follow a different route. No matter how complicated their acrobatic path, the birds always stay close together but never collide. Are they following a leader?

Many species of fish actually spend their entire lives in schools from the moment they are born. Schools are important. When fish travel as a school, it is more difficult for a predator to single out one fish to attack. Schools also allow the fish to find food more easily, and some species of fish travel in schools in order to protect an area that they have claimed for their own.

To quote Reynolds himself:

In 1986 I made a computer model of coordinated animal motion such as bird flocks and fish schools. It was based on three dimensional computational geometry of the sort normally used in computer animation or computer aided design. I called the software boids. Each boid has direct access to the whole scene's geometric description, but reacts only to flockmates within a certain small radius of itself. The basic flocking model consists of three simple steering behaviors:

1 Separation: steer to avoid crowding local flockmates.
2 Alignment: steer towards the average heading of local flockmates.
3 Cohesion: steer to move toward the average position of local flockmates.

In addition, the more elaborate behavioral model included predictive obstacle avoidance and goal seeking. Obstacle avoidance allowed the boids to fly through simulated environments while dodging static objects. For applications in computer animation, a low priority goal seeking behavior caused the flock to follow a scripted path.

Boids – Craig Reynolds' artificial life version of "birds" or "fish": creatures consisting solely of computer software which exhibit behaviors which observers may otherwise attribute to real birds or real fish.

Richard Dawkins in *The Selfish Gene* proposed that pack behavior follows the same rules as those of **boids**. A simple strategy for a predator is to chase the closest prey in its vicinity. This is in order to reduce the amount of energy that it must expend. The strategy for the prey is to keep as far away from its predators as possible. If predators only attack the closest prey, then all of the others should be safe. Each prey can be considered to have a "domain of danger" surrounding it. A lone individual would have a rather large domain of danger, while each individual in a pack would have a small domain of danger around it. The strategy of the prey then is to reduce its domain of danger as much as possible. This is accomplished by creating a pack, where each individual tries to reduce their own domain of danger. But, because those on the edges of the pack have a larger domain of danger than those in the center of the pack, those on the edges try to move inward, thus pushing those on the inside outward.

Simple rules could lead to complex behavior. This much seemed true. But most of the observers overlooked two critical details in Reynolds' description: the model is spatial with a predefined area and he used a "low priority goal seeking behavior" as an input. Leaving out these details leads to promising beginnings but problems in follow through.

The model as a whole – **simple rules interacting within a defined area starting with some goals** – has great promise. So instead of giving you more stories of how to program software creatures on your PC (unless you want a screensaver), we will discuss how to make sense of this model in your business. With luck, it will provide some vital insights.

Great words – what do they mean?

Let's start with the word "rules." In designing boids, Reynolds did not mean to imply that we all must be like children at a military camp. Rules are not to be construed in the "this is allowed, but this other is forbidden" sense. Reynolds was not even talking about computer-type rules – the "if x, then y" of which programmers are so proud. The concept of rules in this instance is more a set of "guiding principles."

To us, the key aspect of rules in Reynolds' sense is that they are totally internalized and have become tacit. For example, "steer to avoid crowding" is a description of behavior as much as it is a prescription of "do this." The boid has internalized the rule and the rule has become part of the boid. They are now inseparable.

Notice that Reynolds used the word "cohesion" for his third rule. Cohesion, as in sticking together, is not only a rule for the flock as a whole, but also for each individual boid. Again, the rule is internalized. Every boid seeks to "cohere." As we prefer to put it: in human organizations, "coherence" is important to the individuals and the group; so too with boids.

Boids use rules that are "simple." As the opposite of complex, this word has a power well beyond its six letters. Notice that the rules are not in an "if, then" format. If they were in such a format, the rules would either have to be nearly infinite in number or infinite in length. How can we possibly describe enough if, thens to tell us (or boids) what to do in every possible situation?

The rule "steer to avoid crowding" does not say "when three other items are within two feet do x." Instead, the rule allows the boid a huge range of autonomy. The principle "avoid crowding" is made part of the boid. The "how" of "steering" is also part of the boid, but the interactions between the goal "avoid crowding," the how of "steering" and any other set of goals and hows which may also be part of the boid are left unspecified. This is the key to simple rules – **underspecify** to allow for autonomy and for a context-dependent reaction to every situation encountered. In the underspecification of a rule lies space for evolution, change, and that complexity word, emergence. Simple rules say something about principles for action but do not specify when to apply the principle, or to what extent, or which principles override any other.

Rules in organizations

Someone once said that the lowest form of a civilized society is one based on the rule of law. Others have suggested that the more rules there are, the less trust there is in the organization. We agree with this, with a caveat. The only time an organization can exist without rules or laws is when complete virtue exists in each of the organization's members. Until that point comes, rules and laws must create a structure of trust and justice. Richard Epstein, in his *Simple Rules for a Complex World*, put it: "government works best when it establishes the rules of the road, not when it seeks to determine the composition of the traffic." In corporate settings, this translates into the idea that managers cannot micromanage all the time without really causing problems. The workers must internalize a few guiding principles and be allowed to get on with their job.

One consultant we know developed a list of rules that he thought would get good results in management if earnestly applied:

1   Attempt to give a lot of credit to the people around you.
2   Attempt to convince the people who work for you that you truly care about their future.
3   Attempt to give your organization clear goals and achievable objectives.

Are these rules simple? We don't think so. The concepts are not quite at the level of guiding principles, and the behavior does not quite get internalized. Notice that each of our friend's rules starts with the word "attempt." Reynolds didn't program the boids with "attempt." He gave them guiding principles and let them carry on.

So let's try a different friend's list:

1   Trust.
2   Respect.
3   Work towards a common goal.
4   Live in harmony.
5   Demand excellence.
6   Work hard.
7   Maintain perspective.
8   Come through.

These are simple. But the behavior they imply is complex. And they follow Reynolds' model. Underspecified to an extreme, they are probably useless if considered by themselves. Their power is in their interaction.

If a rule is to be an internalized guiding principle, it must be exhibited in behavior. Each of us has our own set of internal rules.

Those who know us very well may be able to explicate for us what those rules are, but to relative strangers (including most of the people with whom we interact in the course of doing our work) such knowledge is hidden. If we want to build on the model of a flock of birds, a herd of sheep, or a school of fish, we must take into account the "others" with whom we interact. For all of us in the "flock" to be moving in the same direction, we need to be aware of the simple rules we all are following. So "making" the rules consists in articulating them for the awareness of the others with whom we will interact.

Simple rules work by interaction among numbers (be they of boids, sheep, or people). Complicated formulations of "if, thens" are great for a legal manual, but poor for trying to get a group to act. Action is the name of the game. Organizations are not the legal code expounded by the corporate office and memorialized in the 20-page memos that seem to come down from on high every week or so. **Instead, they are the day-to-day actions of the members of the network – employees, customers, suppliers, partners – doing something**. Simple rules are "made" by allowing those concerned to be aware of them. It does not have to be in words – international road signs work fine in their context – but it does have to be communicated.

Peter Scott-Morgan, in *The Unwritten Rules of the Game*, notes:

> *You encourage people to act in a new way as a means to an end of achieving what is important to them. As they find that the new behavior is valuable in its own right, so the transition is consolidated. Yet the speed of change is far faster than if you only try to encourage people to behave in the new way by attempting to convince them that the behavior is worthwhile in its own right. Try that and they may simply not agree with you.*

Waving a sales sign in a parking lot, shouting about how nicely it is worded or the high quality of the reflective paint on its surface, will not encourage shoppers to leave spaces for the handicapped or for pregnant mothers. Giving them a reason to internalize the behavior pattern (perhaps by showing some poor soul struggling to make their way through an icy lot in a wheelchair while having to play dodgems with the oncoming cars) will not only get the job done but will help it to last for a long time.

⦂ Simple rules lead to meaning only ⦂ through interaction

⦂ What is the "key value added" of Federal Express? As it tells us in commercials, "when it absolutely has to be there overnight." This is a simple rule, but its meaning comes from interaction with other rules.

For example, FedEx could not use the word "absolutely" without both engendering a relationship of trust and asking the same of the customer. Why is the FedEx tracking system so important? Because it allows the customer, if they doubt that trusting relationship, a means of checking up on what FedEx is doing. Respect also enters the picture by means of the Internet interface, which allows the customer **acting on their own** to enter FedEx's computer system and check on a package. The customer does not need to ask for assistance, their privacy is respected, and they are viewed as being able to handle the task. Sure, FedEx was able to save a lot of money because it no longer needed as many operators to handle tracking questions, but the gains it made in its customers' perspective of the company were just as important. The interaction of "get it there overnight," "trust," and "respect" has created a meaningful space in which FedEx and its customers interact.

The *Wall Street Journal*'s Tom Petzinger wrote about this kind of interaction within a Lucent Technologies factory:

Lucent employs no formulas or fixed methods here; constant change is the only constant. But a few simple principles were evident during my visit.

I	Hire attitude over aptitude.
2	Create mission from above, methods from below.
3	Foster feedback.
4	Unite the inside and the outside.
5	Reward teamwork.

Though management establishes the mission, workers fulfill it. "If I give you an endgame," Ms. Mercer [the plant manager] says, "you can find your way there." Teams continually alter the manufacturing process and even the product design itself. A senior engineer named David Therrien, who compiled the original assembly procedures, no longer recognizes them. "My instructions were nothing but a starting place," he says ... The plant follows a one-page list of working principles – not some vague mission statement in a wooden frame, but a contract signed by every employee committing them to speed, innovation, candor, deep respect for colleagues and other plainly stated goals. People cite the document as if it were the Bill of Rights.

And indeed, America's founding fathers treated the Bill of Rights in just this way – as a set of simple rules (guiding principles) that would interact to help shape a new society. It is not that the Bill of Rights is not a complex legal document – it is – but that people tend to internalize it as a quick set of guiding ideals: freedom of the press, freedom of speech, right of assembly etc. Most Americans are not aware of the section of the Bill of Rights which speaks of bills of attainder or habeas corpus or writs of mandamus – those parts are just not relevant to the day-to-day actions on which our attention gets focused.

At Petzinger's example of the Lucent plant, the results of simple rules being allowed to interact are striking:

In the brutal global market for digital cellular base stations, high speed and low cost are everything. So how does this self-directed work force of 480 stack up? In two years it hasn't missed a single delivery deadline. And total labor costs represent an exceedingly low 3% of product cost ... "We solve problems in hallways rather than conference rooms," says production manager Steve Sherman. The process is so fluid that none of the manufacturing equipment is bolted to the floor ... "This business has been handed to us," says technician Tom Guggiari. "This business is ours."

⋮ Interaction happens in context

Recall that Reynolds' boids operate in the space of his personal computer. The Lucent folk are operating within the context not only of their factory but also within a broad network of customers, suppliers, partners and the local community. Context drives how the rules come together and interact. The reason for underspecifying rules is allow the context to drive what happens.

We will come back to this point again and again. Its general name is **"situatedness."** Things happen, people interact, and the relevant part of the environment changes within some context which describes the situation.

Situatedness – the extent to which an interaction or entity is dependent on context.

It is important to remember that while rules may be abstract, situations are not. People care about things that happen, events that occur, and actions that take place; not about steering a boid five degrees to the left in cyberspace.

Knowledge, models, and expertise are co-created by thinking people working in and with their environment. Since that environment is different for every organization, it doesn't work to take something that has been developed in one place and just transfer it wholesale to another place. Consultants and managers have tried that with program after program (BPR, TQM, zero-based budgeting, scenario planning, and the learning organization) and, as a result, have generated a well-earned cynicism among the nation's workforce as it watches these programs come and go without creating the desired change. Today's manager needs something different, something that will engage the whole system of the organization in figuring out what makes sense for that particular system. The answers, the expertise, need to be created by the context that is in need of that expertise. Don't take something that's "tried and true" and apply it in cookie-cutter fashion. If you are to make knowledge work for you, it must be knowledge that is appropriate to the situation and context and not what some book (even ours) recommends.

How do you motivate people? You don't. Instead, you trust that they come with their own desire to thrive. They will make adjustments and do what is necessary for them to flourish. In an organization, you don't have to "incentivize" anybody. You have to create the conditions under which they can thrive, i.e. context. Among the things that human beings naturally seek are the ability to contribute and to make a difference, and the ability to be involved in satisfying social relationships. If you design your organization around these criteria, it will have to be one in which people are not boxed into roles and rules (trapped into inappropriate contexts). The right context is one in which they feel that they can continue to grow, learn, and develop, and in which a variety of relationships are available to them.

Guidelines for using simple guiding principles

The next common sense is about making simple rules interact to enable a coherent viewpoint. Where the old common sense was about dealing with local situations and trying to "sort things out," the next common sense is about adopting a global viewpoint, allowing interactions to happen, which in turn will drive coherent actions.

❖ Always ground your guiding principles in values.
❖ Ensure that these guiding principles are aligned with the purpose, identity and values of individuals and those of the organization as a whole. Don't just cite guiding principles or hang them in a nice wooden frame. The guiding principles must encourage people to act in a certain way as a means to the end of achieving what is important to them. As people find that the new behavior is valuable in its own right and aligned with their values, these principles will be internalized in day-to-day actions.
❖ Use only guiding principles that are allowed to interact, like these two: "management sets the goal, workers fulfill it," and "reward teamwork." Underspecified guiding principles, like "work hard," are useless. Overspecification, like "if..., then..." makes guiding principles equally useless.

Management principles

	Next common sense	**Old common sense**
The world	Complex	Complicated
Management	Guiding interactions	Leading entities
Simple principles	Adopting a global viewpoint, allowing interactions to happen	Dealing with local situations and trying to "sort things out"

Respect Mental Models, Yours and Others

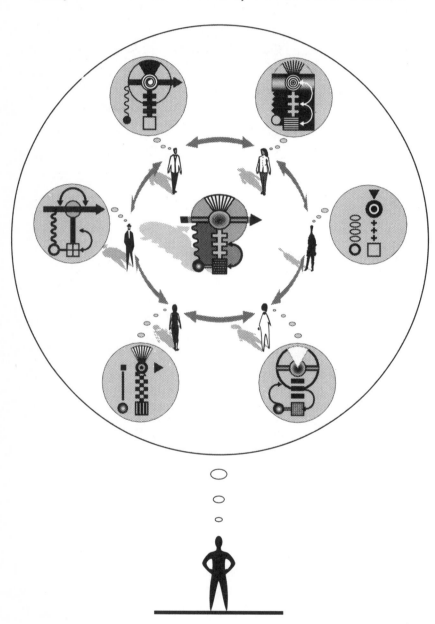

3

RESPECT MENTAL MODELS: YOURS AND OTHERS'

Our friend Mark was working in the African bush with a guide, defining the features and tracing the original names of rivers, hills, valleys and other landmarks. At one point, he said to his guide: "Hey, we are lost!" The guide gave him a withering glance and answered: "We are not lost, the camp is lost."

In a flash, Mark realized a very important aspect of what separated his vision of the world from that of his guide. For Mark, space was fixed and he was a free agent moving around in it, like an actor on a stage, a vast area in which you could lose your way. The guide, however, saw space as something within rather than outside the body, a fluid and ever-changing medium in which he could never lose his way, where the only fixed point in the universe consisted of himself, and within which, although he might be putting one foot in front of the other, he never actually moved. There are cultures where walking is not seen as traversing space but as pushing space under one's feet.

None of us can hold everything we deal with in our heads – we must simplify and edit, otherwise the information demands would be too great. The simple representation we form of something is a model. What matters is how we do the simplifying, how we do the editing. In the modeling process lies the potential for greatness, but also the opportunity to be a goat.

We doubt that the model in your head is a full representation of an actual company, management team or product. Instead, you have only selected concepts and relationships, which you use to represent the real things. These mental models are fuzzy. They are incomplete. They are imprecisely stated. They change with time, sometimes even during the flow of a single conversation. Very often, we are not consciously aware of our mental models or the effects they have on our behavior.

The next common sense is built on a recognition that, in general, things "work out." Where the old common sense insisted that the only "right" way to see things was the boss's way, the next common sense recognizes that my model need not be the same as yours. The uncertainty of the old was reflected in the lip service given to diversity, lip service which contrasted sharply with the incentives given to conformity. The confidence of the new is reflected in respect for others and for their thoughts.

Most of the experts on management and complexity make use of this point to tell you to "shake up" your models. Out with old, rigid thinking, in with a little bit of chaos. As the typical sales pitch might go: "That old model of yours – it was based on structure and order, right? Well, we have a better thought. Creativity is enhanced at the edge of chaos, so it is time to mix things up a bit. Right?"

Wrong. There is nothing in the study of complex systems which suggests, even remotely, that one mental model is, by definition, better than another. What the complexity science literature does suggest is that context and situation will determine which model is more *helpful* than another. Universal models – even management models, such as best practices – have little place in a complex world. Each situation requires its own model. What matters is how we go about modeling. And that process is the topic of this chapter.

Simple rules guide mental models

In a book published in 1997, David Lawrence of the non-profit health system Kaiser Permanente and Robert Bauman of the pharmaceuticals firm SmithKline Beecham discussed what they saw as the reasons for a change program being successful. Their lessons involved shifting mental models by using simple rules which interact.

Bauman tells us that in each of the four phases of SmithKline's change (a total transformation from being a mid-size local British firm to becoming a global player with a number one market position worldwide), the company adopted a simple slogan which served to guide employees on the key value of what was going on around them. Thus, when the British firm which had been known as Beecham merged with the US-based Smith Kline, its slogan and value statement was the "new and better health care company." The emphasis on new and better was both an explanation of the merger and a statement of goals, contained in just six words.

For the next phase, integrating the two operations, the slogan became "Now We Are One." Bauman's goal was "oneness in spirit as well as structure." Again, notice the simplicity of the phrase and its clarity. No two-page mission statement, not the 20-page booklet on "purpose and aspirations" put out by Smith Kline's competitor Novartis, just four simple words. It was hard for employees to be confused about what was intended or what they were supposed to do.

The next two phases of Bauman's program involved values. He wanted the integrated company not only to be one, but to think as one, in a particular way. From six words to four, the slogan became two: "Simply Better." The consultants may tell us about the interplay between the SB of the slogan and the SB for Smith Beecham, but that was not what interested employees. The message was as simple as it gets: improve. One value, one goal, one overriding interest with which everyone could identify.

Once there was a perceived buy-in by the worldwide employee group, the addition of a single word marked the change to phase four. Simply Better became the Simply Better Way. The process of

becoming simply better was now marked by a statement of being –
SmithKline Beecham told the world that "going with us is the simply
better way."

Bauman stresses that these slogans were not just catch phrases to
be casually tossed aside. The company used them as its marketing message both internally to motivate employees and externally to re-orient
customers. Thus, the value statements which these slogans became
were also identity statements. Smith Kline was using simple messages
to tell the world "this is who we are and how we want you to view us."

For his part, Lawrence gives us nine lessons for successful
change. To him, management is about reshaping people's view of the
world:

> *It means shattering their sense of stability, tossing out their old
> standards of success, and prying them loose from the status quo.
> And then it means replacing what you've wiped out with a
> new, coherent, and energizing vision of what you believe the
> future can and should be.*

His advice for others attempting change includes such gems as:

1   Give coherence to the change process. The ability to articulate
     and convey a focused sense of purpose, a clear statement of val-
     ues, and a consistent set of themes is crucial.
2   You have to cement each building block of change in place
     before moving on to the next.
3   Think of change as a campaign. It is not only the content and
     the planning that are important: it is also about how you go
     about winning people over. Successful change – and this
     includes the process of stacking your building blocks – really
     means altering the way people think and act.

Lawrence has a set of principles which revolve around the building
blocks of identity, purpose, and values. Change is not only about
organization charts and budgets, but more importantly about how people think. Bauman shows us a set of such building blocks. By stacking

the building blocks, both Lawrence and Bauman hoped a new and "better" firm would emerge through the shifting of mental models.

Mental models are toolsets

One funny thing about our mental models: we can't operate without them, but we tend not even to notice we have them. Only when an event, or a situation, requires that we pay attention to something do we notice that it is part of our thinking. As a result, most of our models are rather fuzzy, ill defined, and not quite articulated. There is also a growing body of evidence that suggests that the mental representations on which decisions and behavior are based can be highly variable. They depend on subtle aspects of the particular situation or context that decision makers are in at any given time. This makes it difficult to generalize results.

People often do not know what influences their thoughts and behavior. When asked after the fact, people tend not to rely on their memory of recent experiences, but to make inferences based on *a priori* theories and assumptions. When we order a cup of coffee, for example, we judge how hot it is based on what temperature we imagine coffee should be, not on how hot our last cup actually was or on how long it took to take the first and last sips.

When Bill Gates thought that the Internet was only an academic fad, those thoughts, Bill's mental model, guided Microsoft's efforts in creating the Microsoft Network (MSN). Eighteen months later, when Bill decided that the Internet was real (thank you, Netscape), the new mental model guided the development of Internet Explorer. When US Attorney General Janet Reno started making noises about Microsoft's domination, that mental model influenced the speed with which Microsoft was integrating its Internet browser into the Windows operating system. When AOL bought Netscape, once again the mental model shifted.

When the programming language Java was first developed, it seemed as if its only use was going to be to turn on your coffee pot when the alarm clock went off in the morning. Sun came close to abandoning the product several times. It was only when the mental model shifted – when there was a realization that they had something that was operating system independent – that suddenly Java was embraced, and the competitive world of programming took a giant leap forward. We want to re-emphasize this point. It was not the actual development of Java that changed the competitive profile, it was the change in the mindset concerning how Java was perceived. The small embedded controller program became a new operating system. It was the same product, but there was a new mental model regarding it.

Mental models are our "toolsets" for understanding the world. Mental models that are no longer appropriate may prevent managers from sensing problems, delay changes in strategy, and lead to action that is ineffective in a new environment. Metaphors and other mental models provide a means for individuals and, ultimately, organizations to create and share understanding. These mental models establish images, names and an understanding of how things fit together. They express what is important and unimportant. The models must be articulated and accepted in the organization for them to be effective.

In the context of such models, believing is seeing. Managers attend to what they believe is important to their firm's performance. Their mental models will influence attention, and determine what environmental data is noticed and interpreted, all of which together constitute a major factor in guiding and directing organizational activities. The trouble is, of course, that we tend to see what we want to see and hear what we want to hear. It is easy to be unduly influenced by presumptions and prejudices. We tend to make more of the evidence that confirms our beliefs and pay less attention to any evidence that contradicts them.

Conversations and events can alter our mental models. The most potent example of this can be seen during a sporting event when one of those "waves" comes crashing through the crowd. Even the most respectable gentleman of proper upbringing cannot seem to help himself and is up waving with the best of them. Waving is not a part of his normal mental model ("Wave? That is not an appropriate expression for someone of my class and upbringing"), but in the spirit of the moment such formal conceptions of identity get caught, literally, in the wave and fall by the wayside. Perhaps this gentleman will have a different view of a "crowd" once he has "waved." Perhaps he will have a different view of himself. But it is equally likely that he will forget he even stood, never mind waved, once the event has passed. His mental model of himself, if strongly held, will "correct" for such momentary lapses. Only repeated experiences or shared experiences are likely to overcome this built-in resistance to interior mental change.

Actions depend on interpretations

Common sense (both the old and the next) is encountering the world or some portion of it and making sense of it – interpreting it in a manner which allows us to act. Underlying this notion are three others: all behavior is somehow determined (i.e. a decision is made); we may not always know we make those determinations; and our decisions are as influenced by what is internal to us as by the rational external factors that we believe enter into them.

Interpretation is necessary for action. But what is interpretation? Consider Bill Gates. In 1995, Netscape was announced. This web browser seemed to be just a toy, a means for delivering cartoons and pornographic pictures across the academic marketplace known as the Internet. To Bill, the real action was in competing with the likes of AOL and CompuServe. At the same time as Netscape was making its initial deliveries, Bill was launching the Microsoft Network with a grand fanfare. And AOL's Steve Case was asking for government intervention to prevent Microsoft from taking over the online world. As Bill and Steve saw it, the competition was between AOL and the new MSN. Also at the same time, Jim Clark (who had run Silicon Graphics) was busy recruiting Jim Barksdale to give up running Federal Express and join a small start-up called Netscape. Somehow, the interpretation the two Jims had of the online world was very different to that of Bill and Steve. All four took actions – actions that were totally dependent on their individual interpretations of the world around them.

David Lawrence of Kaiser Permanente tells us that successful change requires altering the way people think and act. We would restate this as: change requires influencing how people go about interpreting their worlds so that they can act. If your concept of the world does not change, it is unlikely that you will be changing your actions. Just try to get a pet turtle living in a terrarium to practice standing on its hind legs. Life is good in the terrarium and there is no incentive for this nonsense, so why should it bother? It is a lesson most six-year-olds grasp quickly. If you take the turtle out of the terrarium and only feed it as a reward for standing up – well, life has changed and so do the actions. You now have a standing turtle.

Interpretations can be considered as "having made sense" out of a situation. Having made sense out of it means that ambiguities have been removed, and so action is possible. By contrast, when there is a lack of sense making, when multiple interpretations are flourishing, ambiguity prevails and action avoidance is the normal result. Ambiguity is not the same as uncertainty. Ambiguity can be looked at as "having not quite made sense yet." The "not quite" and the "yet" are important, since they indicate a hoped-for future state when the ambiguity will be abolished and sense will have been made. Common sense will yet prevail. By contrast, uncertainty is the lack of willingness to act. Ambiguity can lead to uncertainty, but you always have the choice of acting. When you act, you act *as if* you were certain.

This "as if you were certain" posture underlies all purposeful action and affects potential actions. For example, Peter Reason argues that for creative learning to take place in the face of an undifferentiated collection of "stuff," some initial structure had to be imposed. Why? To create an island of certainty in the midst of the confusion. The initial structure resolved some questions of interpretation and allowed space. By eliminating some ambiguity, you provide space for action. The actions will change the situation and you move on, but without that initial defining structure, nothing happens.

Lawrence stresses the idea of a team. Bauman speaks of the values of his employees. Both speak to the manager's main dilemma: the manager may desire x or y, but someone else has to actually do it. Since the days of Adam Smith and the pin factory, managers have not had the luxury of doing their own tasks (OK, in the 1990s we type our own letters, answer our own phones, and get our own coffee, but these are not the tasks we mean). If actions are dependent on interpretations and it is someone else who acts, then it is that someone else's interpretations which matter. Mr. Gates interprets antitrust law in one manner and Janet Reno in another. As much as Bill wants the Justice department to issue an "all is fair" bulletin, it is not his interpretation which matters, it is Janet's. Forgetting that was one of the worst PR mistakes Microsoft ever made.

As with Microsoft, so goes the world – at least as far as this lesson goes. Unless you are doing your own thing yourself, you have to align the interpretation of the actual actor with the action you desire. No match, no action – or worse, the wrong action.

Similarly, the notion of family keeps Southwest's employees and executives aligned. The family may be a bit dysfunctional at times – employees do occasionally call in sick all at once – but it remains a family – for example, whenever this mass sickness happens the union adamantly denies that there was any kind of labor action, "just coincidence." Like in a good family, all troubles should be self-contained. And letting the neighbors know – the other major airlines – would be bad for business. A shared interpretation of what it means to be a member of a family is clearly at work. It's the other airlines that have labor problems.

In the same vein, when UPS went out on strike, the labor pool at Federal Express gladly pitched in with longer hours and extra work. Management and labor shared a common interpretation of "let's make the most out of this." FedEx labor would not cross the UPS picket lines, but instead would call their customers to arrange for alternate drop-off and pick-up points. Extra work? You bet. Did they do it without being told? Absolutely. The interpretations matched, and the desired actions were the outcome.

: Exploring the context and
: setting the stage

: How can you tell when interpretations match other than by the benefit of hindsight? This calls for a process of exploring the context of the particular situation. By context, we mean identifying the actors who are going to carry out the action and any relevant decision makers beside yourself. With the parties identified, you then need to explore how each will interpret both the goals you wish to achieve and the present reality, which serves as a base from which to achieve them.

In the abstract, this sounds like an enormous task. And, if you have done no work with goals or values among your employees, it will be. The manager needs to create a readiness for change. Readiness is an attractor; it pulls others into its orbit. Values are yet another attractor. Aligning them can be a powerful shortcut in accomplishing the exploration task. Witness this post from the Internet-based discussion forum on complexity and management which calls itself the "Complex-M list":

> This idea of attractors is a powerful one for me. While I was plant manager I kept track of the amount of time I spent with people who were not direct reports, in the plant and in the community. Over a five year period, I averaged 5 hours a day in this work. I came to realize that in the myriad of conversations, we were crafting the bowl and developing a deep understanding of what things like vision, mission, standards, principles, expectations, values really meant to us. As people more and more internalized these ideas and began to operate out of them, the organization became more open and people could operate with great freedom to do what was needed. The bowl provided order and people operating within the bowl could learn, grow, create and discover their freedom to find their meaning.

The bowl he is referring to is a basin of attraction. Think of it like a river delta or the vortex of an open drain.

In my experience, most questions we ask our bosses are for sanction and/or permission to do what we already know we need to do. If we have a good sense of the bowl, then the answers to say 90% of our questions are already there, before the question. When people understand this, the ability of the organization to move quickly to respond to the changing environment is greatly expanded. The challenge for management in this is to learn to live with the ambiguity. You don't know what people will do next, but it's always within the bowl. It took me several years to learn to have the confidence in this process; I was not disappointed by anyone. Let me tell you a true story to illustrate this.

Background: 1) In the chemical business interacting with the media is usually done by the top management because we are criticized so much and we want to tell our story as well as we can. 2) As we opened up the information flow and people became more involved in everything, they became much more responsible for themselves and the business. We had many teams, including environmental teams.

Story: One morning I got a call from one of our operators who was very active on our environmental teams. She was very upset because, as she was coming into work that morning to start her 6AM shift, she'd heard a couple of guys on a country music show criticizing our plant for all its emissions. That night had been clear and the steam plumes were glistening in the moon light. Because of her involvement on the environmental teams, she knew they were just water vapor, but the guys on the show thought they were chemical emission. After expressing her frustrations, she went on to inform me that she'd called them up, and invited them to visit our plant the next Monday. She had planned the whole visit and told me that my part was to meet with them for about an hour to give them an overview of our environmental work. She had several others lined up to also talk to them about our work. The visit was one of the best we ever had and was done very effectively by her. They spent the next several weeks telling all their listeners about the good work we were doing and all the neat people they'd met. My external affairs guy about had a heart attack over this because it was so out of the box.

I had to have the confidence to know that she was going to do just fine, and she did.

> I hope this brings some sense to this idea of the importance of attractors. I think they're real.

Attractors are an aligning force. They bring coherence to what might otherwise be a confusing process. Bauman's four slogans served as attractors at SmithKline Beecham. "Family" serves as an attractor at Southwest Airlines.

If you have given your employees a small set of powerful images (such as family) to serve as attractors, and if you have lived up to them, then the interpretation process is easier for everyone. Living up to them is important. A contrast between what you say and what you do will only unleash a torrent of interpretation, reinterpretation and second guessing. Failing to live up to an attractor is a surefire way of increasing uncertainty and reducing the potential for activity – especially useful activity.

What is critical in all this is remembering that you are not the one taking the actions. As a manager, all you are doing is enunciating goals. Others act. You can't shape the interpretations of those others; only they can. What you can do is set the stage for how they interpret and thereby influence the process if not the outcome. Traditional management culture with its emphasis on control has never been able to get its hands around this point. But to coerce is not to lead. If you insist on controlling the interpretations of your employees, or customers, or suppliers, you can only do so through coercion. And coercion is just a short-term solution.

Not that companies and managers don't attempt this all the time. We all have worked for a bully who was incapable of listening to anyone but himself. It often was easier to go along than to take issue with his interpretations of the situation and fight about it. But when this happened, did you change your interpretation? No. You went along for the sake of harmony. Often the bully is the last to realize that this is what has been happening. Beware being the messenger of that piece of disturbing news. To interject such a realization into his interpretations may cause the bully an identity crisis. Defensive reactions are all that can be expected.

Lawrence and Bauman stress that leading is the process of creating a "safe" context for change to emerge. Leading is not the process of shoving change down the throats of employees. Both top executives stress that if a safe context is to be created, it is essential to get rid of those employees and managers who are not open to discussing their world view, their interpretations, or to listening to those of others. Being open to discussing world views, interpretations, and listening to others are key ingredients in bringing about alignment.

How can a safe context be created? Well, we have an example from the Internet discussion on the Complex-M list:

Throughout the years, orders for the major products of an assembly department, in a factory I was consulting with, were decreasing steadily. An interchangeable product produced by the same factory was replacing the products of that department. Their workload was decreasing from month to month. Production management was undecided about what to do with the staff of the department. Downsizing and early retirement were being considered. In coordination with the assembly manager, the department arranged the transfer of work from another department, that was overburdened with orders. When the pressure of those orders decreased, the department approached another assembly department, that was also struggling with too many orders, and once more eased matters by taking over part of its work. Soon the department had turned itself into a "crisis dealing" team that took over work from other departments that were having difficulty meeting their order schedule. Production and assembly management began to realize that they were dealing with a new and positive phenomenon that was solving them many headaches. On top of its new function of helping other departments that were under stress, every now and then when orders arrived, the department returned to assembling its original product. The role of the department changed and it organized itself differently, uniting its two teams and arranging the workplace differently. Proud of its new role, the department's self image also changed. Management often made public its appreciation of the important role and unique contribution of the department to the company's ability to meet orders in time.

Notice what the assembly manager did: he allowed the department to create a context for change. He had a choice. He could have said "stick to your knitting," and the department would have been reorganized out of existence. This is an example of what to do.

Let's try another example:

A number of persons are given the task of randomly wandering about the company talking to people. Call them fleabots. They can talk to anybody, have access to all meetings, and to personnel at all levels and in all departments of the organization. The rules are:

1 They can only tell people what they learn from other people.
2 They must honor the company's rules of confidentiality.
3 Their goal is to create more and more communication channels. (These communication channels are not permanent – they randomly open and close.)

Examples: A fleabot might ask things like, "So, what are you working on? So, have you solved any significant problems lately? So, what seems to be screwing up the process? So, do you have any ideas that would help? So, what's frustrating you these days?" A fleabot might tell things like, "Joe in division x is working on this problem. Jack in division y has the same problem. Dick in division z worked something out on this." A fleabot might walk into the CEO's office and say, "Engineer Harry's got idea x and can't seem to get anyone to listen to him," or, "Operator Tom thinks this would work better."

Metastructure:
1 Fleabots meet with each other, a project director and a company project liaison weekly and exchange information.
2 The project director and the company liaison meet weekly to monitor the project.

This is an example of creating human **attractors** – the fleabots. Notice that they are governed by only a few simple rules. Notice too that their first value is to respect confidentiality while promoting open communication. Respecting confidentiality is one required element of safety – the other is the rule that the fleabots can only talk about what others tell them. There are no experts being created here, just a new way of communicating corporate knowledge, in the form of sneakerware.

Attractors – a pattern representing all of the possible states of a system. Note that the pulling force implied by the word is absent; an attractor is merely a passive mapping of the pattern.

Detecting creativity and obstructionism in a mental model

The year is 1989. You are a leader of China. The students have threatened to take over the heart of Beijing. Your mission is to stop this from happening. So what do you do? First, station police everywhere. Second, prohibit gatherings of more than three people. Third, censor all communication. In your mind, mission accomplished. The counter-revolution is over before it has begun.

But wait, something unexpected is happening. Messages are getting through. The students are organizing. Somehow the outside world knows what is occurring and in detail. There must be a leak. Some spy somewhere. Find the spies. But still the information keeps flowing. When the tanks have done their dirty work, you learn the truth. It seems the students had a few fax machines and some cellular phones ... Nothing in your party training prepared you for these new-fangled Western gadgets.

The students in Tiananmen had a different mental model of communication than the party leaders in the Great Hall of the People. But the leaders of China were in good company in not understanding fax machines. When Federal Express introduced ZapMail to American businesses, the very concept of delivering documents across the country in two hours seemed revolutionary. And for a few months it was. But Federal Express, like the leaders of China, had left an important factor out of their mental models – the entrepreneurial spirit. Hey, if FedEx can send these documents around using a fax machine, why can't we? In fact, why do we need FedEx? Less than a year after announcing ZapMail to America, FedEx had indeed revolutionized the way American business sent messages to one another. The fax machine, a technology that had been in commercial use for more than 50 years, began to spread … and business communication was never the same again.

A creative mental model allows us to see what we haven't seen before, it gives a context for creativity and action to happen. An obstructionist mental model casts us into rigidity. We overlook what in hindsight will have seemed an obvious pitfall. We will not see a competitor or a regulator until it is too late. FedEx and the Chinese leadership had bad mental models. How do these "obstructionist" mental models happen? How can we tell if we have one?

Abstraction – the process of leaving out of consideration one or more properties of a complex object in order to attend to others. A general concept formed by extracting common features from specific examples.

Most modeling occurs by a process of **abstraction**. We notice and identify common characteristics from only a few examples and then formulate an abstract concept. Without our ability to do this we would be overwhelmed by new inputs and paralyzed with regard to actions. For example, we need to create the concept "chair" to cover what we sit on. With this concept we do not have to worry about the color of the slip cover, the condition of the leather, the type of wood, the height of the flat surface, whether or not it has arms, or other similar questions. Once we have that concept "chair," we can then judge the "chair-ness" of an object, so that we can decide whether or not it is safe to sit on. Essential to this process are putting aside unimportant features and stressing the important ones. "Chair" in this instance is a model of a whole class of related, but not identical, things. Most of us have a mental model for chair.

The danger inherent in the process of modeling by abstraction is to overgeneralize when it is not warranted. Especially when we have no opportunities for testing our abstractions prior to their application, there is a danger of looking very foolish once hindsight becomes our perspective. Bill learned this lesson and moved mountains to compete with Netscape. The Chinese learned this lesson (albeit with more pain) and have attempted to control their population's use of the Internet. Federal Express gave up and went back to physically delivering packages.

Given an early success, many of us have a tendency to generalize from that. Such a tendency can be dangerous and lead to an obstructionist mental model. Corporate best practices may yield similar results to the failures of most of Tom Peters' "excellent" companies. Federal Express made a massive infrastructure investment based on its early success with ZapMail. The Chinese thought they had the problem licked when they banned public meetings and censored outgoing news reports. Events would soon prove all of these abstractions to be false, but they seemed more than good enough at the time.

Part of the explanation for these obstructionist models lies in the early success of what seems to be an "if, then" rule. When the media were censored, ugly stories about China did stop in the world press. When ZapMail was launched, businesses flocked to use it. MSN stirred up such controversy that Microsoft was forced to limit the potential subscriber base to 500,000 for the first six months. What these successes hid was their situatedness. Some factor other than the "if, then" abstraction of the mental model was responsible for the success. Hindsight would deliver a better analysis, but by then it would be much too late. The general idea is that "deconditionalizing" – idly removing the context from a situation to get at its essence – is mighty powerful whether right or wrong. If you get it correct, the abstraction will serve you well. If you blow it...

In complex systems with many interlocking elements, deconditioning abstractions are dangerous. The effectiveness of an action almost always depends on the context within which it is pursued. A measure that produces good effects in one situation may do damage in another. Contextual dependencies mean that there are few ground rules that we can use to guide us. As we discussed in Chapter 2, those ground rules that do exist are critically important. Outside of those few rules, every situation must be considered afresh.

Those who have a fear of uncertainty prefer to recycle old models. It is not that they have a true belief that the model necessarily applies to each and every situation, but rather that they are comfortable with the old model and afraid of the uncertainty required to reach a new one. On the basis of some minimum of information, they will gladly reach into their bag of models and decide that a particular one applies. No more information is gathered and there is no more questioning. What worked before will work again – after all, isn't the situation the same? Many efforts at getting firms to replicate the "best practices" of others seem to us to be cut from this same cloth.

The opposite mode of behavior is equally as bad. Here, the reaction to uncertainty is never to make a decision. The model is continually to hunt for new information, certain that the critical deciding factor is waiting to be revealed around the next corner or through the next phase of the consulting project. If forced to make a decision, those who fall into this mode often resort either to intuition (I have so many factors to consider, better to go with gut feel) or "emperor syndrome" (I said it and thus it is so). If the latter, they refuse even to process information which does not correspond to their chosen model and course. What matters is not reality but their chosen fiction. Unfortunately, many people of this type seem to occupy executive suites across the US and Europe.

: Creative mental modeling

An obstructionist mental model is therefore one that fails to reflect dependence on a context. You can tell you are in one if you hear yourself using such words as:

> every time, all, without exception, absolutely, entirely, completely, totally, unequivocally, undeniably, without question, certainly, solely, nothing, nothing further, only, never, neither ... nor, must and have to.

By contrast, you can draw some comfort from noticing if your model has some ambiguity in it. Using such words as:

> now and then, in general, sometimes, ordinarily, often, a bit, in particular, somewhat, specifically, especially, to some degree,

perhaps, conceivable, questionable, among other things, on the
other hand, also, moreover, may, can, and be in a position to

is a good sign.

What matters is the modeling **process** and not the model. It is
a mistake to think that creative mental model patterns can be institutionalized. In an effort to tap into the power of ambiguity, GM set up
Saturn and Honda set up its City development team. Both started off
with fresh perspectives and the open language we highlight above.
Two years later, the words being used were very different. Indeed,
today Saturn is just a normal part of GM, and the City development
team represents a force for stability and constancy within Honda.·

The alternative to institutionalizing the creative patterns is to
remain in a state of openness. Percy Barnevik's transformation of
ASEA and Brown Boveri into the cutting-edge firm ABB is one of
management consultants' favorite examples. They stress his slashing
of headquarters to 150 people from more than 3000. What we stress
is somewhat different. Barnevik established a cadre of 500 global
managers to look after ABB's culture. These managers embody the
good mental modeling process. They are a constant source of questioning and stress ambiguity over rigidity.

Barnevik did not pick 500 managers from his native Sweden
and the cadre is not a reflection of his own personality or culture.
Instead, he was careful to select managers from all over the globe,
sensitive to their local cultures and customs, but open to learning the
processes which Barnevik considered important. Their localness
allows for situatedness, at the same time as their ABB-ness ensures the
maintenance of the few simple rules, grounded in ABB values, that are
the guidelines for the whole company. After returning to their home
bases and becoming the local focus for good modeling and processes,
these managers were then ready to take on the balancing act between
situatedness and ABB-ness wherever on the globe Barnevik needed
them. His successor Lindahl maintains these troops, which are integral to ABB's success.

Openness should not be confused with "I have not made up my
mind – please help me." Military strategist Graf von Moltke once said:

If your general is surrounded by a number of independent advi-
sors, the more of them there are, the more eminent they are, and
the more intelligent they are, the worse his situation will be. He
listens to this advisor, then to that one. He follows his first advi-
sor's essentially sound recommendation up to a certain point, then
the even sounder recommendation of his second advisor. Then he
acknowledges the validity of objections raised by a third advisor,
and the cogency of suggestions offered by a fourth. And so we can
safely bet a hundred to one, that thus equipped with nothing but
the best of intentions, he will lose his campaign.

How can you encourage creative mental modeling? Tell enabling stories. These are stories that enhance the key values and simple rules
which to you are an integral part of who you are and what your company is. Meaning is not something we possess, it is something we
make. Making sense of things, finding their meaning, is a task of
leadership. If you are to lead you must attempt to help others make
sense of things ... to find and create meaning of their own. You can
do this with stories.

Every time you tell a good story, you help others to make sense
of who they are. Encourage them to translate that story to their particular context. In doing so, they will articulate how to behave and
what action is appropriate for their situation. Mindless rote repetition
of the corporate legend(s) is not what we mean. Dialogue involving
the local organization members around a good learning story is.

Notice that we opened this section with a stress on the modeling process and now end it with a stress on openness and dialogue.
We have said little about the models themselves. We are not you. We
can't tell you to apply this model or that one. Any good model focuses
on situatedness. So process, dialogue, and openness matter. With
those, we trust you will find your way to your own good models.
Leadership is the creation of contexts in which those you lead can
make sense of their world(s).

Guidelines for respecting mental models

The next common sense is about creating an organizational context for coherent actions. To create such a context you must help the necessary others, i.e. everyone you interact with, in the process of finding meaning and of creating a coherent point of view. Another label for this process is "making sense."

This process of making sense is the key to understanding how each of us goes about acting in the world, not only in our private lives, but in our organizational ones as well. In fact, our mental models guide decisions about future actions – yours, mine, the company's, the work group's.

❖ Remember that you can only force interpretations on others – causing temporarily cohered, but never coherent, actions – at a cost. To have truly coherent actions, you must allow people to make sense for themselves. An organizational context for coherent actions can be recognized by the respect it allows for the necessary others and for their individual points of view. Don't fall in the trap of assuming that coercion has successfully revamped people's mental models. It hasn't, and it won't. The need for context and stage setting will merely lie dormant, waiting for the next crisis to strike.

❖ It is these interpretations (or sense making) that make people act. How much information we need for making sense is up to us. We have the power to decide if it is too little or too much. Beware the overgeneralizations that result from choosing to take in too little information. Equally, beware the escape from reality that can result from taking in too much.

❖ Change your mental models and priorities as the situations you encounter change. At the same time, do not seek to change the mental models of other people. In our modeling, the abstractions we bring out must be open enough to allow for the relevant context. In priority setting, that openness requires a flexibility to allow for the next idea and for the interesting stuff out on the periphery.

❖ Mistakes are essential to developing new mental models and to coherent action. Learn from the daily slogan of the IDEO Design Lab: "Fail often to succeed sooner." The question is how to get enough practice at making mistakes and learning from them without having an adverse effect on the organization of which you are a part.

❖ Help people develop new mental models by creating experiences that broaden their ability to apply their common sense to new circumstances. People can learn from being put into one situation and then another and talking about their behavior and the reaction of the others involved. Through stories people learn to create new mental models and, more importantly, to help others create them too.

Management principles

	Next common sense	**Old common sense**
The world	Complex	Complicated
Management	Guiding interactions	Leading entities
Simple principles	Adopting a global viewpoint, allowing interactions to happen	Dealing with local situations and trying to "sort things out"
Mental models	Recognizing that my model does not need to be yours, and things can still work	Giving lip service to difference, while giving incentives to conformity

Use Landscape Images

4
Use Landscape Images

Humans are good at picturing space. Our ancestors had to hunt and herd on spatial plains, so our genes have programmed us to recognize patterns in space. What we need to do is to make use of that capability to enable us to recognize patterns in business. The next common sense is about using metaphors and images that are aligned with the complexity of today's world. It is *not* about trying to force fit your complex competitive environment into the worn-out models of yesterday's merely complicated world.

Recognizing patterns is not enough, we need to take action. Most of the patterns we find are not directly accessible to action, however. To act on these out-of-reach patterns we need an **interface**, just as we do to make practical use of the computerized world of bits. Manipulating 1s and 0s directly would get a job done, but in years not seconds. Windows is the interface most of us use on our computers. The power of Windows is that it is graphical and spatial. By seeing things, pointing out others, and indicating movement, we can make our computer do what we want (at least some of the time). The interface, the pictures on the screen surface, are the items we relate to, not the arcane programming language of 1s and 0s which lies underneath and actually makes things happen.

Interface – the overlap where two theories or phenomena affect each other or have links with each other. A boundary across which two systems communicate.

The metaphor of a landscape can provide a similar interface for our mental models. Picturing our models as a landscape is reducing them to a familiar space – and relying on the dimension we feel most comfortable at manipulating. The ancient hunter-gatherers within us are landscape based – this is how we found food and avoided becoming prey.

Landscapes are powerful images. Often, for example, we can expend a lot of energy climbing what proves to be the wrong hill. Consider the saga of the PC business. As technology shifted, the hill which was best to climb shifted as well. If you picture time as a landscape of clay made by a child, then the history of major events in the PC world is similar to what would happen if an angry adult came along, picked up the model and gave it a good, hard twist. Up pops a hill where one wasn't before, and the old hills seem to fold in on themselves. IBM once owned 25 percent of Intel, all of Windows, and had the opportunity to buy both Microsoft and Apple. Lost opportunities all, and proof that the discrete events pictured in the mindset of IBM's executives were really connected hills in a landscape of meaning. What if IBM had seized on any of those opportunities? The king of the hill could have captured the power of the volcano. But by choosing to stay on its own mountain, deriding the events as solid hills of granite and not probing for the volcanic forces underneath, IBM found itself overwhelmed.

Framing – to place boundaries (a frame) around a situation for the purposes of interpolation.

Landscape images help us frame, just as photographers create powerful images by framing each image with their lens. **Framing** is the process of calling attention to some pieces of a puzzle and ignoring others, for the purpose of making sense out of what is occurring. All of us frame, all of the time.

Why do we frame? To be able to act. Unlike a computer, which can deal with vast amounts of data, we have a limited ability to deal with multiple pieces of information. There is a theory of the "magic number seven," regarding the number of items we can cope with simultaneously. By framing, we can restrict our attention to a quantity of data with which we can deal. The frame creates a boundary – what is critical is how we draw that boundary.

Why landscapes?

The use of landscape metaphors as a thinking tool started in the 1930s. Back then, "landscape thinking" was marketed only to a specialized group, biologists. But you don't need complexity scientists to think for you any more than you needed FedEx to fax for you. By using the thinking tool of a landscape, the world takes on new meanings.

Let's begin with the story of Apple computers. When Steve Jobs and Steve Wozniak built the Apple I, their target market was the hobbyist. Computers on the scale of the Apple were a toy. To enter data required manually altering the physical configuration of each machine. A real computer processed reams of data entered on punch-cards and used miles of whirring tape to record what occurred. Jobs' and Wozniak's Apple II was a milestone. Suddenly hobbyists could input data using a keyboard and see what resulted directly on a monitor. The hobby market loved Apple.

If we think about the competitive world of computers at this time, the landscape was the familiar board game known to generations of MBAs and business strategists. IBM was high on a mountaintop, the maker of serious computers, and scattered about were foothills, the makers of microcomputers such as DEC, but the game was still "king of the hill." DEC and the others were occupying the foothills, waiting for the forces of the empire camped on the mountaintop to fail. No failure, no advance. Apple was a small outpost scattered somewhere in the hinterlands. The lords of the mountain did not take note of such an insignificant player. To the DECs and others in the foothills, the outpost was like an alien from another world, not worthy of attention.

Jobs' next move was not rational or well thought out. Instead, it was the result of **serendipity**. Xerox PARC invited a group from Apple to come take a look at what the researchers there were playing with. On this visit, Jobs spied two items that changed his mental models for ever – the mouse and the

Serendipity – making a fortunate discovery of something you were not looking for, accidental sagacity.

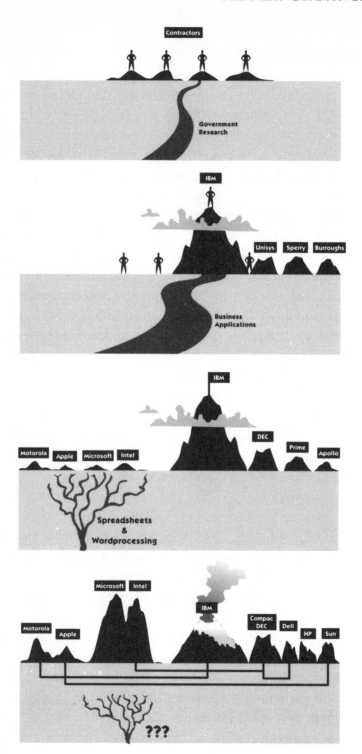

graphical interface. With these ideas in hand, the race for the Macintosh had begun.

What Jobs seized on, Xerox had ignored. The use of small computers was for the hobbyist and Xerox was "the copier company." It occupied its own mountaintop on a landscape vastly different from computerland. Apple was not even an outpost here. Jobs and crew could be safely entertained because in Xerox's mental model they were not only not competition, but not even potential competition. It was like letting the local ladies' auxiliary from the hospital in for a plant tour – good community relations and harmless to long-range plans. This was the mental model, and thus this was the reality ... at least as far as Xerox, IBM, and DEC were concerned.

As the Macintosh crew went about building a graphical interface and making use of the mouse, another non-player appeared on the landscape. Dan Bricklin was tired – tired of recalculating columns of numbers every time even one of them changed and tired of being asked to do numerous calculations to answer the question "What if?". Bricklin invented the computer spreadsheet. VisiCalc would suddenly change the way that numerical analysts did their work. Goodbye reams of accounting paper. Goodbye the need to check and recheck every addition. Suddenly, the hobbyists' computer had a practical purpose. Unbeknownst to IBM, Xerox and DEC, the landscape had acquired a small volcanic force underneath. The fixed playing field was about to change for ever, and a new, molten one was to take its place.

IBM announced the PC at about the same time as the Macintosh was born. Bricklin's VisiCalc created a whole new demand. The hobbyists weren't the ones seeking small computers – instead, it was the analysts toiling at corporate desks. This demand needed a new mental model. Careers would be made or ruined over whether a mind was capable of such a shift. But, more importantly, the landscapes had been altered.

Picture a set of mountains, each a distinct subset of the competitive world. IBM on one, Xerox on another, AT&T on a third. They are connected only by difficult-to-climb mountain passes, and the only transport is donkeys. Suddenly, two changes occur. The Swiss tunnel through the mountains and the automobile is invented.

Transport that took weeks now takes only a day. Minds must shift and the scale of the landscape has been altered, though physically every-thing looks pretty much as it did before. After the automobile comes the airplane, and now things are shifting again. And then, before you adjust to the airplane, the video conference arrives. Just yesterday trekking from IBMland to Xeroxland was the journey of a lifetime, now it is summoned up by a button on your desk and can be ended in an instant. Where is the landscape now?

The graphical interface introduced by Apple (that little out-post, remember?) would now seize the mental model of the king of the hill. IBM wanted a graphical interface for itself. Render unto Caesar the things which are Caesar's. In the process, it created Bill Gates – no good deed should go unpunished. In deciding that the toy was indeed a computer and that analysts and secretaries were legitimate sources of demand, the world had undergone another shift. Now the landscapes were merging as well as shifting. IBM's mountain was being eroded from underneath. The failures that DEC was hop-ing for would happen, but they would be a lack of water on DEC's hills and a volcanic eruption from within the camps. Intel and Microsoft, two lowly suppliers, were transforming the landscape by sheer force. The good lord IBM was blind to what it could not see. From the top of the mountain, the clouds all looked the same. Why bother looking down at the lowly earth?

With Windows 3.0, Mount St. Helens erupted. IBM's hilltop was no more. The hill itself was still there, but it was lower by a few thousand feet and had a large crater in its midst. IBMers used to look-ing up at clouds and down at earth suddenly had earth on all sides and a long donkey ride back to the transport system. Volcanoes are powerful things.

By picturing this business story in terms of the evolution of a landscape, the notion of competition in the computer world takes on a multitude of new meanings. If someone could have sensed the tran-sition that the landscape was about to undertake – from fixed to molten, from static to dynamic, new mountains forming – perhaps they would even have been able to outfox Bill Gates. The strategic moves seem much clearer from a landscape perspective than from the staid numbers and charts used by most business forecasters and historians. Grab the outpost about to become a mountain, block the strategic tunnel, build a funicular railway. And if you are king of the hill, take a lesson from the Pope – escape routes to safer ground should be continually maintained. The US strategic air command maintains a "safe base" inside a mountain for similar reasons.

Gaps and bridges

Brenda Dervin offers us a vivid picture. She suggests that we could picture individuals as continually making sense as they move through time and space in an ongoing life journey. We would add that this journey is in and on a landscape. In the metaphor, the person is moving through space and time, taking steps through experiences. A new step is taken with each new moment. Even though the step may be a repetition of past action, it is a new step because it takes place at a new moment in space and time. Movement is accompanied by the person continually making sense of their actions and the environment. For as long as the person is able to construct meaning, movement ahead is possible.

However, from time to time movement is blocked by a perceived discontinuity. The person is stopped in a situation where movement forward is prevented by the perception of some kind of gap. They have run out of understanding and need to create new sense. They define the nature of the gap and, based on this interpretation, select tactics to bridge that gap. Finally, the person crosses the bridge they have constructed in order to continue on their journey.

Research using this approach has revealed general categories by which people perceive and bridge their cognitive and information gaps, and has found that the way the individual perceives a gap is a good predictor of how they will go about bridging that gap and therefore of the kind of information they will need to help them. For example, a set of categories could describe how the way ahead is being blocked. These categories include:

❖ Decisions: having two or more roads ahead.
❖ Barriers: having one road ahead but something blocks the way.
❖ Spin-outs: having no road.
❖ Wash-outs: being on a road that suddenly disappears.
❖ Problematic: being dragged down a road not of your own choosing.

Other categories depend on perceptions (how foggy the road is), situations (how many intersections are on the road), and association (how many people are also traveling).

The staff members of Tripod, an Internet company, used this very approach to describe how they were reacting to changes in the web market. In two years of a researcher asking for descriptions and illustrations, the Tripodians kept coming back to this metaphor of a journey with gaps and bridges.

The image of gaps and bridges recurs in many contexts. Consider, for example, the notion of parts and wholes. We are constantly presented in life with spatial configurations in terms of wholes: the road ahead of us on the literal highway is there as a whole. We also know when to look at parts and when to look at wholes: examining a space or two in a parking lot tells you nothing about how full the lot is. By contrast, time configurations are not perceived as wholes, other than in historical terms. When they are half complete, we are less than comfortable about filling in the missing pieces. It is also difficult in the thick of developing events to leap back and forth in time, now looking into the future to speculate on what is likely to happen, and now looking into the past to review what has occurred.

The difference becomes heightened when information is missing. When we are shown an incomplete spatial pattern we often have some idea of how to fill in the missing pieces. But businesses must pay attention to trends in sales, markets, and production in order to try to see the way the pattern is moving. The very idea of planning is forecasting events in relation to time.

The business community is chock full of stories about those who took advantage of another's inability to calculate the effects of time. We live in time, but we have trouble picturing it. Events seem discrete and isolated. In order to fill in the missing pieces we have to project a set of new wholes. The very idea causes us discomfort and we are bad at it, unless we have specialized training or an odd personality. Instead, most people extrapolate from the given movement, either relying on immediate past events or on a theory we have clung to from some lesson previously learned. As we mentioned in the previous chapter, in such practices lie the roots of many a famous error. While we are programmed to recognize spatial patterns, and do it naturally, an entire set of professions has developed to assist us in seeing patterns over time. Strategic planners do for business what psychologists do for individuals – create meaningful patterns.

Patterns of meaning are even more difficult. This is the specialty of the academic and the myth maker. If we see events as discrete in time, we are even less likely to connect the meaning in those events, even though we long for such connections. Journalists sell millions of newspapers and hours of television by addressing this longing, but theirs is instant analysis. It is a rare historian who makes millions and an even rarer bishop, but history is still a required subject at school and for much of the world religion is a necessary part of life. Longer-term analyses are thus part of our mental models, for we are exposed to them both early and often.

Models of meaning are the hardest for us to deal with. Either we are confronted with some interesting set of words, usually encoded in jargon, or an obscure mathematical formula, devoid of actual content. The alternative to this is the 500-page dissertation explaining a set of events. None of these is simple enough to allow us to conduct a dialogue about it nor complete enough to make us comfortable in manipulating it. Sure, if you are one of the privileged few who coined the jargon or have an advanced math degree some dialogue is possible. But how is the assembly line worker supposed to deal with being told that the pattern of his emotional up and down swings is a third-class differential equation and please take five minutes off when the second coefficient is in the negative part of the saddle? To plot the course of meaning over time or space or people some other kind of model is needed – at least if we want to use it as part of management and not just write prose.

⋮ Using landscape images

⋮ By shifting our thinking to landscape images, we can convert our discomfort with time and meaning into the comfortable world of geographic space. We already do this, for example, with some of our emotions. When something special happens, we say we were moved. We describe people's mindsets as expansive or narrow, using those terms to refer to some metaphoric place of unknown dimensions. We "give an inch" sometimes, and others "take a mile." We come to believe, implying a journey, and arrive at a conclusion, though the welcome is uncertain. Landscape as interface serves the same purpose as the interface on your computer screen or telephone, to induce a comfortable metaphor so that you can forget about the tactile qualities of the model you are manipulating and pretend instead to manipulate the things modeled. Landscapes of time, of space, and of meaning can give us similar access to manipulations of mental models.

Contrast the usefulness of the landscape image to the usual 2 × 2 matrix drawn by consultants, or those nice bubble charts drawn by the business press. It is much easier to tell a meaningful story based on a landscape. Our minds can more readily create pictures of landscapes than such terms as "key success factors" and "value chain." A value chain creates an image of steel links, not of a vibrant, interrelated network of you, your suppliers, and your customers. How much easier is it to picture that network as the landscape surrounding a big city, where the farms and transportation system keep the city fed? This kind of image has much more of a story to it.

To return to the Apple example, Steve Jobs is once again at the helm. He has learned from the lessons of the past. What does he do? First, get rid of outsourced licenses. If Apple is to control any aspect of its co-evolution with the landscape, it must control what gets labeled as an "Apple product," which hills become mountains.

Second, bring in the enemy. Microsoft made a nine-figure investment in Apple. The rivalry was over. But in landscape terms a tunnel was opened to the new mountaintop. Apple may no longer

have the volcanic force to challenge the leader, but there is good business in being a supplier. The mountaintop needs food and workers.

Third, find a focus. On the selling side, concentrate on resellers
who matter. Forget the 300 or so sellers who didn't have Apple at
heart. From the landscape perspective, narrow the web, make better
and heavier use of arterial connections, the interstate highway system
(your main resellers), to strengthen both them and your interdependence. The smaller roads required too much maintenance. On the
product side, forget the Newton and other such devices. Resources
are limited and not every opportunity that presents itself can be
chased after. Palm-pilot had won this hill, so cede it. Marshal the
troops to work on the main goal.

In Apple's case, survival is dependent on getting the competitive
landscape to co-evolve with the company. The first time around Mr.
Jobs thought this was automatic; this time he knows it requires work.
To let Apple evolve in one direction and the environment in another
is to allow disaster.

Notice that Jobs' actions are not based on the concepts of discrete events and discrete worlds. The old Apple believed that the
graphics and education markets were worlds unto themselves and
that the installed base of Apple users would accept time shifts as
Apple defined them. The new Apple understands that markets are
interrelated, that what happens in the Windows world affects the
Mac world and its subparts, and that time is determined by Andy
Grove (of Intel) and Bill Gates. When Microsoft tries to buy Intuit
– a developer of personal finance and accounting software such as
Quicken – that has meaning in Apple's world (i.e. there is a bur-
geoning market for money-related software) and blissful ignorance is
an inappropriate response. The earthquake signaled that a volcanic
eruption was on its way.

To hold on to a prior mental model, to frame the world only
from within pre-existing concepts and images, to assert a sense of
control over empty words – these are signs of permanent encamp-
ment in the village. Staying in the village and ignoring the shifting
land and flows of lava is not healthy. The old Apple did not understand this; the new Apple lives it every day.

The image of the lava flow and the village forms a picture of shifting mental models. These shifts are a constant part of the new economy. Take Nike. When Phil Knight first began making and selling running shoes, his mental model was that of the "concerned athlete." Phil's shoes were made and sold for one purpose – to help his fellow runners run a bit better, jumpers to jump a bit higher, and the hurdlers to have a slightly easier stride. Thirty years later, the Nike logo assaults us everywhere. No longer is the concerned athlete the mental model – Nike has become big business and the target is us.

A similar story can be told about Prince, the inventor of large-headed tennis rackets. Or about the man who invented Big Bertha, the large-headed golf putter. In all these instances, what happened? The product was invented, a target market conceived and gone after, and contentment reigned at the house of the inventor. Within the original mental model all was well. Then along comes a shift in models. The causes vary, but the effects is the same. By shifting the context of the invention, by changing the landscape, the new mental model opened up vast new markets.

Nike recognized the consumer. Prince found delight on the face of every tennis player over 50, and Bertha delighted the same people when they shifted their play from a clay court to a leisurely walk among the greens. From sales of thousands came sales of millions.

Ray Kroc told a similar story when he was alive. He began by selling milkshake machines to a collection of roadside stands. He found one customer who needed more and more machines. This customer had a simple formula: only burgers and fries. The proprietors of that original restaurant could not buy into Ray's vision – hundreds of restaurants doing the same thing. Take the formula and spread it widely. They sold out to the milkshake machine guy, but their name – McDonald – lives on. Some 12,000 McDonald's restaurants later most of us have forgotten Kroc's name, but his vision, his mental model, lives on under the name of those who rejected it.

In each case, the shift in the mental model was what mattered. Think of Federal Express and the fax – 50 years passed between the introduction of the technology and the shift in mental model. Most of us don't realize that microwave ovens have been used in restaurants since the 1930s. Or that color television has been with us since the 1920s. Instead we think of the consumer appliances of the 1970s. Same technology, just a different mental model.

Landscape imagery is a useful tool for describing these shifts because we all recognize landscapes. If the new market is to be created, if some new action is needed, it is not enough for one person to have an idea – it must be conveyed to others. While there are many tools for this kind of communication, landscapes are the most potent.

Landscape images can create coherence

In *The Leadership Engine*, Noel Tichy provides one of the most striking examples of the power of the landscape metaphor.

> One day in April 1992 at 6:00 A.M., forty manufacturing workers climbed aboard a bus at General Electric's range-building plant at Appliance Park in Louisville, Kentucky, and headed for the annual Kitchen and Bath Show in Atlanta. They were setting out on a crucial reconnaissance mission. Appliance Park, a sprawling old 1,100-acre complex, had once employed more than 23,000 workers. By 1992, the company had closed down one of its six large production buildings and stopped making room air conditioners and microwave ovens. Employment at Appliance Park had dwindled to 9,000. The range line was losing $10 million a year, and the jobs of everyone on the bus were in jeopardy.
>
> The trip was the brainchild of Tom Tiller, who had arrived ten months earlier to take over as manager of the range plant. The plant had a history of antagonism between management and the union. At 29, Tiller was one of the company's 5 youngest plant managers, and within two weeks of his arrival, he had laid off 400 people. "The building was in a fair bit of trouble," says Tiller, putting it mildly. Even worse, it seemed unlikely to Tiller that anyone outside of Appliance Park was going to do anything to make it better. GE wasn't investing in the business, it hadn't

produced a new generation of products in twenty years and Jack Welch, GE's hard-charging CEO, was not known for his fondness for money-losing operations.

"The bus ride," says Tiller, "came from a sense of Somebody's got to do something here, and we can either wait for them to take care of it, or we can do it ourselves." The trip was both a signal to the workers about how serious Tiller considered the problem to be, and a concrete first step toward solving it. "We had to figure out how we were going to turn this business around. So we got on a bus and we rode down to the Kitchen and Bath Show in Atlanta," explains Tiller. "For a lot of them, it was the first time they were together ... design engineers and people off the shop floor and so forth. We played some cards, we drank some beer and got people kind of comfortable together," says Tiller. Then "we went through every product that was offered down there, and we said, 'Well, we could take this idea, we could take that idea.'" By the time the trip was over, says Tiller, "There was a very clear sense of 'We've got to do something. We've got to do it fast. We don't have 142 years to do it, and we're going to do it.'" And they did.

Within eighteen months, the people on the bus had spearheaded an effort that had three new products designed, built and delivered to the market. The plant went from a $10 million loss in 1992 to a $35 million profit in 1994. "There are two new production lines over there as a result of that bus ride, which is a big deal for the people in that building," Tiller told me four years later. "It's the difference between that building staying open and closing." Even today, he says, "Everybody knows what the bus ride was, where we went, why we went there and what came out of it."

The bus ride has become a metaphor for the revitalization of the plant: "Everybody knows what the bus ride was, where we went, why we went there and what came out of it." It is the symbol not only of a journey through the landscape but also of the co-evolution of that landscape. The GE workers did not just accept the landscape as given, as they saw it out the bus windows, but by taking the ride they were able to *change* the landscape. They reconnected with the evolving world of which they were a part. The new products and ideas which developed as a result of the bus ride process changed the competitive landscape for an entire industry. Tiller's leadership evoked the use of a powerful landscape metaphor to begin the task of organizational transformation, of shifting mental models.

Why is the bus ride story so powerful? It is a reflection of what leaders do best. As Tichy says:

> *They see reality by sizing up the current situation as it really is, not as it used to be or as they would like it to be, and mobilize the appropriate responses. This is a lot harder than it sounds. Seeing reality requires that leaders remove the filters that screen out the things they might not want to see, acknowledge their own and their companies' shortcomings and accept the need for change. When you miss a delivery, it's easy to blame a supplier for not getting the parts to you on time, or to blame the customer for having demanding specifications. It's a lot tougher to admit that your procurement system is messed up or to accept that the failure to give the customer what he wants is your failure to deliver and not his failure to be satisfied.*

A clue to this power is in one derivation of the word "lead," from the Latin *lira*, meaning a "furrow." This analogy evokes the image of a leader creating pathways that direct natural processes to flow along them. Leadership in this metaphor is the creation of conditions under which action can occur. Leading in this sense is like conducting. The conductor (con – with, duct – connect) forms connections which create the context which allows for action.

Storytelling is like a bus ride – furrowing a path through the ever-changing landscape. The path will be returned to again and again. Symbolically, it is the path not just of any journey but of a successful journey through the landscape. It is a source of strength and comfort, since it implies that success can once again be attained no matter how much the landscape itself evolves.

Leaders use dynamic stories about where they are taking the organization to excite people about the future and spur them to act.

There are three types of these stories. The first are "Who am I?" stories, which tell about not only the person the leader is but, more importantly, how they see the existing landscape and how it evolved from recent history. The second are "Who are we?" stories, which provide some sense of identity for a group, through common experiences or values, by describing the group's place on the landscape as the leader sees it. These are really stories about we fit in, what our place is, and what is going on around us. Finally, there are "Where are we going?" stories. In these, the leader provides a description of why the group must leave the place they are now, where they are going, and how they will get there. Tied together, these three stories are what Tichy calls a leader's "storyline." The consistency that runs from story to story gives the leader legitimacy. A landscape perspective can be a set of concepts that are seemingly disconnected, until they are brought together in stories that help people make sense of the present and take them forward to the future.

A further thought emerges from this use of landscapes that may be frightening or hopeful, depending on your perspective. Those of us who are not part of the "computer generation" think about landscapes as fixed. We need the notion of a volcano or an earthquake to express the dynamism that is increasingly part of the competitive environment. Perhaps people who fly or sail are somewhat better equipped, because the navigation of seascapes and airscapes is dynamic. But our children are still better prepared. In the virtual reality of computer worlds and video games, landscapes are dynamic – and dynamic across space, time, and meaning. Only in the virtual world can we get a simulated experience of wormholes, time tunnels, meaning connections, multiple universes, and the like. Yet these very landscapes are the models of what the evolving competitive environment holds for us and our children.

What we now consider mainstream – the trends, the fads, the gadgets, the styles, the tastes that have become popular – often comes from the visual, sensory, emotional cues of those who are considered "the fringe" or "the underground." As two of the "fringe" put it in a recent book, *Street Trends*:

We're getting more philosophical, more theological, more politi-
cal, more creative in what we speak about, because the ghetto
doesn't only exist in a physical environment, it also exists in our
mentality – it's a mind state – that's where things are going.
Instead of looking out to feel for things, it's going in – into our
imaginations to speak about things that we never thought we
would speak about ... We of the younger generation took the first
step when we seized the technology from the exploding technolog-
ical era which we were born into, and we empowered ourselves
with it. But we didn't empower ourselves like those who came
before us. We didn't buy into the dominator culture, the rat race,
violence, or mass-media pop-culture cheese ... we said "f--k all
dat!" We took voice mails, computers, our internet, turntables,
amplifiers, the ancient art of trance dancing, and we made them
our common ground, a creative sign of unity, rebellion, and
responsibility. So now we're linked up, we all have the means of
doing some major networking and supporting each other.

We dare not speculate as to the types of landscapes they will create.
All we know is that we and our landscapes will have to co-evolve with
them. Sort of like Rome facing the Goths.

Guidelines for using landscape images

Take advantage of our natural propensity to think in landscape
terms. Landscape images align with today's world – just look at the
ascendancy of the landscape motif in numerous book titles, articles,
conferences, and media events. Landscapes are part of the next common sense because they provide context we all can relate to. They
work much more easily than jargon, and are better descriptors than
the game and race metaphors of the old common sense.

❖ Ask yourself and your organization landscape image questions:
Does your landscape hold together? Does it have a sense of
integrity and coherence? Fragmented, disconnected landscapes are

difficult places to traverse and to use as a base. Examine your land-scape for integrity. Poke around to discover what is missing about missing pieces. Treat every hill as a potential volcano.

❖ Remember that viewing landscapes is an act of framing. Like the artist of old or the photographer of today, the business manager must choose which items, situations, or events will be captured within the frame of view. Integrity is a function of the frame. What rules are you using for framing? Do they fit the landscape or do they feel forced? Is there a natural coherence to the values you are applying, or have you force fit the jigsaw puzzle piece? Do your rules encourage examination of the landscape and of adjacent land-scapes, or have you retreated to a village and exiled the world?

❖ Recognize the mediums in your environment – the transmitters or carriers of information or emotion. Like the oils of a painting or the phone wire of a telephone call, the vehicle that transports information has an existence that will affect the perception of the information itself. Travel on landscapes and transformation of landscapes both require mediums – tools or vehicles. People, too, can be mediums for the exchange of information. Speaking of the members of one's network in this way conveys a sense both of how important each member is and of what actions each member can take. It is important to realize that we often see through mediums (indeed, that is why they are mediums) but that they play vital roles on the landscape. Recognizing them means talking about them and not letting them remain unseen. Ask the following: How do your employees see the landscape? How do they see where they and you fit in? Do you talk about it? Do they?

❖ Frame landscapes of space, time and meaning. Then have a dia-logue around these images.

❖ Some of the best business lessons can be neatly captured in land-scape idioms, e.g. Don't build a village in the future caldera of a volcano.

Management principles

	Next common sense	**Old common sense**
The world	Complex	Complicated
Management	Guiding interactions	Leading entities
Simple principles	Adopting a global viewpoint, allowing interactions to happen	Dealing with local situations and trying to "sort things out"
Mental models	Recognizing that my model does not need to be yours, and things can still work	Giving lip service to difference, while giving incentives to conformity
Landscape images	Thinking about ecosystems	Thinking about a car race or a football game

Combine and Recombine

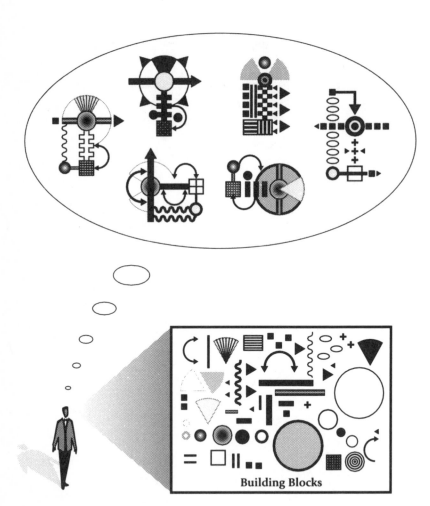

Building Blocks

5

COMBINE AND RECOMBINE

When August Roos (Johan's son) jumps up each morning, energized by a night's sleep, he runs out to his LEGO "workshop" and starts building new models or taking apart an existing one. Often, he does this while passionately explaining to his parents how he dreamt about another way to make the race car go even faster, or how another kind of building would make more sense to him. The workshop corner is scattered with LEGO pieces, partly deconstructed old models, half-made new models, and what he feels are really good models that "deserve to be kept" (at least for a few days). August has no hesitation in taking apart an existing LEGO-designed model and adding his own bricks that did not come with that particular set.

Lately, August's exuberance for LEGO has been reinforced by the LEGO Creator CD-ROM. Here, children can create and play in their own imaginary world of LEGO people, animals, buildings and machines. His adventures in the imagined world of LEGO Creator on his PC often get interrupted by his need for a more tactile experience of what he just imagined in the virtual world. Running to his 10,000-plus supply of LEGO bricks, he often grabs a bunch and starts to combine them in new ways in front of the PC. The tactile field makes up for the frustration which ensues from the unfortunate fact of life that five-year-old hands are nowhere near as fast as a five-year-old mind. And, by the way, the last thing he does before going to sleep is talk about his latest model…

As with LEGO, so too with ideas, knowledge, products, services, and the day-to-day activities that make up the modern organization. The next common sense is about increasing your ability to recognize parts and imagine how they might be recombined.

An organization's ability to adapt to change is greatly enhanced by a concurrent ability to recognize parts and imagine how they might be recombined. New knowledge is formed by recognizing that a particular thing is made up of components and combining those components in new ways. Old knowledge is recycled when systems are labeled as non-decomposable wholes or when possibilities for combinations are limited by perceptions of what is and is not "allowed." Thus, developing new knowledge is inhibited if our ability either to perceive components or to combine them is constrained. Henry Ford first capitalized on this idea when creating the assembly line and manufacturers have seized on it ever since. Yet in the coming era, such decomposition and recombination will be all the more important in the worlds of ideas and relationships.

Building blocks are integral to how we think

Imagine how confused and frazzled we would be if we had to treat everything we saw, every visual input, as a separate element. Imagine if we had to figure out connections anew each time we opened our eyes or moved them from one point to another. We don't see the world this way – instead, we see patterns. We have detectors to notice lines and boundaries. The world is organized in our eyes to highlight contrasts, before any information reaches our brains. We have other powerful organizers to frame the world, so that we group things together that are close to each other.

When a flock of birds flies overhead, we see it as one flock, sharing a common fate. Each time the flock shifts direction, we don't have to track the trajectories of each bird individually. If one bird flies off on its own, that is the bird we notice. It has broken the pattern of the common fate, and it commands our attention. The items we pay attention to tend to number seven plus or minus two. The seven change all the time, but are for their brief moment in the spotlight the building blocks on the basis of which we understand the world.

Even infants organize the visual world through patterns. Show an infant several dots moving together, and they will treat them as one unit. Send one dot off by itself, and they will be surprised. We recognize the surprise because the infant stops drinking their formula at just that instant.

Our catalogue of building blocks is vast and ever expanding. It is built up by the domains in which we move and affected by our experiences. What the novice sees and what the expert sees are two different worlds, even when they are sharing a common experience. When the experience of experts lets them see a situation, even a non-routine one, as an example of a prototype, they know the typical course of action right away. Their experience lets them identify a reasonable action as the first one considered, and usually they don't bother thinking of any others. By contrast, novices have a much smaller catalogue of prototypes. They can see the same experience but may lack a category to put it in. Instead of acting, they will first search for a reasoned understanding of what they see. Then they will act. The difference lies in the building blocks available to the expert and the novice.

The notion of what kind of building blocks and how many reveals itself in the kinds of plans we adopt. A stable environment permits more precise and detailed plans, because the stability means that we don't need to keep changing the building blocks. A rapidly changing environment favors modular plans, those that look at the situation activity by activity and not the whole at once, because these permit rapid improvization. Each module calls for its own building blocks and you don't need to deal with the requirements of the other modules. In contrast, the old, resource-limited environment favored integrated plans, which involve the building blocks of experts – full of combined prior knowledge – because using such building blocks (and not the novice's need for new searches) will be more efficient.

With building blocks in place, the unexpected can be exploited. A good example of this occurred at Japan Railways (JR) East, the largest rail carrier in the world.

> JR East never anticipated that constructing a new bullet-train line through the mountains north of Tokyo would lead it to a new and very profitable business – in beverages. The new train line required many tunnels. In the tunnel through Mount Tanigawa, water began to cause problems, and JR East engineers drew up plans to drain it away. But inside the tunnel, construction crews had found a use for the water – they were actually drinking it. A maintenance worker, whose job was to check the safety of the tunneling equipment, thought it tasted so good that he proposed that instead of pumping it away into runoffs, JR East should bottle and market it as premium mineral water. His idea was implemented, and soon the water appeared on the market under the brand name Oshimizu. Within a very short time the water became so popular that JR East installed vending machines for it on every one of its nearly one thousand platforms in Tokyo and eastern Japan.
>
> Advertisements for the water emphasize the purity of Mt. Tanigawa's snow pack, the source of the water, and the slow process by which it percolates through the mountain's unusual geological strata, picking up healthful amounts of minerals such as calcium, magnesium, and potassium. A JR East subsidiary now offers home delivery of it in cases or twenty-liter containers, and the product line has grown to include juices as well as iced and hot teas and coffees. In 1994, sales of Oshimizu beverages were $47 million. (Robinson and Stern, *Corporate Creativity*)

Think of the building blocks necessary to make this story happen. The engineers recognized the need to be rid of the water. Serendipity intervened and one of them tasted it. That taste would have been for naught, but for a critical building block – employees felt free to make even "unusual" suggestions to management if the suggestions seemed to be coherent with JR East. Central management was prepared to deal with the suggestion that the waste water could be sold. More than that, they were ready with a consumer marketing approach that did not involve selling rail travel. Their advertising department knew what images would be appealing precisely because of the travel opportunities they normally sold. Central management, knowing that they were in the transportation business and that consumer sales of beverages was a different field, had the building blocks in place of "let go" and "allow expertise to flourish." As a result, they were prepared to establish a separate subsidiary to carry out the entire task, and ultimately to become a water company all its own.

Notice that the building blocks were already there and that JR East was able to recombine them to create something both new and profitable.

Compare this to IBM's experience with the ubiquitous consumer barcode. More than 15 years before RCA made a splash with the first trade show display of barcode technology, IBM had hired the inventor of the codes. Tom Watson (then CEO) had been attracted to Joseph Woodland precisely because he held the patent to the barcode. But Watson wanted Woodland as an engineer to work on problems that IBM considered important. Ten years after hiring Woodland, IBM allowed him to sell the barcode patent to Philco, which never used it but instead sold it to Ford, which never used it and in turn sold it to RCA, which finally recognized the inherent value and committed resources to its development.

When the IBM staffers attending the trade show first saw the barcode display, they were impressed and determined to build a similar product for IBM. Imagine their surprise when in the midst of the patent search they discovered that the very inventor of the barcode was already on the payroll and had been for 15 years. They felt odd calling the executive office to request the man's reassignment to work on a product that IBM had once hired him for and then abandoned. As the new head of the barcode group phrased it, "Joe's pride of ownership was very strong at all times. Actually he sort of invigorated the whole group, because all of a sudden we felt that we really had a resource that could bring us great success." It was the nineteenth anniversary of Joseph Woodland's hiring by IBM and the twenty-third anniversary of the patent.

Here the building blocks were also in place, but they were invisible to those to whom they would have mattered.

Context is the most important building block

Clearly, there is something very different about the corporate cultures of IBM and JR East. In fact, something is not nearly a strong or inclusive enough word. Clearly, *everything* is different about IBM and JR East. The context – the setting in which the members of each of these two organization's networks find themselves – is so different that they might as well be different worlds.

Building blocks need a context which serves as a foundation on which they can rest and a set of constraints so that they do not wander while the mortar is drying. In LEGO bricks, both the foundation at the bottom and the interlocking surfaces are composed of a "clutching force" (not the mortar which holds regular bricks but an alternating pattern of circles and gaps which fit together to create the "clutching"). The surfaces themselves will not clutch a finger (infants excepted), but will clutch other LEGO with which they are aligned or cohere.

The physical configuration of the LEGO which emergently creates the "clutching" has its metaphoric counterpart in the worlds of ideas, knowledge, perceptions, and emotions. The setting of the organization is both the base on which all behavior rests (like the plastic LEGO foundation) but also the provider and reinforcer of the social norms which emergently act as the "clutching force."

At JR East, the foundation allowed an "odd" idea to be carried to management, and the context – JR's set of cultural and social norms – led to the activities which resulted in the water company. At IBM, the foundation was the overriding imperative of the mainframe computer and the context – IBM's set of cultural and social norms – was "do not question, do not challenge, do not raise the flag of a potentially competing priority." JR East makes money from its waste water, and did so from the beginning. IBM gave up a 19-year head start on barcode technology. Who could calculate how much money it didn't make?

Both the JR East and IBM contexts were consistent, but when viewed in hindsight, one was obviously more functional than the other. Your objective as a manager is to avoid creating a dysfunctional context. While the lessons of history are interesting – and we will continue with a few more – your object is the here and now.

The point to pay attention to is that **context matters**. The right context can be very enabling and the process of combining building blocks will flourish. The wrong context will be dysfunctional. In it, building blocks will be cast adrift, materials needed for construction will go begging and be hunted for, and, in the end, what might have been created will not be built. (This is what happens to August Roos on a bad day or when the wrong person makes a few discouraging comments.)

Pascale illustrates the power of a dysfunctional context with a revealing quote by a middle-level GM executive:

When you look at GM as an outsider, it seems that some of the things we're doing are crazy. But if you look closely you discover that everyone here is in a lifeboat, and no one is courageous enough to jump out. You have to realize that the system we've got today has been good to everybody. It rewards managers very, very well. In addition, all of our inefficiency means that during boom times the hourlies double their salaries with overtime, which takes care of them, too. We have hourly employees at GM making $40,000 a year, and they need that income to support the standard of living they have become accustomed to. In fact, one of the few worker complaints from our venture with Toyota in Fremont, California, is that they really have to live on their straight-time salary. They don't work overtime.

Another factor: When you truly empower employees, and initiate from the bottom up, it takes away the legitimacy of privileges. For one, it reduces the importance of the salaried ranks – and arguably even their numbers. It casts doubts on the appropriateness of a variety of management's perquisites. Managers have mahogany offices not bullpens. They park in heated garages in the winter. They have separate cafeterias with catered services. And they have large bonuses. I'm quite sure that if you took a survey among GM executives at all levels, you would find that they would not wish to give those things up, and yet those are the very things which are at stake, and which would have to be relinquished if we were to adopt a system analogous to those which we see at Toyota or Honda. In summary, the inefficiencies of the General Motors system are very beneficial for people. They do a lot of "good" for us.

This type of context tends to depress the utilization of whatever building blocks the organization has in stock. Contrast it with the type of context urged on corporations which embrace Open Book Management (from www.openbookmanagement.com).

People should see themselves as partners in the business, the pioneer figures, not on opposite sides of some labor–management fence. When the company does well, everyone should do well. And when things are tough, everyone should know it. People should be empowered – not just to ensure quality, not necessarily as part of a team, just as part of their regular daily job. Managers are responsible for setting directions, as in any business. But employees voice ideas, take part in decisions that affect them, and help run their workplace. The idea of specialized work – do your job and nothing but your job – goes out the window. And then, the most important innovation: if people are going to see themselves as partners in a business, if they're empowered to help run things, they have to understand what the business is all about. They need information – a ton of it, and on a regular basis, just as a manager does. They need a basic understanding of the financials, so they can evaluate and act on all that information. Without information and understanding, the pioneering companies believe, empowerment is just an empty word. Ignorant employees are always dependent on someone else to tell them what to do. Without information and understanding, profit sharing or stock ownership is at best no more than a nice extra benefit. Unless you act and think like an owner, you don't feel like an owner.

So at the GM of the 1980s you did what you were told, stayed within your narrow niche, learned not to ask questions, and never to volunteer information unless it was needed as part of a command. In the open book companies, by contrast, information sharing is the guiding principle. People are free in the open book context both to make use of the building blocks they have and to acquire new ones. In the GM context that Mort Meyerson described, such behavior was risking serious bodily injury, at least at a metaphoric level if not in reality.

What gives these corporate contexts their insidious power is that we generally do not distinguish between what's being thought and the context in which it's being thought through. Thus it is worth delineating some of the differences in context so as to highlight their very existence. We can summarize these contrasting contexts. The context of the old common sense is marked by 10 points:

1   Capital, technology, and labor are interchangeable and can be managed.
2   Items are discrete and rational analysis can be applied.
3   Business is separate from the rest of life; leave your home at home.
4   Profit is the ultimate measure of business performance.
5   Chains of command, spans of control, centralization and decentralization are the key dimensions of organizing.
6   Focusing on bottom-line results is far more important than paying attention to process.
7   Organizations are the personification of their leaders: Jack Welch (GE), Ace Greenberg (Bear Stearns), and Bill Gates are role models.
8   Compensation systems should reward top executives at dramatically higher rates than other employees.
9   There is a consistent tendency to see alternatives as binary choices such that "either/or" dominates lines of thought (as contrasted to "and/also").
10 The language of management sounds like war, sports, the Wild West, sex, chess, a board game, mountain climbing, and Newtonian physics.

These can be contrasted to the guiding principles of Dentsu, the largest ad agency in the world. Dentsu's ten principles were articulated by its first Chairman, Hideo Yoshida, who titled them "The Ten Rules of the Demon":

1   Initiate projects on your own instead of waiting for work to be assigned. Take an active role in all your endeavors, not a passive one.
2   Search for large and complex challenges.
3   Welcome difficult assignments. Progress lies in accomplishing difficult work.
4   Once you begin a task, complete it.
5   Never give up.
6   Lead and set an example for your fellow workers.
7   Set goals for yourself to ensure a constant sense of purpose. This will give you perseverance, resourcefulness, and hope.
8   Move with confidence. It gives your work focus and substance.
9   At all times, challenge yourself to think creatively and find new solutions.
10 When confrontation is necessary, don't shy away from it. Confrontation is the mother of progress and the fertilizer of an aggressive enterprise. If you fear conflict, it will make you timid and irresolute.

These principles are more in line with the next common sense.

Seeing is the first step

Returning to our earlier examples, Tom Watson saw the value of Joseph Woodland, but not the value in his idea or product. Management at JR East saw both the value of the maintenance worker and the value of his idea. Context matters, and what you see is a function of where you stand.

Seeing **leverage** points in business situations is critical. Leverage points play an important role in a wide variety of domains.

It is not that your context will allow you to see a leverage point as a leverage point – that would be like suggesting that you always should be able to predict the stock market – but rather that your context either facilitates or blocks your ability to see opportunities. Once you see them, you can act on them. If you don't see them, you can't. Thus seeing is the critical first step.

Leverage – the strategic advantage, power to act effectively, a way to amplify potential gains.

Consider the realization by Boeing engineers that commercial jetliners would have a big advantage over propeller-driven planes. Although Boeing's engineers had not designed such a plane and did not have a ready market for one, their context allowed for exploration, whereas the Douglas Corporation (now incorporated into Boeing) lacked such a context. Rival airplane manufacturers were not prepared to handle the market that opened up after Boeing introduced the 707.

Henry Ford's realization in 1907 that he could manufacture affordable automobiles using mass production to cut costs is a well-known example of a leverage point. At the time, Ford was just one of 30 competing automobile companies. In the early 1960s, Thomas J. Watson, Sr., at IBM, realized that a state-of-the-art system (to become the IBM 360) could change business in the way that Henry Ford's standard model automobiles changed transportation.

We have already discussed the importance of seeing parts and wholes. Now we want to focus on how what you see changes with experience and context. For example, intuition simply depends on the use of experience to recognize key patterns that indicate the dynamics of the situation. Articulating this fact removes a good portion of the mystery and fear surrounding such intuition. Because patterns can be subtle, people often cannot describe what they noticed, or how they judged a situation as typical or atypical. Their lack of ability to describe pattern recognition does not negate the recognition itself.

Recognizing a building block means seeing its parts and wholes. The recognition of goals, cues, expectations, and actions is part of what it means to recognize a situation. If managers recognize a situation as typical and familiar, they can proceed to take action. With recognition, they understand what to build (which priorities to set), which cues matter from the context (thereby preventing an overload of information), what typically to expect next (preparing themselves for both that action and for noticing surprises), and the usual ways of responding. They also recognize a course of action likely to succeed (notice we didn't say the best course, just *a* course).

If the situation does not clearly match a typical case or maps on to more than one typical case, the manager may need to gather more information. Information gathering takes time, and raise the risk that the situation will be altered by the time the information is gathered. Patterns observed then disappear and new patterns emerge. What managers in this situation frequently do not see is the likelihood of such change and its consequences. Many decisions to search for more information assume that time stands still and that information acquisition is free. It is critical to any decision that full account is taken of these complications.

Managers use metaphors as other building blocks for seeing. For most managers, the effective metaphors are those which help to organize action. These use well-learned behaviors, such as flying in formation, driving on a highway, or moving folders on a desktop, so that the new task could be performed smoothly using coordination skills that have already been developed. Metaphor does more than adorn our thinking. It structures our thinking. It conditions our sympathies and emotional reactions. It helps us achieve awareness of the real situation. It governs the evidence that we consider salient and the outcomes that we elect to pursue.

When there are anomalies or ambiguities, managers often check several interpretations to discover which best matches the features of the situation. It is at this stage that the differences between experts and novices become most obvious. Experts not only have a greater stock of interpretations (cognitive building blocks) from which to draw, but also greater experience at sorting which features are salient and which are not. Experts truly see differently as a result.

Both novices and experts build stories as a means of increasing their stock of building blocks and their ability to discern salient features. Stories are complex because they are composed of interwoven building blocks. Hiding facets of a story (making it complicated) is a successful strategy for suspense, but a miserable strategy for explanation and understanding. Thus, business stories are not the same as a mystery novel or a Harvard case study. To be coherent, a business story must aim to explain and elucidate, not to mystify or confuse. You tell stories to provide yourself or others with the benefit of an experience – giving them the ability to see a building block of which they may have otherwise been unaware. Don't spoil your ability to grant them new vision with a deliberately inserted curtain. (Curtains, of course, have many folds and are complicated – stories are told to simplify the complex, not to fold it up and hide it away.)

There is, however, one curtain which most of us construct all the time, and which a good manager tries to take down – the curtain which prevents us from seeing the functionality of a component as a component in itself.

Functionality is an important component

Think of the IKEA experience. You can go to the warehouse of this furniture company and help select the actual piece of stock you will take home. Delivery is not an issue – you take it with you. How do you know it is properly assembled? Of course it is, you've done it yourself. And if it isn't, you've only yourself to blame. At the same time, the store needs fewer stock clerks, fewer delivery people, no assembly workers. Funny how much money a store can make by seeing things a bit differently.

IKEA succeeded in rearranging the building blocks. The quality of "making deliveries" was separated from the delivery van. The quality of "assembly required" was separated from "sell a complete product." These qualities are examples of that mysterious component "functionality."

Sony recognized a style functionality when it began to market 20 different models of Walkman each year. Swatch recognized a similar style functionality and markets hundreds of different watches each year (these even have the exact same movements). The fact that people will queue solely for the privilege of buying these products is evidence that style is valuable.

But style is easy. The entire fashion industry is built around the idea that we will recognize and give value to style functionality. Designers go one step further. They often recognize that their very names can create a style functionality separate from their designs. One building block becomes two (or more if you have multiple subsidiary lines). Donna Karan sells not only her own brand but also DKNY and then licenses both to others.

Recognizing functionality and being able to separate it out as a new building block is a key to innovation and to ongoing corporate success. Much like the designers recognized the value in separating their name and their designs, it is critical to learn to see *how* something is used as separate and distinct from the thing being used.

With people, there is defensiveness about such a separation. If my job is a garbage collector, I am resentful and worry if you try to tell me that I am a truck driver and an object lifter, and that the processes of track driving and object lifting which I have mastered may be better deployed for a different purpose. (And wait until I tell the union, boy will you be hearing about this.) What do you mean by suggesting that perhaps garbage could be compacted or composted on site and that there is a need for school bus drivers?

You probably have not thought of your secretary as a travel agent (who could be earning a decent supplement to her (or his) income while booking others over your Internet connection whenever you are out on the road), nor as a librarian (who could earn lots of money for her skills at ferreting out obscure information from corporate databases or the web), nor as an events coordinator (those people to whom resort hotels pay good money to prevent expensive affairs from having that "fatal" problem which keeps the client from returning next year), nor as a transcriber (research programs pay good money for transcriptions, as do medical hospitals for recorded doctors rounds), nor as someone who performs a myriad of other functions.

Do you hope that your secretary does not start thinking of herself as capable of doing these things? Would you prefer to think that she is a "secretary" and not a person with a bundled set of process skills? Would prefer your secretary not to know that the processes may each have a greater value than the complete package? Sorry to be discomforting (especially if you have a talented and underpaid secretary). Functionality is often hidden and not seen, yet recognizing it as separate and distinct liberates both the item which is engaged in the process and the process itself so that they can be recombined in new ways to achieve greater value.

Coherence has building blocks too

Coherence has its own building blocks: purpose and identity. In a context where these two are aligned, you may not see them as distinct and it may not matter. In a context where they are not aligned (or not aligned for all concerned), seeing them separately is the crucial first step to trying to attain that alignment.

Victor Kiam of Remington (the electric shaver company) did not see the distinction. He offered employees a ten-dollar bill if they could recite the company's mission statement when he asked them. Having each employee able to recite a canned speech was an exercise in identity, but said nothing cogent about purpose. (Leaving aside the employees' desire to get the extra $10.)

The GM example of forcing the junior executive to give a presentation which he could not buy into was the opposite. Purpose was confused with identity. The executive was told get in line or get out. Tom Watson made a similar mistake with Joseph Woodland. Watson saw Woodland for what Watson wanted him for, not for who Woodland was. It took 19 years for Joseph Woodland to arrive in what for him was an aligned position.

Such mismatches between purpose and identity may have been tolerated by the Joseph Woodlands of the 1950s, but they are not so easily tolerated by the baby boomers and Generation Xers of today. Without alignment, it is too easy for this generation to take a pass on the definitions of others and a demand that they fit themselves in. They think they're entitled to a job that is fun, a job that is cool, a job that lets them discover who they really are. Work is not about paying the rent; it's about self-fulfillment.

Corey Thomas, a senior at Vanderbilt University in Nashville, is only 21, but he understands how the new game is played:

> *My mother tells me to no end that she thinks I'm self-centered in my job hunt. But the way I see it is that while I want a company that's good for me, I truly believe that if I don't perform they'll get rid of me in a heartbeat. My dad worked for Sears for 19 years as a security guard, and then he was laid off. I have to position myself so I can constantly watch out for myself. I have to be self-serving.*

Jon Bond, chairman of a New York ad agency, notes:

> *People used to do anything to get a job. A couple years ago a guy came in and stenciled every square of toilet paper with the words, "I'm willing to start at the bottom." Another guy sent me a plastic mannequin's leg with a note that said, "Now that I've got my foot in the door, check out my resume." Today everyone thinks they're entitled to a job. Last week a woman we didn't hire sent me a note letting me know she was hired elsewhere. The note read: "You lose."*

Again, what you see is a product of where you stand.

Guidelines for combining and recombining

In the complicated world to which the old common sense was attuned, it seemed self evident to deal with apparent complexity by trying to break things apart and then deal with the pieces separately. This was a sound strategy when entities mattered more than interactions. But the interactive world of relationships and processes is very different.

The beauty of pieces, of building blocks, is that they can be combined and recombined to create new things, new ideas, and new ways of relating and interacting. In a world where wholes are not simply the sum of their parts, it is critical to train ourselves to think about deconstructing and recombining. The philosophers may call this postmodernism – we call it the next common sense.

❖ Treat ideas as if they were LEGO bricks. Recognizing parts that can be used as building blocks is the first step to creating a context for new actions. Combining the parts is the second step. Stories are a tool for helping yourself and others to recognize what is a part, what is a whole, what is salient, what is not, and what kinds of combinations make sense.

❖ Look for recombinations. LEGO and its competitors have appeal precisely because they encourage combinations and recombinations in a limitless fashion. They cohere around the idea of "see parts – combine – make wholes – bust into parts – recombine – make new wholes." To make new things we first have to recognize that those that already exist are made up of separable parts. Then we recombine those parts. In computer science this is known as object-oriented programming. In the home it is known as gourmet cooking.

❖ Recognize functionality as an important component and separate it out as a new building block. This is key to innovation and to ongoing corporate success. Much like fashion designers recognize the value in separating their names and their designs, it is critical to learn to see how something is used as separate and distinct from the thing being used.

❖ Ensure that combinations and recombinations are aligned with the two components of coherence: purpose and identity. If not, it is inevitable that you will lose your best people – to the coherent place next door, around the block, or a URL away.

Management principles

	Next common sense	Old common sense
The world	Complex	Complicated
Management	Guiding interactions	Leading entities
Simple principles	Adopting a global viewpoint, allowing interactions to happen	Dealing with local situations and trying to "sort things out"
Mental models	Recognizing that my model does not need to be yours, and things can still work	Giving lip service to difference, while giving incentives to conformity
Landscape images	Thinking about ecosystems	Thinking about a car race or a football game
Combine and recombine	Asking about how parts can be combined into new and better wholes	Segregating parts to be treated as their own self-sufficient wholes

Recognize Your Multiple Roles, Don't Hide From Them

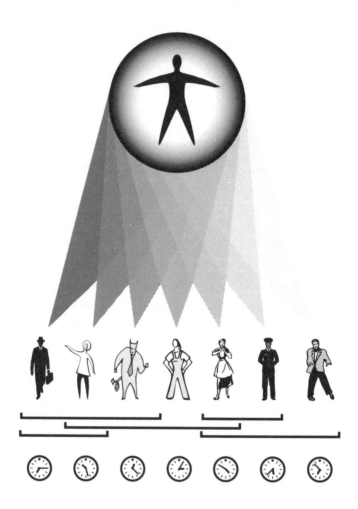

6

RECOGNIZE YOUR MULTIPLE ROLES, DON'T HIDE FROM THEM

It has been another typical day for Lisa Stevens. At 7 a.m. when she left for work, the alternator blew on the car and she spent a miserable half hour at the service station patiently explaining to the mechanic that no, she did not need to talk to her husband before authorizing the repair. Once at the office (and by now a full hour late), she was so harried that she nearly missed the early termination clause in the $1.3 billion contract she was signing for the firm, but she saw it in time. Her team of assistants was subjected to the wrath she could not quite dish out to the mechanic (after all, he had her car captive, but she was their boss). "Early termination ... when was the last time I authorized an early termination clause? ... get it out and today ... I want to sign this afternoon." In the middle of this angry speech, there's a phone call from Harvey Rund, her most important client. Anger is tossed aside, sweetness and light are all that can be heard from Lisa's side of the telephone. Relieved, her staff slip out quietly.

At 11 a.m. crisis hits. Josh has a fever, says the school nurse, please come and get him. Harvey Rund is due at the office for lunch. Jeff, her husband, is in Tokyo and can't just swing by to pick up Josh. Lisa tries to reach her mother, but it's Tuesday and Lorraine is on the

golf course on Tuesdays. Can she ask Mark, her secretary, to go get
Josh? Not a great idea. Mark gets huffy about non-job-related tasks
(as he defines them – get coffee, yes; make copies, yes; drop the client
at the airport, hell no). What could she do?

Mark buzzes that the school has called again. Today of all days.
Can't they just give him an aspirin and tell him to lie down? Wait,
what am I saying, this is my eight-year-old I'm talking about. The
perfect child – except when he gets sick right before Harvey is coming to lunch. How will the contract get signed (without that damned
early termination clause) if I'm not here to remind Harvey that we
never sign early termination clauses? If I leave it up to Jim and
Rhonda, the contract will have us paying Harvey for the right to stay
in instead of him paying for the right to leave early. Josh, Josh, why
today of all days?

If this sounds all too familiar, it is because everyone has days
like Lisa. Whether we like it or not, we each occupy a multitude of
roles and they have a nasty habit of making conflicting demands just
when we don't want them to. In the workplace of today (at least in
America and most of Europe), the issues raised by the roles of work
and family have moved to the forefront of employee/employer relationships. The old command-and-control model of "Josh will just
have to wait" may have worked fine when father was at work and
mother was at home, but the 1950s picture of the perfect family has
not been true for decades (if it really ever was). In today's corporate
environment, the demands placed on Lisa are not uncommon. But,
knowing what to do, having a coherent understanding of which roles
take priority when, is not yet a part of the corporate landscape.

The notion of multiple and conflicting roles is important if the
goal is coherence. While each of us is a single person (and while our
organizations like to be thought of as a single entity), in reality within
the structure of this one self lies a creature who must fit into many
different roles and who bears many different responsibilities. Who
among us has not felt torn between the demands of a sick child at
home, and a business deal that will fall apart if not attended to yesterday? The tension from conflicts among these roles works to dissipate a sense of coherence, while resolving such conflicts enhances

coherence and its related qualities. Multiple levels and roles are in some sense a separation between being a part of one thing and a whole of something else – e.g. a subordinate and yet a product team leader.

The old common sense says that work comes first. Work is whatever the company says it is. As new tasks appear or as conflicts occur, then answers are there waiting to be revealed, i.e. do what the boss tells you. In a world of complication, it is not surprising that facets remain hidden, to be unfolded and revealed by the boss or corporate headquarters, as necessary (and only on a need-to-know basis). Under this scenario, Lisa's choices are simple. Don't waste time with the mechanic, Jeff will deal with it when he gets home, so take a taxi to work. Josh will wait – the school will understand that work is more important and so will Josh. Lorraine will accept a scolding for being unavailable and will tell Lisa in turn that if she were a good mother she would be home for Josh and not playing footsie with Harvey to help the boss land that big contract. But in that world Lisa couldn't be the boss.

In the complex world of today, Lisa is the boss and Jeff (reachable by videophone at a moment's notice) still can't get to the school to pick up Josh. Lisa's multiple roles have all reared at once: boss, mother, supplier, spouse, daughter, parent, and consumer. And it is only 11 a.m. The next common sense recognizes the multiple roles and understands both that they will conflict and that each has its place. This understanding will not solve Lisa's multi-lemma, but it can shed light on how not to get into the trap in first place.

Lisa's mistake is to have assumed that she could handle all the roles at once. Like the rest of us, she is only human and it is hard to express several roles at the same time. We can *have* several roles at once, that is to be expected. But expressing them is a horse of different color. The issue is one of attention.

Concepts such as foreground and background come in handy in assessing how to "be" multiple things at once and yet to "do" only one or two at a time. The scene, the context, captures all of our roles with some more prominent (foreground) than others. The scene itself is background. What we choose to do when, that is foreground. Notice that we often say we "take things out of context," yet never do we say we "do things out of context." We do what we do, but it is our choice to recognize that the context – the multiple roles, the background – exists, or to pretend that it does not. The old common sense argues for pretending – the next common sense urges that we accept the entire picture, warts and all.

⋮ Success through multiplicity

⦂ Recognizing and respecting multiple roles is a speciality of some very successful companies. Whole Foods, a US supermarket chain, is a firm believer in local stores having autonomy for local decisions. Though centrally owned and making use of central shipping and purchasing, each local Whole Foods store has a definite community feel. Food choices, layout, and timing of price specials are decisions made by the store team and not headquarters.

Global conglomerate 3M encourages not only its researchers but also its managers to take 15 percent of their time to "explore." The company recognizes that scientists are at their most creative when working on projects of their own choosing. The creativity unleashed carries over into their assigned tasks as well.

Perhaps the best example of multiplicity is an American firm known as Thermo Electron. Thermo Electron was founded in 1956 by Dr. George Hatsopoulos, a Massachusetts Institute of Technology researcher and professor of mechanical engineering. His original plan for Thermo Electron was to develop commercial applications for thermodynamics – the study of converting heat directly into electricity – an application still unrealized by the company. By the early 1980s, Dr. Hatsopoulos was looking for a way to continually renew the energy of the business, and the company needed funding to further development of its heart-assist technology. The solution was to "spin out" Thermedics, one of the core businesses. Spin-out, as Hatsopoulos conceived it, is the opposite of spin-off. With spin-off a peripheral business is cast aside; with spin-out a core business is given access to the public capital markets while retaining a strong affiliation with (and long-term part-ownership by) the parent. Thermo Electron only spins out strong core businesses when they are ready to stand on their own and when a continued dependence on the parent for capital is a detriment.

By recognizing each role (creating it as a separate, stand-alone company) and respecting the role (allowing the subsidiary to spin out and gain its own recognition, capital, and master plan) Thermo Electron was honoring the many roles of the employees and business units within it. In the process, a very strong set of incentives were created for both employees and the parent company. To employees, success meant the chance to do one's own thing with the support of but not the constraints of the parent. To the parent, as subsidiaries grew and prospered, managerial attention could be allocated to the start-ups and to the weaker siblings. The strong would both take care of themselves and contribute to the well-being of the Thermo family. Wall Street has reacted well to this strategy and so have employees: Thermo has one of the lowest turnover rates in the high-tech field.

This sounds like decentralization, you say. And it is. But it is decentralization only of the units that are able to be decentralized. The stronger your unit is in the Thermo system, the more likely it is to be spun out. By contrast, most corporate decentralization strategies and structures begin with a philosophic statement, "we should decentralize," and so they do, everything. But decentralization works well for some and not at all for others. That corporate America has spent a fortune hiring back its own laid-off executives and middle managers as employees of "outsourcers" is a testament to the failure of a broad-brush approach to decentralizing. Thermo Electron said no to the broad brush and instead puts in the effort to identify the right time for each unit to be spun out and with how much autonomy. The underlying concept "decentralize" may be the same, but the application and focus are very different.

Holon not synthesis

When you think of a successful computer-related company, which ones come to mind? Intel and Microsoft, the Wintel duo, are a likely choice. But in the excitement over the Internet and low-cost PCs, few seem to remember the dark days at Intel – days that reflect multiple roles and their conflicts as much as does Lisa's story above.

Intel was a memory company. That's right, memory, the cheap $1 to $3 per Mb chips you now stuff into your computers 64Mb at a time. The founders of Intel (Moore and Noyce, Grove came later) were convinced that there was a market in replacing expensive mainframe magnetic core memory with cheaper semiconductor memory. And they were right. So right, that Asian factories did the same and nearly destroyed the company. In a commodity market, those with the lowest costs win, and Intel did not have the lowest costs.

Noyce and Moore were noticeably luckier than Lisa, because the company had many other product lines that had been overlooked. Senior management may have seen it as a memory company, Wall Street may have seen it as a memory company, but Intel was more than that. It made processors as well as memory. Processors in the early 1980s were not what we think of today. Volume was much lower and there was competition. Intel had the 8086 and the 80286, but Motorola had faster RISC chips and Apple was still a big thing. But, even more importantly, Andy Grove saw that the microprocessor was not a commodity. The skills of Intel's workforce could be used to produce a money-losing commodity (DRAM memory) or a not-so-sure product, the specialized microprocessor. Grove made his choice and we all are living with the results. (The machine we typed this book on proudly says "Intel Inside.") Intel was rescued by its own multisidedness. Contrast this with Zenith (yes, Zenith was once in the memory market too).

The Romans had a god for this type of reasoning. Janus was the god of beginnings and endings, the guardian of doorways. He had two faces, one that looked in and the other that looked out. Arthur Koestler took the idea of Janus and coined the word "**holon**." This word concisely expresses the idea that everything (like atoms, cells, solar systems, cars, and people) is simultaneously a whole in and of itself and a part within larger systems. The holon is a central principle of general systems theory. It is the idea

Holon – as coined by Arthur Koestler, something that is simultaneously part and whole, and that has multiple roles simultaneously.

that life, and the universe, and everything in between structures itself in levels, subsystems comprising systems within supersystems.

We use the holon idea when we "go up a level" to a higher authority, broader scope, and more abstract view. We also use it when we "go down a level" to more detail, narrower scope, and more concrete views. It is useful to picture people's multiple roles as holons, for example:

1 The self (Josh).
2 Members of groups (Josh and his classmates).
3 The groupings of groups – the company, the organization, the community, and so on (Josh, Lisa, Mark, and Harvey, who got dragged along to pick Josh up, lunch will just have to wait).

Though a new word for most people, holon can stand for organizations, small groups, and individuals. It is logical (if a bit strange) to say: "a team is a holon composed of individual holons that are part of a larger organizational holon." An autonomous individual is transformed into a member of a team; then there is the transformation of individual members into the group as a whole; and finally comes the transformation of a group of individuals into a new level, an organization, or even a community. (And as part of that community, Lisa told Mark stop whining and keep Harvey entertained while she put Josh to bed.)

What we draw from the story of holons is the importance of recognizing and respecting multiple roles. The context we find ourselves in determines which facet gets the focus of attention. This is no different than trying to take the perfect photo while on your vacation in paradise. There is the beautiful landscape and there is your spouse. Where do you focus? Who is the picture for? The in-laws? That's one photo. The kids? Another. Joe, your neighbor who always shows you his 1000 perfect slides from his picture-perfect trip (of which he takes three a year)? Or perhaps the guys you play basketball with at the gym? Maybe for them, you forget the spouse and get the cute blonde on the beach. (If you do this, try to keep in mind which one of you is picking up the photos from the photo shop. No need for an argument, the guys at the gym aren't worth it.) It's the same trip, despite the awesome variety of photos that could be taken. Just as you are the same person, despite the many roles you find yourself in.

Synthesis – the putting of two or more things together, so that the combination becomes a whole.

The opposite of recognizing and respecting multiple roles is to synthesize them into one. The very word **synthesis** has the same root as synthetic – fake and artificial. There is a time for fakes and reproductions. It is much safer to walk down the street with a 10-carat cubic zirconium ring than a diamond of similar size – but don't wear the fake to an auction of Impressionist paintings, the folk at Christie's may choose not to let you in. The joy of a reproduction, a fake, a synthesis is its simplicity. No longer do you need to be concerned with many things (neither folded, i.e. complicated, nor woven, i.e. complex) but just with the essence, the simple truth. But truth is rarely simple and life seldom still. Unless you are confronted by simplicity, it is doubtful that extracting a oneness from the multitude of possibilities is a fruitful long-run strategy. The following story from our friends Philip Kirby and David Hughes may illustrate what we mean:

Dylan is five years old. Typically, he's in constant pursuit of his nine-year-old brother Chad. And Chad, like most older brothers, is always picking on Dylan. Chad and two of his buddies are hanging out in his room one day when Dylan comes wandering in.

Chad says to his buddies, "Hey guys, wanna get a laugh? Watch this." His friends eagerly gather around. "Dylan, come here."

Dylan, pleased with the invitation, breaks into a big grin and looks up with great anticipation.

Chad sits down on the edge of the bed and holds out his hands, palms up. In his right hand is a dime and in his left a nickel. He glances back at his buddies and whispers, "Watch how stupid Dylan is." Turning, he flashes a know-it-all grin at his brother's innocent face. "Hey Dylan, which one of these coins do you want, the big one or the small one?"

Dylan's eyes ponder his choices for just a moment. "This one!" The little guy shoots out his hand, grabs the nickel, jams it in his pocket, and leaves the room.

Chad triumphantly closes his hand on the dime, breaks into a smug smile, and turns for approval from his buddies. Both boys are in stitches. Chad stops chuckling long enough to say, "Is that stupid or what? And he does it every time. I can't believe it – he always falls for it."

"He's so stupid," chimes in one of the buddies.

A large shadow fills the doorway. The laughter is cut short. It's Chad's and Dylan's father. "Chad, your brother is not stupid, and I don't want you playing that trick on him again. Do you hear me?"

He gets a guilty reply. "Yeah, okay. We're just playing, Dad. Dylan doesn't care. He likes it."

His father interjects sternly, "Well, I'll have no more of it, and I'll speak to Dylan, too." He turns and heads for Dylan's room.

"Hi Dylan. How're you doing,"

"Hi Dad." Dylan, sitting in the middle of his bedroom floor surrounded by LEGO blocks, hardly looks up.

"Dylan, I want to explain something to you." Lowering himself on to the floor, he leans back against the end of the bed.

"Okay Dad."

The father then spends the next five minutes putting the value of nickels and dimes into context for his son. Using pennies, nickels, dimes, and quarters, he shows his son that the size of the coin does not always represent the value of the coin. Throughout the chat, Dylan listens carefully and his continual head nodding seems to indicate that he understands.

"So, do you see the difference between a nickel and a dime?" asks his father.

"Yeah. A nickel is 5 pennies and a dime is 10 pennies," he answers proudly.

"Good. So the next time Chad asks you to pick a coin, which one are you going to pick?"

"The nickel," came the quick reply.

"No Dylan. Not the nickel, the dime – it's worth twice as much."
Exasperation is all over the father's face.

Dylan reaches under his bed and pulls out an old sock. He takes
a handful of nickels out of the sock and holds them up to his father.
"Yeah, but if I take the dime Chad will stop playing the game with me ...
and look how many nickels I've gotten from him!"

The father's synthesis works if the game is to be played only one time.
Younger brother and father both gain respect. Older brother learns
not to tease the younger. But if there are multiple plays of the same
game, that changes everything. Dylan clearly is the wisest of the
three, since he is accumulating the nickels. The role of accumulator
was more important to him than the cost of being labeled as stupid.
In common parlance this is known as being dumb like a fox. Intel succeeded by capitalizing on the right role at the right time. Synthesis –
we make DRAM – would have been the trap of death. For Lisa,
synthesis – I am my company – is what got her into the 11 a.m. crisis.

Failure in artificial unity

Our holonic natures need to be recognized in deeds and not
merely in words. This is what we mean by "respect." Its absence,
despite propaganda to the contrary, can tear an organization apart just
as its leaders are proclaiming its inherent unity to the world.

Consider Allegis Corp. You don't recognize Allegis? Perhaps
you know its parts: United Airlines, Hertz, Westin and Hilton Hotels.
Allegis was supposed to revolutionize the way we travel and achieve
synergies among the flight we take, the car we rent, and the bed we
sleep in. As a vehicle for delivering value to consumers, Allegis was a
great idea, but about 10 years ahead of its time. Where Allegis and its
architect, UAL chief Richard Farrell, failed was in addressing the
roles and expectations of its employees. United's pilots did not like
losing their perceived status as the "important ones" at the company.

Other airline employees wondered about being made comparable to "mere" car rental people. The reservations clerk stationed at the Hertz drop-off booth resented being "off airport." Then there was the diversion of revenues into making property improvements at the hotels rather than buying new planes and flying new routes. Senior management at Allegis had a unified idea, but they failed miserably in getting it embraced by their organization. The very unity they proclaimed was undermined by the fractures and divisiveness that management did not want to recognize. Less than a year after Allegis was born, hostile takeover offers forced it apart.

Consider the recent break-up attempts at Andersen Worldwide, a global accounting firm married to a management and technology consulting firm whose mission is "to help its clients change to be more successful." Such change was not accomplished within the two halves of Andersen. Formed from a common base, the consulting and accounting arms each went their own way, bonded by a common name, a revenue-sharing arrangement, and little else. Andersen Consulting was supposed to be a spin-out à la Thermo Electron, but it was a spin-out without communication and without strong parental ties. Employees had little sense of what Andersen Worldwide was, while they did have strong identification with their unit. When push came to shove and there was a fight about money, all that was left of the unity was a hollowed-out name.

From a different domain, witness the evolution of the large for-profit hospital chains and HMOs (health maintenance organizations). While there is constant pressure for cost savings from patients and insurers, there is also a sense of place that attaches to the local hospital and doctors' offices. The large chains saw the local "niceties" as an easy answer to higher profits and lower costs. The localities involved saw a loss of local institutions and the substitution of McCare. The backlash has forced the chains to devolve, to put back more autonomy at the local level and to rebuild both community and doctor relations.

The contrast between the operating style of Whole Foods and the operating style of these "proclaimed unity" corporations is like night and day. Decision making at Whole Foods is located where it will make a difference, local for some things, national for another. At the unity companies, the proclamations say "we care" and the actions say "only about ourselves." Or, as one of our friends puts it, "The lips are flapping but the feet ain't moving." Failure to respect the multiple roles of employees, citizen, customer, and supplier has cost these firms dearly.

Epitomizing this type of decline is Apple computers. The cutting-edge technology spirit of Apple, its "all for oneness," was undercut once the project teams charged with developing the Macintosh and the Lisa (a little remembered, very powerful and too expensive failed product line from Apple) went into competition. The Mac team was even allowed to fly its own flag above its building on the Apple campus. The Apple hardware model – we build it, you buy it – was the very opposite of the PC makers, who had clones and clones of clones. The Apple world was a closed system. It proclaimed unity to the world and drove out those who could not buy into its enforced synthesis.

And what happened is that the world quietly passed Apple by (although by 1998, Steve Jobs was back – a coherent force – to attempt a final rescue). Customers who had their needs ignored or who were told "we know better" went elsewhere. Innovative software programmers switched platforms – not that they liked Microsoft better, but at least Microsoft did not tell them what to do. But what one hand giveth the other taketh away. As this chapter is being written, Microsoft is disclosing its own versions of Apple's sins. Apple enforced a false unity internally, Microsoft is enforcing one externally. Where Apple declined as the market moved on, it remains to be seen what happens when the coerced unity of the Microsoft world shatters in light of antitrust pressures.

To ignore holons and assert false synthesis is to risk fracture.

Why Richard Branson doesn't knit, or using multiple roles as building blocks

Tom Peters has made a lot of money telling companies to stick to their knitting. Richard Branson has made much more money ignoring that very advice. A record label and a cola seem very different from a bridal shop and an airline. What they have in common is

Richard Branson and his team of entrepreneurs.

Richard Branson founded Virgin as a mail-order record retailer and shortly thereafter opened a record shop in Oxford Street, a prime shopping area in London. During 1972 a recording studio was built in Oxfordshire. The first album of the newly created Virgin Records went on to sell over five million copies and over the years many household names, including Steve Winwood, Paula Abdul, Genesis, Phil Collins, Peter Gabriel, and The Rolling Stones, helped make Virgin Music one of the top six record companies in the world. The equity of Virgin Music Group – record labels, music publishing, and recording studios – was sold to Thorn EMI in 1992 in a $1 billion deal.

Virgin Atlantic Airways, formed in 1984, is now the second largest British long-haul international airline and operates a fleet of Boeing 747 and Airbus A340 aircraft to New York, Miami, Boston, Los Angeles, Orlando, San Francisco, Hong Kong, Athens, and Tokyo. Virgin Holidays, formed in 1985, is one of UK's largest long-haul tour operators, specializing in East and West Coast USA.

The interests of the original Virgin Group have expanded into international "Megastore" music retailing, book, and software publishing, film and video editing facilities, clubs, travel, hotels, and cinemas through over 100 companies, including Virgin Direct Personal Financial Services, a joint venture with Norwich Union established to sell financial services by telephone, Virgin Vie, a cosmetics and beauty care company, and Virgin Bride.

The various Virgin companies and their joint ventures currently employ over 15,000 staff and operate in 22 countries. In 1998 there were eight main divisions: Virgin Communications, Virgin Retail, Virgin Travel, Voyager Investments and Virgin Hotels Group, Virgin Radio, Virgin Entertainment Group, and Virgin Direct, each of which operates autonomously. Virgin is one of the UK's largest private groups and has achieved organic growth (without any major acquisitions) from sales turnover in 1983 totaling £50 million to sales turnover in 1995 (excluding Virgin Music) of over £1.5 billion.

When the multiple roles have a strong identity behind them which is respectful of the separate worlds in which it operates, there is the opportunity for brand extension and profit. Analysts claim that

Branson is expert in none of the many areas in which Virgin operates, despite his profits. So what is his means of success? He looks for business fields where change has been slow or non-existent and where the current leaders have synthesized their positions.

Take the UK market for cola as an example. Both Coke and Pepsi assumed that large advertising dollars were a barrier to entry in the field. No other cola could make an inroad because of the expense involved in matching the advertising and promotion budgets of the top two. Surprise – both Branson and supermarket retailer Sainsbury's challenged that wisdom. Within three months of their entry, the cola market had been redivided. The two "low to no" advertising brands (Branson's Virgin and Sainsbury's Own) had captured more than 30 percent of the market.

Branson and Sainsbury's both capitalized on a holonic perspective. Each was perceived by the British public as standing for "quality" and "value" and "truth." So if they say "we will give you a quality cola," the public believes them. The Virgin name, until then an airline and a record shop, was now a soft drink. The link was the image of quality and the strong identity that that image captured for the public. Virgin's ability to recognize that the perception of value held by the public could be activated in new arenas and new roles is an example of the next common sense. Insisting on a narrow focus – only one market that will reinforce the Coke or Pepsi name – was old synthesis.

The contrasting perspective also applies. When Virgin extended its quality franchise to rails, the point got lost. The image of quality could not overcome the reality of rails, which are anything but. Quality image and reality are easier to converge in a new field than when taking over an old one.

Separate out the foreground

The perspective we are suggesting on multiple roles can be seen as analogous to allowing a symphony orchestra the opportunity to play modern jazz. The orchestra is used to playing in harmony, most of the players in the background or all together, occasionally a soloist doing their part. With jazz, however, each player has the opportunity if they want to take a forefront role and improvise, with the remaining players serving as backup. The forefront role is likely to move around the orchestra, and even more so once its members have gotten used to this new freedom. The orchestra as a whole remains the same. Ask for Beethoven and the sound will be as sweet as before.

The portfolio of roles in an orchestra is like the portfolio of roles we all face. The players function as individuals, as team members, as orchestra members, and as symbols for the community or school of which they are a part. Each player represents a potential – in the orchestra for sounds; in your life for situated actions. In classical music the forefront roles are few and well restricted; in jazz they are many and free. In both types of music, the potential is there for foreground, for gaining the spotlight, for attention.

Another analogy might be the "Magic Cube," a device sold in novelty stores or through catalogs. Inside a ball or cube with a small translucent window floating on a gel-like substance is an eight- to twenty-sided solid. On each face of the solid is written a piece of advice or a directive for action. If you are confused about making a decision, just consult the Magic Cube. Give it a good shake, then set it down. After a while, one of the facets of the solid will step into the forefront. Your decision will now be visible in the little window. All the other possible decisions or actions remain in the cube, in the background. Any of them could have stepped to the foreground, but only one does so. (If you don't like the answer, just shake again!)

Notice how different this notion of foreground and background is from that of *separating* roles. If you have one self at the office and one at home, what do you do when the two roles collide? You are not Dolly the sheep. Cloning is not a viable solution. What you do is ensure that for each of your many roles, you have a grasp on foreground and background – what steps up for attention and what recedes to the background. What you must also do is realize that it is still the same overall scene and that it is you who switches where attention is directed. The scene is your life and the spotlight control lies in your hand.

Richard Branson is self-aware of the control switch in his hand. Andy Grove was well aware of his for Intel. Steve Jobs lost sight of the control switch and tried to keep a single spotlight shining on first a dividing scene and then a fading one. At Thermo Electron, not only does Hatsopoulos know that he holds his switch, but he makes sure that his best employees know that they too are holding one. Spin-out is a way for their units to take the forefront, and then to develop their own units for spinning out.

Guidelines for recognizing your multiple roles

We question whether it was ever common sense to insist that the company always comes first, but clearly that has been a norm in big corporations for years. In the next common sense it is critical to allow people to be themselves. Only by acknowledging the many sides of each person can a company hope to obtain maximum benefits from that person over the long run. Most firms recognize this for their CEO – it is time they recognized it for the troops in the trenches.

- ❖ Visualize your multiple roles. You are not a many-headed Hydra, but a different version of you is needed for various situations. They are all you, but acknowledge and respect their differences. Whenever possible, you want to embody Janus. (And no, we do not mean go to a spa and pretend to be a Roman god.) The notion of a holon tries to capture this many facetedness of you. After you have visualized this about yourself, try to remember that it applies to everyone else as well.
- ❖ Think about those multitudes as alterations of foreground and background. Your visualization should not be separate selves in separate settings. There is only one you. But you have many facets that you can call on as the situation demands. The facet up front is foreground, the others recede into the background, but they are still there.
- ❖ Be flexible in altering what is foreground and what is background. The great picture may be the sunset, but your spouse wants to be included. The camera of life is flexible enough to accommodate

both within a short timeframe. If Kodak can do it, so can you. If you like, think of it as flickering a diamond's many facets to catch the light best.

Management principles

	Next common sense	Old common sense
The world	Complex	Complicated
Management	Guiding interactions	Leading entities
Simple principles	Adopting a global viewpoint, allowing interactions to happen	Dealing with local situations and trying to "sort things out"
Mental models	Recognizing that my model does not need to be yours, and things can still work	Giving lip service to difference, while giving incentives to conformity
Landscape images	Thinking about ecosystems	Thinking about a car race or a football game
Combine and recombine	Asking about how parts can be combined into new and better wholes	Segregating parts to be treated as their own self-sufficient wholes
Multiple roles	Allowing people to be themselves	Insisting that the company come first

Create Canyons, Not Canals

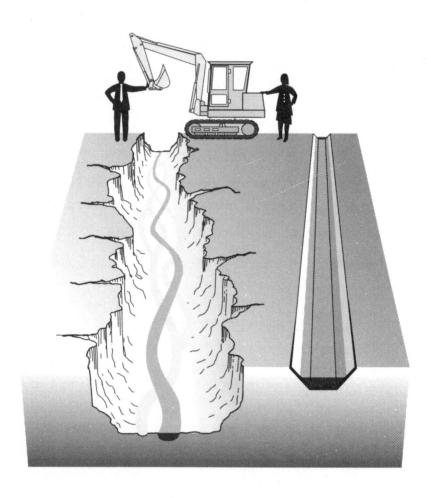

7

CREATE CANYONS, NOT CANALS

When Leo Burnett stepped down as chairman of his ad agency in 1967, he offered words to work by in his departure speech. More importantly, he told employees that if they didn't hold true to his basic values, he would insist they take his name off the door. "And, by golly, it will be taken off the door. Even if I have to materialize long enough some night to rub it out myself on every one of your floors. And before I dematerialize again, I will paint out that star-reaching symbol too. And burn all the stationery. Perhaps tear up a few ads in passing, and throw every goddamned apple down the elevator shafts. You just won't know the place the next morning. You'll have to find another name." Leo had created a canyon and would be da*ned before he would let his company leave it.

Water flows downhill. Energy is like water and follows the path of least resistance. Our friend Max Boisot calls this the **"least action principle"** – whatever method requires the least amount of energy expended to accomplish the stated purpose, that is usually the method employed. The old common sense involved a lot of canal building – ignore the idea that water flows downhill, we can move it to where we want to go. Locks and dams have their analogues in such things as corporate dress codes, "the way we do things around

Least action principle – Max Boisot's term for the concept that the method employed will be the one that requires the least amount of energy expended to accomplish the stated purpose.

here," and the organization chart. The analogue of the Russians reversing the course of a river is the resistance we all have encountered from our company's bureaucracy. The next common sense is about not fighting the least action principle but taking advantage of it. To take advantage we need canyons not canals, and free-flowing water not locks and dams. The analogue of the canyon is basic values. The analogue of the flowing water is ideas, knowledge, and actions.

Following the least action principle

For a moment, assume that people follow the least action principle. Actually, bear with us and please assume it for the rest of this chapter. What does this mean?

Think of Lisa (the executive in the previous chapter). If we analyze her potential actions from the least action principle, the short-term answer would be to hang up the phone when the nurse calls and then to instruct Mark (her secretary) not to put through any more calls from school that day. But that would be a truly short-term perspective. Josh would stay at school feeling miserable. The school would label Lisa a "bad parent." Lisa would be worried throughout the day and might just screw up that lunch negotiation with Harvey.

From an intermediate-term perspective, least action does not say "hang up the phone," it says "drop what you are doing and go get the kid." The long-term outlook probably suggests what Lisa ended up doing. To risk missing Harvey at lunch may require a huge expenditure of energy later to fix it, so it would be better to bring Harvey along. Besides, triggering the "concerned parent" image in Harvey's mind might be good both for negotiations and future business dealings.

All of this sounds fine, but like Lisa you usually have to make decisions on the spot. Decisions involve trade-offs and choices. If you begin with complication, the choices are many and the options seem discrete. If you perceive matters from the viewpoint of complexity, those many choices all have interwoven strands. Plucking one choice immediately shifts the context for all the others (foreground moves and background gets rearranged).

Corporations have sensed that such a context is important. They write mission statements in an effort to provide it. Take the card company Hallmark. As with many other companies, by the late 1980s growth and change fueled the need to codify its beliefs and values. John Hall told Patricia Jones and Larry Kahaner for their book *Say It and Live It*:

> *The primary reason we wrote [the mission statement] was that Hallmark was increasing in size and complexity. More employees, more locations, more products. When this happens, you can't assume everyone automatically understands the corporate beliefs and values as they did when the company was smaller. This is particularly true when the beliefs and values have not been written down. We have acquired a number of companies over the years, and their employees need to know what Hallmark stands for.*

Today Hallmark Cards, including subsidiaries and international operations, has about 21,000 full-time employees and 14,000 part-time employees and annual sales of approximately $37 billion. Hallmark dominates the US card market and produces cards in 20 languages and in more than 100 countries. Hall said:

> *During this time we also were engineering an organizational transformation. We were flattening our structure, developing interdivisional teams, speeding up production, and emphasizing continuous improvement. Beliefs and values are a touchstone in such times of transition, the unchanging foundation on which everything depends.*

The authors of *Built to Last*, Jim Collins and Jerry Porras, tell us that vision is the key to managing both continuity and change: "Vision provides guidance about what core to preserve and what future to stimulate progress toward."

Why do people attempt to write mission statements? The stated reasons usually go like this:

❖ To focus the organization on winning.
❖ Motivating people.
❖ Calling attention to specified "targets."
❖ Leaving room for contributions "from the bottom up."
❖ Creating and sustaining enthusiasm.
❖ Guiding resource allocations.

Unfortunately, the unstated reason is often: "Tom's company just finished their mission statement and it's hanging all over the walls. Maybe we need one. Besides, I can't stand Tom's ribbing me over this topic, it is screwing up my golf game."

In our view, mission statements are an attempt to provide context. The goal (when sincere and not motivated by golf) is correct – context is critical – but the vehicle is weak.

Consider this mission statement we found on the Internet:

Mission Statement:

We are Intense Moments, a clan of surfing professionals dedicated and empowered by the strength of our people. We seek extreme challenges to create and innovate. We make statements that reflect our actions, demonstrating our commitment to excellence. As we explore and grow into the future, we shall continually focus upon customer satisfaction, employee wellness, environmental responsibility, and sensitive balance between personal and professional fulfillments.

Afterthought:

An intense moment is a powerful lapse of time, a furious instant that may have severe consequences. An extreme blink of an eye that no matter how vicious or severe, it ends up being an unforgettable experience of great magnitude.

You can recognize the surfers that have experienced these excessive flashes of time by the look in their eyes, their forceful calmness, their untamed spirits and colorful personalities. They are strong, passionate

---

characters, determined to ride the unthinkable in an impressionable deci-
sive manner.

INTENSE MOMENTS is a company run by such surfers. People
who enjoy these heavy situations that the ocean has to offer. All the
members of our staff, our shapers and team riders are seriously active in
developing the equipment and clothing that represents and endures these
experiences.

The reflection of these occasions are on the images of our products and the power of our hardcore equipment.

Mission statements, strategic intents, visions (that thing Lou
Gerstner couldn't get into and George Bush couldn't get enough of),
and the like do not substitute for attaining and promulgating a sense
of coherence among the members of the organization. In the case of
Intense Moments, we suspect that the coherence is attained by surfing and not by making money (thus we would not want to be the marketing manager for these folk, but then again no one asked us). The
lure of selling surfboards, wetsuits, t-shirts, gear and shoes is just not
as intense as the lure of the wave. On the other hand, the fact that the
members of Intense Moments have such a strong common bond will
probably get them past watching the WalMart vice-president drive
away, contract unsigned. The surfers will remain true to their values
– catching that perfect wave.

The next common sense involves both knowing what those values are and creating enough room to allow them to be embodied (carried out more than just expressed). Mission statements, an expression
of the old common sense, just do not go far enough. They stop at
expression, as if the mere statement of something were enough to
cause it to exist.

In the complicated world of yesterday, stating things stood
alone. It was yet another element among many discrete ones. The
mission statement was a symbol, not quite as poetic as the Williams
College line "Climb high, climb far, your goal the sky, your aim the
star," but imbued with the same sense of being a target. In the complex world of interwoven interrelationships, expressing such goals, if

not accompanied by action, causes nothing but problems. Dilbert knows this only too well.

The next common sense involves coherence. Coherence, in turn, is about values. **Individually held values that are aligned in a sense of common purpose – now that is coherence**.

Mission statements are supposed to be a corporate effort at channeling those effects around one critical item: values. But values are held by individuals and are very local to each person and the situation(s) they face. To codify the values, to render them in some permanent and abstract form that is to apply to everyone, is to make them meaningless at best or just plain wrong. And the effort to do so may be more corrosive to the sense of coherence in an organization than leaving them unarticulated.

This is not to say that values do not matter. Values do matter. But what matters about them is how they are enacted – carried out in day-to-day activity. Enactment and articulation are two very separate processes. It is unfortunately a common mistake to equate the two. This happens when we give out commands. Just saying "do *x*" does not mean that "*x*" actually happens (though we all have worked for bosses who make that assumption and act accordingly). The problem with mission statements is the reverse. Setting out a set of values and goals does not render them "believed in" by the members of an organization's network, nor does it make them more likely to be believed in the future.

Create canyons

Sitting at lunch the other day, our friend Paul remarked on how important it is for artists and designers to be given a fairly direct brief on what they are being asked to do. "Some people think that the way to get the best work out of an artist is to just let them do their own thing, give them total freedom to produce whatever it is they desire. Well, this isn't true. The best thing is to present the artist with a series of constraints against which he can challenge himself, and give him the freedom to go about meeting those challenges as he sees fit. To give an artist total freedom is to invite him to produce a mess."

Paul claims that artists use the brief they are given as a set of **constraints** (what we call context) and then implement these as they see fit. Authors of good mission statements write them in the same way. Authors of bad mission statements attempt the reverse – recipes for implementation with no sense of context.

Constraint – a device that holds someone or something back from action, a strong binding force.

For example, Novartis (formed from the merger of Ciba-Geigy and Sandoz), in attempting to "explain" what the company "stood for" to its newly assembled workforce, produced more than 20 detailed pages. This is not context, it is a foolish attempt at a blueprint. Length is not the only way to make this mistake. "We are a positive influence in people's lives. We produce quality. We serve the customer. We wisely manage corporate resources. We value our employees." That is the mission statement of one of the Fortune 500: not a lot of context.

This chapter is titled "create canyons, not canals." Why? Because canyons are a "capturing" feature of the landscape. A river will not (without a cataclysm) escape its canyon, but *within* the canyon it has freedom of movement. The canyon is Paul's set of constraints. The river wandering therein is the freedom to implement.

Canyons embody Max's least action principle. The river is faced only with the set of choices within the canyon. And within the canyon an entire ecosystem can develop, perhaps oblivious to what goes on outside the canyon walls.

A river left undisturbed, especially on level ground, will change its course chaotically, but it will do it within certain **boundaries**. If humans try to take a river outside its 'remembered' boundaries, it will at every opportunity 'snap' back to its boundaries.

Boundary – indicating or fixing a limit or extent, a real or imaginary limit.

It's like some desktop publishing programs where you draw frames on to guides (boundaries). You have an option of "snap to guides," where the frame will automatically snap back to the guides once you pass a certain point as you're drawing.

Creating canyons helps produce alignment. Alignment is about ensuring that the interests and actions of all employees are directed toward a company's key goals, so that any employee will recognize and respond positively to a potentially useful idea. Alignment is often overlooked; it is intangible and elusive, and as far as corporate creativity is concerned, its effects are readily visible only when a company is either extraordinarily well aligned or misaligned. Companies can function with relatively poor alignment, but they cannot be consistently creative unless they are strongly aligned. As Collins and Porras tell us:

> *A visionary company creates a total environment that envelops employees, bombarding them with a set of signals so consistent and mutually reinforcing that it's virtually impossible to misunderstand the company's ideology and ambitions ... Far and away the biggest mistake managers make is ignoring the crucial importance of alignment.*

Canyons work best when they are deep and wide. Shallow canyons can overflow. Narrow canyons can flood. Within the organization the employees, the customers, the suppliers, and the stakeholders are the flowing river. Your job as a manager is to create the canyon for them to flow through. Make it deep and wide.

Depth comes from values

Collins and Porras point out that if you "listen to people in truly great companies talk about their achievements – you will hear little about earnings per share ... You discover core ideology by looking inside. It has to be authentic. You can't fake it." Jack Welch concurs when he says: "everything we do [at GE] focuses on building self-confidence in people so they can be simple."

Where does this sense of self-confidence come from? From alignment of the actions you are asked to do with your deeply held values. When the actions and values are aligned, the descriptions can be simple, and the canyon will be deep and wide enough to contain and channel future opportunities.

Values are embodied by the individuals who are members of an organization's network. They are articulated by the actions we carry out day by day. They can only be meaningfully observed from the outside and in practice. Those we speak about may be very different from those we actually perform. In a different vocabulary, values are tacit not explicit. Their tacit nature is why shallow-sounding mission statements are not the way to capture what employees believe or how they act. As Welch points out, the aligned can produce simplicity. We have to add the thought that simplicity itself is not a sure sign of alignment.

What values matter? Here we are at the dawn of the twenty-first century and we are asking much the same question as was asked 4000 years ago. The answers do not seemed to have changed all that much either. Integrity, self-consistency, being "good," not doing "evil" unto others, ascribing respect where appropriate, appreciating the efforts of others and the notion that valued things are the product of effort themselves ... these were core values to the ancients and they are just as applicable as core values today.

What has changed are the situations in which these values find application. (None of us has the task of figuring out how to replace a chipped block of stone from the Great Pyramid and thankfully does not have to face the labor problems such a task in the modern world would present. How would the union react to the incline of the ramp or the temperature of the work site?)

Some corporations already embrace the notion that deeply held values are key. Consider the mission statement (overleaf) of Sharp Corporation, a Japanese consumer electronics giant. Conspicuously absent are such words as profit, earnings, or even "value."

Notice that you are presented with a list of values, the consequences of which are expressed, and you are invited to partake. The values and actions of the individual are preserved, as are autonomy and self-actualization. The statement coheres because it provides the space necessary for the individuals reading the statement to find their own way.

The same type of thing can be accomplished by saying very little. Nike's line "Just Do It" may not seem the most ethical of

---

Sharp Corp.'s Business Creed

Sharp Corporation is dedicated to two principles: "Sincerity and Creativity."

By committing ourselves to these ideals, we can derive genuine satisfaction from our work, while making a meaningful contribution to society.

Sincerity is a virtue fundamental to humanity ... always be sincere.

Harmony brings strength ... trust each other and work together.

Politeness is a merit ... always be courteous and respectful.

Creativity promotes progress ... remain constantly aware of the need to innovate and improve.

Courage is the basis of a rewarding life ... accept every challenge with a positive attitude.

---

corporate missions, but it certainly demands of individuals that they find their own way. Similarly, the line "Tripod: Tools for Life" (see Chapter 11) says both nothing and everything at the same time.

The complexity of modern situations is all the more reason that the pathway you create has to be deep. There are many interrelated challenges to our values and there are conflicts among them. What we put at forefront or back may carry us up near the canyon's edge or may propel us further downstream, but we need to be prepared for either event. Lisa found a solution to her conflicts of multiple roles by calling on deeply held values to establish the correct context. A shallower person may have left Josh stranded, Harvey angry, or the contract lost.

"The only way to change people's minds is with consistency," Jack Welch says. "Once you get the ideas, you keep refining them and improving them; the more simply your idea is defined, the better it is.

You communicate, you communicate, and then you communicate some more. Consistency, simplicity, and repetition is what it's all about." Find your values, express them, live them ... consistently and often.

Width provides opportunity

Serendipity is the art of making discoveries of things that were not being sought. As originally defined by Horace Walpole in 1754, it combines a fortunate accident with sagacity. Although the word is widely used, few people know of its unusual history and that its original meaning has been lost. The modern usage of serendipity puts the emphasis almost totally on accidents and leaves out sagacity. The latter is derived from the Latin noun *sagicitas* ("keenness of perception") and means, according to the *Oxford English Dictionary*: "gifted with acuteness of mental discernment; having special aptitude for the discovery of truth; penetrating and judicious in the estimation of character and motives, and the devising of means for the accomplishment of ends."

When this meaning is restored, the actions that companies can take to promote serendipity become clear. Creativity often involves recombining or making connections between things that may seem unconnected. The more abstruse the connection, the greater the intellectual distance that must be traversed to make it, and the greater the role for the unexpected. Serendipity helps to bridge distances.

Width in focus means promoting the opportunity for fortuitous events. Too narrow a focus, be it on implementation, operations, or marketing, can mean missed opportunities and missed evolution. If you are going to have the flexibility to adjust foreground and aft, you have to look at the scene without the camera as well as through the viewfinder.

Evolution takes full advantage of serendipity. Evolution has proved to be creative, and the engine of its creativity is randomness and redundancy. For species that are subject to natural selection, zero redundancy is not a recipe for survival. Corporate creativity is no different. If companies were to have no redundancy whatsoever, they would be optimized for their present environment and would limit themselves to doing only what could be planned.

An often cited example of such unused potential for change is a heron's wing. The heron uses its wings not only to fly, but also to shade a patch of water from the sun in order to better see the fish it is trying to catch. The question is: how did the heron's wing evolve? A wing is useless, it seems, until it is fully developed. Diminutive wings are too small to fly with or to serve as much of a sunshade.

How did evolution take birds from no wings to full wings, with every stage of development conferring even more advantage than the last? Darwin himself suggested an answer. Since a fraction of a wing is useless for flying, it must have originally sprouted for some other purpose. The prevalent theory is that the feathers help to retain warmth. Moreover, the need for warmth was greatest for the small dinosaurs that would evolve into birds, because they had the largest surface volume ratio and so were most prone to heat loss. Over millions of years, as feathers covered wings and enlarged through stages of evolutionary advantage, new and unanticipated uses emerged. Once the wing reached a certain size, herons could fly and shade the waters to catch more fish. But in the beginning, the feathers certainly had unused potential for change. And they still do – but who knows what it is?

So serendipity occurs when fortunate accidents happen to sagacious people. There are three approaches a company can take to promote serendipity. First, increase the frequency of accidents that could turn out to be fortunate. One way to increase the frequency of accidents is to promote a bias for action, toward tinkering, toward empirical research work. Second, increase awareness of the accidents that do occur. Serendipitous events happen in companies more often than people realize. Perhaps there is a tendency to downplay their importance because people feel uncomfortable depending on accidents that come from a source they feel powerless to control. It is important for everyone to know that when accidents happen, they are driven by underlying phenomena that it is worth understanding further. Finally, the general principle of "don't overlook exceptions" needs to be instilled in everyone.

An exception, however small, may be the fortunate accident that sparks a serendipitous discovery. When John Vaught of Hewlett-Packard (the inventor of thermal inkjet printing) saw a hot soldering iron touch his syringe and ink spurt out, he quickly pulled out a high-speed camera to learn what had happened. Millions of offices since have benefited. Fortunate accidents are rarely "one-shot" events. They arise when people interact with each other and their work. They are often a continuous drizzle of tiny, almost imperceptible events that may escape the attention of all but the most alert and motivated observers. Occasionally, a cloudburst comes along and makes these events easier to see.

The existence of wide and deep canyons of values work to increase the company's domain of sagacity to turn more accidents into fortunate ones. A company can also take positive action to raise the chances that these accidents will turn out to be fortunate – that they will meet with sagacity. To do this, an organization must enlarge the domain in which it is sagacious and deliberately create unused potential for change, that is, redundant capacity in human potential for change. Sometimes a company can have so much focus that it can miss the opportunity that is right next to it. At some point, every company must be able to move away from what it already does.

There is value in being able to look and move in directions other than straight ahead. When a company strategically uses randomness and redundancy, it opens itself to serendipity. Some companies believe in training people only for what they need to know to do their current job. This amounts to optimizing for an existing or predetermined situation. Employees should be encouraged to take classes that are not directly related to their work, to go to conferences where they are not making a presentation, to take study leaves or sabbaticals with the purpose of learning something different. One can never know when new knowledge will become useful. Until it does, like the heron's wing for flight, it represents an unused capacity for change.

That unused potential capacity is a keystone of any group. When combined with deeply held values, there is the potential for a powerful flow of energy. Rivers use it all the time. Intense Moments uses it to catch a wave. For those surfers the wave may be WalMart or it may be the ocean. They have left themselves the potential for both.

⋮ Dams are obstacles (not, as your CFO ⋮ would tell you, a revenue source)

⋮ In the canyon of your company flows a river of energy. What can hinder the river? Our perspective has already been given away. Unless you are the electric company, don't decide to create revenue on your river by building a dam. Dams are obstacles. Obstacles block the flow and allow valued items to picked off by predators. That is why beavers build them.

Barriers to entry, that vaunted business school idea, work in two ways. They represent a cost to potential entrants who buy into the paradigm, or they function like the beaver's dam allowing the cola market to be picked off by the likes of Branson and Sainsbury. Coke and Pepsi did not quite have that in mind, but then again they are the ones who built the dam.

Similarly, bureaucracies can be efficient mechanisms for carrying out orderly tasks or they can be major obstacles to the river of creativity and innovation in a company. Every bit of energy spent fighting with the internal bureaucracy is energy not spent in a creative moment. Dams can thus take many forms: the high level of expenditure on such things as advertising, the multitude of forms and budget approvals that only bureaucrats and regulators love, and even the very words articulated by management.

Consider the notion of a mission statement from this perspective. In an organization that believes in autonomy, self-actualization, empowerment, and decentralization, the very act of saying so in a mission statement is an indication of the opposite. Including it says that management is so distrustful of the network members' abilities to exercise autonomy, self-actualization, empowerment, or decentralization that they feel a need to assert the primacy of those values in writing. In organizations that do not believe in these values, it would be inconsistent to mention them; but then there would be a strange hypocrisy in proclaiming that centralized control is valued above all. If you believe in control, why bother with a mission statement? There are easier ways of evoking Big Brother.

Mission statements are found in the day-to-day actions of the members of an organization's network. The critical task is coherence. It will not be magically accomplished by writing down some set of "first principles." But it can be affected by communication. Shaping the values can only occur in the context of shaping actions, as the members of the network go about their tasks, observe one another, and discuss what they will.

Values are not represented by mere words on a piece of paper. They are embodied by actions, exhibited by behavior, and tested by experience. When senior management goes through the process of articulating those values in a mission statement, it is as if the values have acquired the status of objects. The statement has been written with hammer and chisel, and Lord help the unfortunate soul who attempts to alter what has been ensconced in granite.

When mission statements are created, the values, goals, and plans of some set of people have been abstracted into a few short paragraphs. If the process of creation was an inclusive one, then the multitude of meanings which the values had for the many people affected get reduced to some lowest common denominator of words with which they all could agree. If the process was an exclusive one, then the words represent solely the meanings of the small group empowered to draft the statement. Either way, once written down the words take on a life of their own ("reified," as we have said in Chapter 10). They can become like rocks – small obstacles blocking the path of the river – or, if there are enough of them, a dam.

Dams do to water what fences do on land: they block things. This is the other main obstacle that the free-flowing river of innovation and knowledge faces – parts of the organization building a fence around themselves or even trying to dig a canal to "steal" part of the river.

Fences may help those inside the fence or may create a false confidence that the barbarians have been excluded. Just as the Great

Wall only created the challenge which spurred the Mongolians on to rule China, so too can corporate fences and the fiefdoms they create work first to frustrate those who are blocked out and then inspire new creativity to make the fence irrelevant.

Side canals only confuse

When was the last time you read about a new conglomerate being formed? That phenomenon of the 1960s does not work in today's complex world. It is hard enough to gain an understanding of a coherent set of interweavings. It is requiring the wisdom of the gods to demand that an executive (or a stock analyst) understand a series of such interweavings grouped together without rhyme or reason other than "it was available at a good price."

Warren Buffet may invest in many industries, but he doesn't try to run them. Mutual funds work on the same principle. The main canals of St. Petersburg and Amsterdam are designed to speed freight on its way. The side canals are designed to lure invaders into a trap. All that poor Lisa needed was an obnoxious copier salesman showing up in her office at that fateful 11 a.m. We only have so much energy and so much attention. To divert it into side trips and away from our coherent viewpoint is a mistake.

This is not an argument against exploration. We will talk about scouting parties in Chapter 9. It is an argument against institutionalizing diversions.

Multiple pathways within the canyon are fine. Canals out of the canyon are not.

Guidelines for creating canyons

Canyons are not about the command-and-control culture of the old common sense – they are about the guiding values of the next common sense. Canyons are an analogy for the guiding viewpoints that managers of interactions need to be effective. Canals are the comparable analogy for the manager of entities who issued commands in an effort to manage outcomes.

❖ Think of the values you express and enact as forming a canyon in which ideas and action, just like a river, are free to seek out the most appropriate route. Remember that your canyon needs to be as wide and deep as your values. Narrow allows too little freedom of movement. Shallow is too easily overrun. Thus, don't fall into the trap of overspecifying actions or values.

❖ Keep ideas and action flowing: obstacles can block their flow just like a river's. Shoals are dangerous whether in a river or in the open ocean. When fully flooded over, no problem; but as obstacles, look out. Organizational dams – either of the fiefdom or the frozen images variety – block the free flow of ideas and innovation.

❖ Create your canyon of values wide enough and deep enough to feel no need for diversions. If you do feel a diversion is needed, make your canyon big enough to accommodate it. One canyon is simple and direct. Many side canals are confusing.

❖ When the water is flowing, get out of the way. So too with ideas and actions in your organization.

Management principles

	Next common sense	Old common sense
The world	Complex	Complicated
Management	Guiding interactions	Leading entities
Simple principles	Adopting a global viewpoint, allowing interactions to happen	Dealing with local situations and trying to "sort things out"
Mental models	Recognizing that my model does not need to be yours, and things can still work	Giving lip service to difference, while giving incentives to conformity
Landscape images	Thinking about ecosystems	Thinking about a car race or a football game
Combine and recombine	Asking about how parts can be combined into new and better wholes	Segregating parts to be treated as their own self-sufficient wholes
Multiple roles	Allowing people to be themselves	Insisting that the company come first

Canyons not canals	Guiding viewpoints not controlling actions	Controlling actions in an attempt to control outcomes

Tell Stories

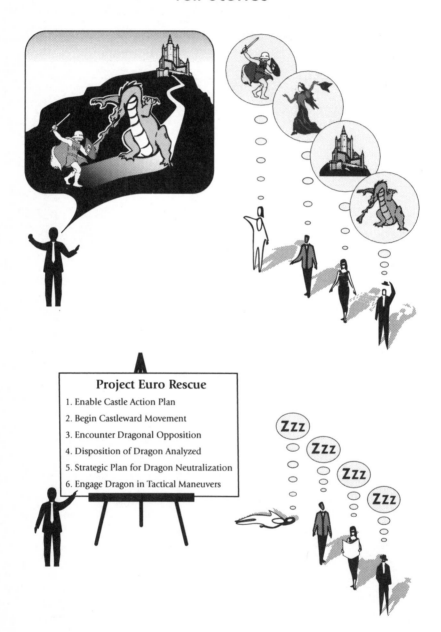

8
TELL STORIES

S tories are narratives that elaborate on explanations of what
has happened, what is happening, or what might have happened. Much of what people know about the world comes
from stories supplied by friends, relatives, teachers, journalists, and
officials. Stories are powerful sense-making devices because they posit
a causal sequence of events that lead to an outcome, and because they
provide a rich, multilayered representation of an episode that evokes
understanding and empathy.

The construction of shared meanings in organizational life uses
myths, symbols, rituals, and stories – the means by which people
understand the history of their actions, and their place in that history.

Myths are real or fictional stories, characters, or actions that
embody the organization's ideals and sensibilities. For example, many
organizations maintain creation myths of how they were founded,
complete with mythic heroes (technical wizards, financiers), events
(competition, market uncertainty), and explanations (superhuman
effort, carving a market niche). Symbols are things, signs, or behaviors that link organizational experience to feelings and values. Thus,
meetings symbolize thought, language symbolizes status and power,
and mission statements symbolize solidarity. Rituals are ceremonial
activities that preserve traditions and sustain meanings. The development of a business plan is an example of a common ritual that signals

the legitimacy of the meanings and interpretations that are linked to it. (And, when it is good, gets money to flow, but that is for a different book.)

To develop a coherent viewpoint regarding any particular experience, we recount the experience in detail (without summarizing or labeling it). Thus, if I act on the basis of my understanding of a common experience and you act on your different understanding of that same experience, we have some common origin of those understandings. If each of us is quizzed separately as to why we did what we did, our answers are likely to flow from the same experience. Such commonality is what binds our viewpoints together and makes it possible for each of us to understand the sense that the other has made.

We title this chapter "Tell Stories." We do not mean to your children. In western cultures the word "storytelling" immediately makes 95 percent of adults dismissively think of children. But if they can be persuaded along to a show for adults they are astounded at the quality and magic of what they have been missing – those Grimms' fairytales weren't originally meant for kids at all. Storytelling festivals and local groups are full of appreciative adults. In many cultures which have more of their traditions and extended family life intact, storytelling is for all, and even by all. You may think that stories are just an entertainment device, but you are wrong. Stories are the best tool we have for making sense of our environment and getting comfortable both with what has already occurred and with what is yet to come.

Storytelling is how we make sense. We tell them to ourselves and to each other. With stories we can develop a coherent viewpoint. Without them we can only exchange mere words as symbols or icons. If we all had precisely the same set of experiences, the mere sharing of words and icons would be enough. One word would have just one exact meaning. But in our complex age, not only do we all have divergent experiences, but for each of us those experiences are woven together in a multitude of ways. Our mental models, multiple roles and the present foreground and aft dramatically affect how we interpret what we see and encounter. We need stories to make sense of it all, for ourselves and for all those we wish to communicate with.

Look at the illustration that begins this chapter. Once there was a knight, Sir Euro. Noble knight Euro was madly in love with Princess Prosperity. They often walked in the enchanted garden of Fiscal Stability. But one day the evil Prince Unemployment tricked Princess Prosperity and took her to his moated castle – Inertia Land. Inertia was guarded at all times by the terrible dragon Minister and his family of yeah-saying, currency-speculating dragons, the politicians. Euro the noble knight set out to rescue his princess. Would he succeed? Would he slay the dragon? Or, perhaps even more clever, get the dragon to join his team? We may never know. Surely this story does more to impress itself on you than the dry pages of an economist's report or the summary bullets of the evening news. The story may be fanciful, but it engages. In such engagement, in its ability to capture attention, lies its potency. So too with any good story.

Sense making

Organizations are often viewed as vehicles for solving well-defined problems. But organizations also provide sets of procedures through which participants arrive at an interpretation of what they are doing and what they have done while in the process of doing it. From this point of view, an organization is a collection of choices looking for problems, issues and feelings looking for decision situations in which they might be aired, solutions looking for issues to which they might be the answer, and decision makers looking for work. Meanings are always multiple and ambiguous, and understanding must continually be struggled for and won anew.

People in organizations are continually trying to understand what is happening around them. They first have to make sense of what is happening in their environments, in order to develop a shared interpretation that can serve as a guide to action. Sense making suggests that people in organizations are continually engaged in interaction and talk in order to find out what they are thinking and to construct interpretations of what they are doing. The recipe is "How can I know what I think until I see what I say?"

One could say that sense making is a continuous, social process in which individuals look at elapsed events, frame packets of experience, and select particular points of reference to weave webs of meaning. The result of sense making is an enacted or meaningful environment, which is a reasonable and socially credible rendering of what is taking place. The central problem in sense making is how to reduce or resolve uncertainty and ambiguity, and how to develop a shared coherent viewpoint so that individuals in the organization may act collectively.

The noted organizational theorist Karl Weick suggests that organizations are "loosely coupled" systems in which individual participants have great latitude in interpreting such questions as: What is happening out there? Why is this taking place? What does it mean? Such sense making is done retrospectively. We cannot make sense of events and actions until they have occurred. Only then can we glance backward in time to construct their meaning. Weick notes: "a sensible event is one that resembles something that has happened before. Sensemaking is an effort to tie beliefs, and actions more closely together ... taking whatever is clearer, whether it be a belief or an action, and linking it with that which is less clear."

A general metaphor for sense making is that of people and organizations "looking backward," retrospectively making sense of events and actions that have already taken place by enacting and selecting meaningful interpretations. The sharing of experience assists the sharing of meaning. What is being shared are the actions and conversations that constitute the experience, as well as the opportunity to talk about that experience soon after it occurred. Such sharing allows people to collectively develop a common vocabulary which encodes the experience and renders it meaningful.

We learn by doing

Remember Alexander the Great and the Gordian knot? The lesson of cutting through the tangle is much better told by recounting the short story than by repeating its conclusion. But think of how much more vivid a lesson it was for Alexander himself. When next confronted by what seemed an impossibly complex task, Alexander could draw on his personal knowledge of having cut the knot.

As with Alexander, so too with all of us. Try explaining how to ride a bicycle to a four-year-old. You utter a few hopeless sentences and then lead the child outside to try it. Yes, the next step is to go buy a set of training wheels and some gauze bandages, but the only way your child will learn to ride a bike is by riding a bike. The same applies to catching a ball, and using a knife and fork or chopsticks. What gives Bauman and Lawrence of Chapter 3 the confidence to give advice to others attempting major corporate change? Not the hubris of a sales pitch, for these executives do not want to sell you anything. Instead, it is the coherence that stems from experience.

Doing is different from saying. Our minds process nearly 1 billion "bits" of neurological data each second. Our consciousness is aware of less than 100 of these. We can only speak of that small piece of which the conscious is aware, but we experience all of it. When we do, we activate more than 10 million times as many inputs as when we say. When academics speak of the importance of "tacit" knowledge this is what they really mean. Leave all the vague academic phrases aside, the simple truth is that 1 billion is a whole lot more than 100. Is it any wonder we learn more by doing than by reading, or listening, or by nodding yes?

When Nike tells us "Just Do It!" we should. Dylan (of nickels fame from Chapter 6) certainly knew this better than his father and had a sock full of nickels to prove it. We learn by doing.

Stories are verbal simulations

We can't all do everything. So as much as we learn by doing, we don't have time to do it all. Stories are the next best thing. (Phone calls come third, sorry Ma Bell.)

The power of a story is that it allows the listener to recreate an experience in their mind. Too many details, too fine a point on things, removes the potency of the listener's imagination. Long before we had computers to run fancy simulation exercises, we had our brains. Long before Disney, we had the Brothers Grimm. The power of a good story is in the experience it evokes in its listeners.

The power of intuition enables us to size up a situation quickly. The power of mental simulation lets us imagine how a course of action might be carried out. The power of metaphor lets us draw on our experience by suggesting parallels between the current situation and something else we have come across. The power of storytelling helps us consolidate our experiences to make them available in the future, either to ourselves or to others.

Gary Klein, in his *Sources of Power: How People Make Decisions*, focuses a great deal of attention on stories. He notes:

A story is a blend of several ingredients:

❖ *Agents, the people who figure in the story.*
❖ *Predicament, the problem the agents are trying to solve.*
❖ *Intentions, what the agents plan to do.*
❖ *Actions, what the agents do to achieve their intentions.*
❖ *Objects, the tools the agents will use.*
❖ *Causality, the effects (both intended and unintended) of carrying out actions.*
❖ *Context, the many details surrounding the agents and actions.*
❖ *Surprises, the unexpected things that happen in the story.*

In a simple form, a story ties these and other ingredients together.

His list resembles the instruction list for the designers of SimCity and other computer simulations. What this highlights is the idea that if a story is good, the listener will be able to build an imaginary world and project action in it. Just like a simulation.

What makes good storytellers great? They tell stories of the type or in the style that suits their personalities the best. They develop an almost instant rapport with the audience. They have a highly developed sense of flexibility and timing. They really like what they are doing, are comfortable in front of their audience and engage with them. They have stage presence. Perhaps this can be defined as confidence, assurance, audience rapport, a sense of knowing they are good and could take the audience with them wherever they went.

Another part of stage presence is good use of pacing, facial expressions, and pauses. Often a pause, a lifted eyebrow, and a look all around the audience can accomplish more than any number of words. These tellers know it and use these techniques well. Stage presence is just a term, borrowed from theater – many storytellers don't think of themselves as performing on a stage, but that doesn't preclude us using this term. They tell from the heart, to the heart – honestly, openly, and without trying too hard.

Without trying too hard also means using less, not more. The key is to let the listener fill in from the billions of unarticulated bits flowing though their brain. John Carroll at MIT and his associates have shown that this principle works for instruction manuals. Users of complicated equipment gain proficiency faster by being told less and having to experiment more. They learn by doing and use the stories in the instruction manual as a verbal simulation for the experiences they have not yet had in real life.

Stories reinforce images

August Roos and Dylan have LEGO in common. When they build a LEGO model, one of the first things they do is to weave a story around the item they have constructed. The story gives the model context and the model gives the story a link to real life. LEGO took this concept and created the LEGO Creator CD, a collection of interactive stories (built Chinese menu style by interactions with the child). The stories told on the CD reinforce images of models the child has built or would like to build (and, as Johan will confirm, images of expensive models the child wants the parent to purchase).

When the CEO tells war stories, the purpose is to reinforce some set of values and choices for the rest of the organization. Herb

Kelleher uses many stories of incidents occurring around the Southwest system to illustrate his values that employees come first and "we are all a family." The stories mean more than mere words in a letter from the chairman. When Herb tells a story, the employees can create the scene in their minds and picture what occurs. Such pictures get reinforced each time the story is told and each time the message is recounted in conversation. Having the mental picture means a lot more than merely having "at Southwest we care about our employees" in a wooden frame in the employees' locker room. (Herb hates words in frames like this, and Southwest employees we know even have a picture in their heads of Herb bashing the first one he found. Another important image.)

Most stories are set into a context by their tellers. That context reinforces images of place and time. By activating the listener's mental model for a time and place, many details need not be told, and the room is created within which the listener's imagination can roam. In effect, the storyteller has carved out a canyon and the listener supplies the river of meaning to run through it.

Because a story (at least a good one) is a canyon and not a canal, the listener is encouraged to make their own interpretations. The context set out by the storyteller will conjure up a new set of "related ideas" in the minds of each listener. Meaning emerges from the combination of what the storyteller supplies and what the listener's mind adds. Stories suggest recombinations.

Since context triggers images of place, time and experience, the listener is able to trigger the recall and use of a much larger portion of the 1 billion bits per second in their head than the 30 or so derived from the words of the storyteller. Whatever images get triggered in the listener become building blocks for the meaning they weave.

Stories are not a set of labels. If they were, then as the labels got triggered a predefined set of images would be unfolded by the listener. Every listener would hear and construct the same story. Children learn that this is not true when they play "telephone" or "operator." Corporate managers, however, tend to forget this childhood lesson. The children's game illustrates the new things that can emerge as stories are told and retold. The corporate chieftains tend to expect the same meaning to be evoked by their story as they retell it from audience to audience.

What matters about a story is what the listeners do with it, not the smile it brings to the face of the teller in its one hundredth reincarnation. Listeners use the images evoked to create meaning ... meaning that goes on to inform actions. Those actions are what we think the corporate chieftains should be interested in.

Not icons, not symbols, not commands: stories

Isolated words, phrases and pictures do not convey nearly as much meaning as a story. Unless the standalone text or picture is accepted in the community as a "code" for some oft-told story (e.g. a communion wafer and all it implies), the mental pictures triggered are just not rich enough to channel a creative flow on the part of the receiver. Coherent viewpoints are not made up of isolated words. They too must evoke deeply held values and images. To offer up isolated words is to evoke a shallow stream of water in a hot desert. Whatever value there is dries up quickly.

Consultants are all too aware of this phenomenon. While a good consultant concerned with client relationships will want to evoke and implant stories, the more task- and project-oriented consultant will tend to view the richness of such material as their own. To share it would be to diminish the unique value that they bring to the table. It is an unfortunate fallacy that is repeated as often as the empty war stories of the corporate chiefs. Its mistake lies in thinking that the value is in the story and not in what it evokes in its audience.

Gary Klein tells this story of how threatening the power of stories can be:

A friend is organizing a large conference and asks if my company can help. She had put on a previous conference and had gone to the effort of preparing a volume of proceedings. All the presenters had submitted abstracts of their talks. The document was tedious to read and not very useful. Now as she prepares for another conference, she asks if we can attend the sessions, listen to the stories, and compile them as a record of the conference. It sounds interesting, so even though we will not be interviewing anyone, we agree to do it. Five of us go over to the center where the conference is taking place, one for each of the five concurrent sessions. Each time a presenter puts on a slide about the major ideas, everyone in the room starts writing furiously, but we observers just sit back. Every time a presenter gives an example or tells a story, we are writing furiously and the others sit back.

By the end of the two days, we have accumulated a wonderful set of stories. We know that all the official viewgraphs listing the five key steps to do this or the seven ways to do that are fairly useless. You can exchange these slides from one session to the next, and no one would notice. Their slides are filled with useful tidbits like, "Keep the lines of communication open," and "Don't wait too long when problems are building up." Presumably these bits of wisdom are going to help those who keep trying to close lines of communication and who insist on waiting too long whenever a problem is detected. We are confident that in recording the stories of line experience during organizational crises, we have captured the real expertise.

I gather all the stories and incident accounts and write them up into a short, thirty page conference "proceedings." The incidents the presenters have described are funny, and tragic, and exciting, with many useful ideas, lessons learned, and cognitive modeling. The other people in my company who see the document are also enthusiastic. We send it to the conference organizer, and she is even more enthusiastic that we are. She wants to get some additional funds so we can expand this into a book. As a formality, the conference organizer sends a copy of the document to each presenter to make sure each is comfortable with the way he or she is represented. That's when everything falls apart. Most of the presenters are disappointed. Some are furious. The problem is that each presenter wants to be remembered for the dry viewgraphs on "twelve essential keys to a happier relationship between management and labor." They had worked hard on these presentations and are shocked that the official record won't show any of their thinking, any of their viewgraphs, any of the important conclusions they had presented. Instead, they are going to be remembered as people who just swapped stories and anecdotes.

We want to explain to them how meaningless these slogans are in contrast to stories, such as the one showing how they had kept the lines of communication open during a difficult incident in which a plant was shut down. We had included some introductory material for each story to identify the main points, but that is not enough for the presenters. It is going to be a losing battle.

We withdraw the document, and add it to the set of stories we tell.

Daniel Dennett, the philosopher, has said, "Our ability to interpret depends on our confidence in predicting." That confidence can be assisted by good stories. If the story helps to create a canyon, the canyon walls provide boundaries and the canyon's path suggests an outcome. Good stories thus reinforce our abilities to interpret still more stories. The trite notion "chance favors the well prepared" seems only too apt.

Guidelines for telling stories

Stories are about context. The old common sense may have encouraged the use of bullets as a means of avoiding context. The next common sense is about telling stories that are open enough to allow listeners to draw relevant conclusions and authentic enough to convey their context in metaphors.

- ❖ Only tell stories that you can tell from your heart. These are the ones you can tell most easily and the ones that will evoke canyons.
- ❖ Tell stories that reinforce the basic values shared in your organization. These are the ones that lead to coherent action.
- ❖ Always ask your listeners about the images your stories bring to mind for them.

Management principles

	Next common sense	Old common sense
The world	Complex	Complicated
Management	Guiding interactions	Leading entities
Simple principles	Adopting a global viewpoint, allowing interactions to happen	Dealing with local situations and trying to "sort things out"
Mental models	Recognizing that my model does not need to be yours, and things can still work	Giving lip service to difference, while giving incentives to conformity
Landscape images	Thinking about ecosystems	Thinking about a car race or a football game
Combine and recombine	Asking about how parts can be combined into new and better wholes	Segregating parts to be treated as their own self-sufficient wholes
Multiple roles	Allowing people to be themselves	Insisting that the company come first

Canyons not canals	Guiding viewpoints not controlling actions	Controlling actions in an attempt to control outcomes
Tell stories	Providing meaningful context and allowing employees to draw their own conclusions	Providing bullet lists of conclusions and demanding that employees fill in the necessary details

Send Out Scouting Parties

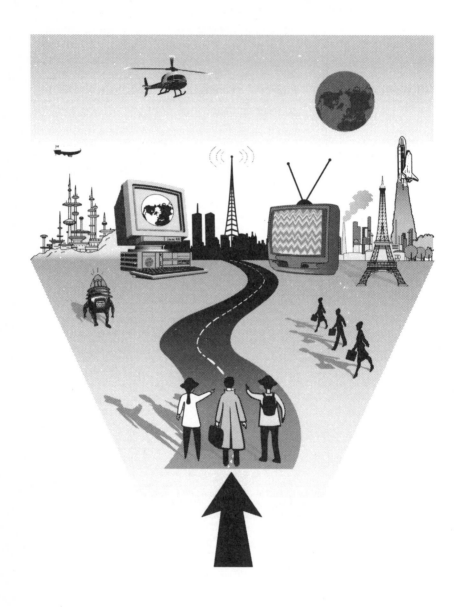

9
SEND OUT SCOUTING PARTIES

Don't let this happen to you. The scene is the Gobi Desert in the Jurassic era. Two dinosaurs locked in combat did not even notice the approaching sandstorm that buried them both. Their fossils, with their jaws still clasped around each other's neckbones, were not discovered until the summer of 1994. What a wonderful symbol: two dinosaurs so intent on mutual destruction that they were oblivious of the impending storm. Sounds a lot like Ford, GM, and the sandstorm of small Japanese cars in the 1980s. Or like the luxury car market in the US in the 1990s. Or TV networks in the era of cable and satellite. Or landlines in the era of wireless. You get our point.

The message of this chapter is "send out scouting parties to probe the environment." Send them out far and wide with the goal of finding stories to bring back. The old common sense reflected a now tired academic line: "An unexamined life is not worth living." To that line, all too many replied, "Yes, but an unlived life is not worth examining." The next common sense is about finding a way of balancing both these points.

To the Nikes of the world who "just do it," the next common sense replies but resources are not unlimited, so please choose what you are going to do. To the "cash cow" resting on past laurels and uninterested in exploring new frontiers, the next common sense replies, "and what will you do when Mohammed comes to you?" It is critical to send out scouting parties to explore the environment, but it is equally critical not to devote so many resources to exploration that your main activities are left to atrophy. The next common sense preaches balance.

Scouts need to be sent out both within the canyon and beyond. They need some guidance of what to look for, and they need to report in regularly. And the stories the scouts bring back need to be discussed and, if possible, brought to life. Allowing the reports to pile up on a bookshelf, or in a file cabinet, or worse in the "to be read" folder on your PC, will not help you or your organization know what is going on around you.

Think of your favorite restaurant. How is it that the chef keeps the menu appealing? It isn't by keeping everything the same. When items get stale or go out of season, the menu undergoes at least a subtle change. The chef is often out and about, visiting the farmer's market, talking with other chefs, even apprenticing at a more "famous" chef's kitchen for their "vacation." The chef acts as a scout. There is a need for scouting parties no matter what your business and no matter how comfortable you may be with how things are. A sandstorm could be just around the bend.

Where to go –
Part 1: Within the canyon

The strategy literature suggests that there are two main strategies for surveying and using the competitive landscape – one can explore and one can exploit. Some corporations exploit primarily (Harley Davidson and GM come to mind), some explore primarily (3M and Thermo Electron), and most switch between periods of heavy exploitation and periods of heavy exploration. Sending out scouts within the canyon is part of the exploit concept. Sending them beyond the canyon is part of explore.

Exploiting is about making the most of the situation you are presently in, thus our analogy of scouting within the walls of the canyon. Climbing those walls and moving to a different place requires a much greater expenditure of energy than trying to capitalize on the situation within the walls. The canyon is your value set, your industry, your competitors, your customers, and your employees. A great deal of value exists within the canyon – the question is how to exploit it. Exploiting it requires you to know about it, and this is where the scouting parties come in.

Microsoft's basic business strategy is to exploit its position and to scout its canyon thoroughly. (There are those who might argue that Microsoft also spends a lot of resources making the canyon bigger, but we will leave that argument for now.) Despite Bill Gates' talk about innovation, most of the innovating that happens in the Windows world occurs at third-party developers. These folk – usually located a few bends down the river from Microsoft's present position – put nearly heroic effort into defining and then defending some small niche of possibilities that Microsoft has overlooked. Thus, companies such as Norton and Symantec made small fortunes by providing utilities which would look after your PC and clean up after Windows. RealAudio makes its money by improving on sound transmission. Creative Labs does the same with soundcards and the technology which Intel does not include on its chips.

But what do both Microsoft and Intel do once the developer has found a successful niche and identified a product need? First comes the co-option approach – work with us before we swallow you – then the purchase approach – you might as well sell now while you still have a market – and finally the OK, let them drown approach – where the full marketing and financial muscle of the firm is unleashed to overwhelm the poor developer.

Notice that your web browser and wordprocessor now come with a spell-check program, that your spreadsheet can make fancy outputs, and that even your calendar program will print mailing labels. In the Wintel world, first a small developer finds a niche and makes the most of it, then Microsoft or Intel has a scout who reports back "this is selling," and then the niche product gets incorporated into the Microsoft or Intel product line. Recall that this is what AOL complained about when MSN was launched and what the FTC complained about when Microsoft wanted to buy Intuit, the makers of Quicken. The Justice Department claims that this is *modus operandi* for all of Microsoft's efforts, thus the case regarding Internet Explorer and Netscape. Philippe Kahn, the former president of Borland Software, claimed that he exited the software business just to escape the continual feeling of being swallowed up.

What works for Microsoft and Intel can work for you. The first step is to know what's out there. You created your canyon wall, now explore what is within it. Is there a tangential product you haven't focused on? Is there a customer need you haven't been meeting? Are there others in the canyon providing services that you are not? The way to do this is simple: send out scouts to report back. The local five and dime sends comparison shoppers, the local newspaper reads its competitors, and most good companies attempt to purchase their competitors' products so that they can sample the experience being offered to their customers. If you don't attempt to discover what is out there, you will be caught by surprise.

Within the canyon the most effective scouts are real people, with eyes, ears, and a good sense of smell. Within the canyon you are perceived as a real entity with real characteristics. The stories you want to obtain about the rest of the canyon should be of a similar nature. Merely collecting data, by whatever means, will not substitute for the experiences of a live person. This does not mean we are suggesting that you should send your secretary to Paris (unless shipping items to Paris in airplane seats is part of your business), but it does mean having people poking around. You will be surprised at what you can learn.

Where to go – Part 2: And beyond

Knowing your canyon is not enough. There is a whole world out there. This is the second part of the strategy lesson: explore.

The noted psychologist Donald Winnicott described the ideal setting for human development as being a "secure holding environment" from which the individual can venture forth to explore the world, but which always remains nearby for the individual to return to if they get frightened. The canyon is your secure holding environment. Yet you need to know about more than just the canyon itself.

Organizations can learn about events on other landscapes through some kind of remote sensing, and build models of what the events there mean for them. Remote sensing means things like the Internet, databases, reading the trade press, going to conventions, and even hiring consultants. Remote sensing is but a start. Even better, organizations can send out scouts (real people) to explore other landscapes and come back with their findings. Notice we said scouts and not the whole company. You send scouts to explore, and the mothership remains safe in the canyon.

Why are you exploring? Think of the following sequence and whether it may apply, if not to your company then to the one down the road:

1 There is some "marginal" or out-of-the-ordinary activity happening (a) in the mainstream activities of your own company, or (b) in other companies or relationships in the industry or related industries, or (c) somewhere on the fringes of the company, the industry, or outside of the industry (such as the activities of engineers or hackers toying around, or academics, hobbyists, and artists).

2 Someone in the company draws a connection between the marginal activity and a looming crisis or recurrent problem.

3 Some person or company interested in innovation makes a commitment to explore the marginal activity to see whether it could be a promising source for resolving the crisis or recurrent problem.

4 If the exploration uncovers a stable connection between the marginal activity and the prevention or correction of the recurrent breakdown, then someone institutes a new program to turn this connection into a product or service that can be marketed or some new internal business process that can confer an advantage.

5 Someone markets the new offer of a product or service or institutes new roles, processes, and practices in the company.

6 Competitors arise with improvements in the product or service, or copy the advantages of the company's new internal operations. Complementary industries arise, and new industry performance benchmarks are established.

We strongly suspect that organizations that are able to build a exploration process will create several competitive advantages simultaneously. One is the capacity to anticipate critical changes coming to the industry before they become competitive necessities. This will allow the organization time to shape change in its own favor, rather than being forced to react to it. Equally importantly, a process of constant exploration and reporting within the company will lessen anxiety and help people build a sense of serenity and stability as environmental change becomes the normal order of things. The organization will be able to implement changes more quickly and with less loss of productivity. This in turn will allow it to take advantage of the sometimes very brief windows of competitive opportunity as they arise.

ˣ "Future planning is too slow," says Skandia's Leif Edvinsson. It's not enough to plan ahead. To get ahead, organizations must look forward, outward, and faster. "The ambition is to move from the driving forces for the future to tangible indicators in a short period, thereby turning the future into an asset rather than a liability and a threat."ˣ

Edvinsson built his Future Teams on a model of organization he calls "3G": a mix of generations – called 25+, 35+, and 45+ – functional roles, organizational experiences, and cultural backgrounds. Skandia's aim is to do a more explicit job of managing conversations within the group and to create intellectual capital from the dialogues. The idea is to make the organization more transparent and thus reduce the leadtime from learning to teaching. Some of the most potent lessons come from those normally excluded from the discussion of strategy – the young and untenured. To quote Edvinsson:

> We need someone who can understand the archeology of the future. That's why we have these 25+ individuals in our program. They already have that vision – they carry the icons of tomorrow with them. They are going to be the leaders of tomorrow.

Navigating the landscape is not a game of tic-tac-toe, and IBM and *E.coli* explore their possibilities in fundamentally similar ways. The nature of exploration, at one scale or another, may be to explore first and decide later the value of what we've found. Diversity, be it in nature or among competitors, is the expression of a basic drive to explore for new niches throughout the landscape as one of the most important ways to extend sustainability for companies and for natural species. Yet any business that tries to explore in too many directions simultaneously will soon run out of cash. Exploration out of the canyon is expensive. Thus, we suggest a regular program of remote sensing (data services and the Internet are cheap) with focused use of real live scouting parties.

What to look for

Psychologists tell us that humans are better at discriminating significant trends from noise when they are looking or listening for something. So the question is: what should the scouts be looking for? Scouting reports differ between the nearby in canyon search and those from beyond the canyon walls. Within the canyon you want to know every surprising thing, regardless of whether you can see the immediate connection to your business. Surprise within the canyon walls must be dealt with sooner or later and usually sooner is better. Outside the canyon walls lies perhaps too much information. The question is not only what to look for to bring back, but what to focus on to justify sending the scouts to look. Here two types of reports are helpful: the truly surprising and the unexpected tangent.

The **truly surprising**: picture those dinosaurs. The sandstorm was a true surprise and not at all related to their then present fight. The invasion of Kuwait, the Indian nuclear tests, Sadat's trip to Jerusalem, Nixon's to Beijing, Monica Lewinsky, the Fed raising the interest rate, the fall of the Berlin Wall, and Diana's auto crash all are examples of surprises that may very well have affected your business despite their being well outside the canyon walls. The point of exploring for true surprises is to gain a time advantage on reacting.

The **unexpected tangent**: when your scouts observe something that seems to be a product extension, a market extension, a functional extension, anything that extends your current base or which looks like it may prevent the extension of your current base, these too should be reported. The value here lies in the combination of surprise and tangency. You want to gain early warning of new directions to turn in (turn in, not jump to) and tangential paths to take.

The rest of what gets reported on is nice but not what you should be seeking, unless you have excess resources to spend and the time to process what returns. In our observation, the critical resource is time. Scouting reports are valuable information for an organization's most senior decision makers. The issue then becomes one of focus. More here is clearly not better. Too much and you lose your audience.

Consider this story from *Fast Company*:

The setting is ancient: A 400-year-old castle in Northamptonshire, England. The participants are young: 23 fast-track employees from German computer giant Siemens Nixdorf Information Systems. The talk is about the future: The breakthrough technologies, demographic trends, and competitive forces that will define the computer market in the year 2005. CEO Gerhard Schulmeyer launched the new planning initiative at Europe's largest computer company. The idea was radical, even a bit subversive: give young people – those most enthusiastic about new technologies and closest to the company's next generation of customers – a genuine voice in shaping corporate strategy.

"Our role is to challenge the board," says Stacy Welsh, who, at 29, is one of the youngest FutureScape members. "The management board is saying, 'We don't understand the buying patterns of 16-year-olds, the kids who are watching MTV. We're nowhere near that generation.' They look to us for perspective."

FutureScape members are "sparring partners for the board," says Richard Roy, an executive vice president of SNI. "They should challenge us to look beyond today's boundaries and shape our thinking about the market, technology, social change. The young generation has a different model of how it thinks about things. FutureScape gives the board views it would not otherwise get. It also gives people in the organization a greater chance to influence the board. It encourages people to offer ideas. That's not always easy in a big German company, where the culture says, 'Wait to be asked.'"

⋮ Bring back stories

Bring back stories, not bullets. The normal thing for most MBAs is to prepare a bullet list. It fits the way we are used to writing and presenting information in company settings. It seems to be economical when examining the ratio of ink to white space. It reduces complex business situations to a few apparently clean points. It gives the presenters the opportunity to move, modify, clarify, and revise on the fly while presenting. It mirrors the cultural position of "reduce complexity by simplifying." And it throws out the baby, the bath water, and the bassinet. You are only left with baby odor (be that good or bad, newborn or one-year-old). As Gordon Shaw of 3M said, "Bullet lists present only an illusion of clarity and it can be an expensive illusion."

Stories, by contrast, allow listener and teller alike the opportunity to get excited. Stories have passion where bullet lists have bullets. Stories allow listeners the opportunity to interpret. Bullets only provide that opportunity to the presenter. Remember Gary Klein's saga from the last chapter. The observers collected great stories really useful to the audience; the presenters wanted to distribute only bullets and overheads, reserving power to the presenters and removing all utility to the audience.

Edvinsson asked his 3G teams to develop and act out stories about the questions they felt top management should be asked. Developing and acting out stories is a far cry from presenting a "not more than one page" memo with bullets. More ink is spent, more paper too, but the participants leave with an emotional reaction as well as a rational one, and it is the emotional we will remember next week never mind next year.

The stories are great – but beware the diehard who won't bring them back. You don't want members of the scouting party who think: "At least for me the zest is in the search more than in the conquest. I like looking more than I like finding." Voyeurism is not what scouting is about, returning with stories is.

:Discuss them

When the stories come back they need to be discussed. Notice that both Skandia and SNI have regularly scheduled discussion sessions with their scouts. Discussion can take many forms, but a simple one follows the formula: Scan, Focus, and Act.

Scan means just what you'd imagine: looking about for different options, or to gather information in a broad sort of way. Scan also implies a vantage point of some sort from which to view. The original meaning of the word means to climb or mount. In the Scan phase you are building mental models.

Focus implies choice. The majority of the opportunities presented in the Scan phase are discarded in favor of only one or several, which are scrutinized and evaluated more rigorously. At length, a decision is made and action follows.

The actions themselves will lead to more stories, more tangents for the scouts to use when exploring and a trip further into the canyon, thus moving the sites you seek to exploit. If the information gleaned from the scouts' stories is used, movement occurs. By contrast, if the stories are merely recorded in a paper file or discussed at the water cooler...

When discussing the stories, don't let them get you upset, no matter how much they challenge either your mental models or sense of identity. The CEO of one company we know is notorious for hiring consultants to explore problems and then yells at them when they present findings he doesn't like. This is upsetting to both the consultants and the rest of the staff. It discourages exploration. Any corporation that makes the lives of its explorers dangerous is one that won't last very far into the next quarter century, much less the next millennium.

A company that systematically practices this kind of discovery and exploration of weirdness in the business will, over time, generate a very different mood about innovation and change. Members of front-line units that are involved in such explorations are typically given authority to "break the rules" of the organization, and they have more frequent conversations with company leaders than do their colleagues. Anxiety and cynicism begin to evaporate as people participate in the process of changing the identity of the company, rather than having change pushed down to them by the corporate organization. But especially at first, it is difficult to operate as a semi-autonomous unit within a larger corporate culture.

However, it is practical to send out "explorers" to the new area and begin to populate its slopes – the explorers are funded by the continued income from the old businesses, so they have enough cash to sustain them until the new technology generates earnings in the marketplace. Over time, if the explorers are successful, more and more investment (people, money, management attention etc.) will be shifted to the new arena and away from the old.

Guidelines for sending out scouting parties

The old common sense, which may have justified a closed mind, not-invented-here syndrome, just does not work in a world of interactions. The next common sense asks what we can learn from the environment. Preparation is the key to attaining advantage.

❖ Always be prepared for surprise (yes, we were both boy scouts). Only by being prepared can you deal with serendipity.
❖ Balance exploitation with exploration. Your canyon demands to be exploited and the outside world (beyond the canyon walls) explored, but resources are limited. In the canyon exploit all surprises, outside it explore the truly surprising and the unexpected tangents. Ignore the vast middle.
❖ Bring back stories that challenge, not bullet lists that put you to sleep.
❖ Be open to discussing the stories and their implications.

Management principles

	Next common sense	Old common sense
The world	Complex	Complicated
Management	Guiding interactions	Leading entities
Simple principles	Adopting a global viewpoint, allowing interactions to happen	Dealing with local situations and trying to "sort things out"
Mental models	Recognizing that my model does not need to be yours, and things can still work	Giving lip service to difference, while giving incentives to conformity
Landscape images	Thinking about ecosystems	Thinking about a car race or a football game
Combine and recombine	Asking about how parts can be combined into new and better wholes	Segregating parts to be treated as their own self-sufficient wholes
Multiple roles	Allowing people to be themselves	Insisting that the company come first

Canyons not canals	Guiding viewpoints not controlling actions	Controlling actions in an attempt to control outcomes
Tell stories	Providing meaningful context and allowing employees to draw their own conclusions	Providing bullet lists of conclusions and demanding that employees fill in the necessary details
Scouting parties	Asking what can be learned from the environment and, on finding a good idea, using it	Asserting that we know best and that all good ideas are invented here

Post and Attend to Road Signs

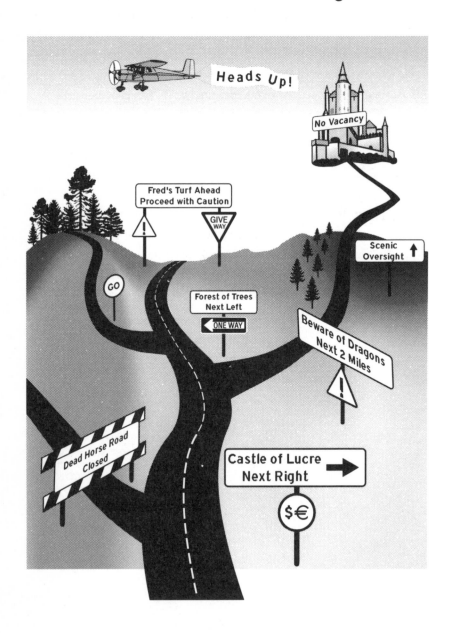

10

POST AND ATTEND TO ROAD SIGNS

Why was Jerry Michalski one of the most desired men in the world of technology? For most of the 1990s, Michalski was managing editor of *Release 1.0*, the high-tech computer trade journal. A mention by him in *Release 1.0* could do for a software or hardware company what a line in Walter Winchell's gossip column did for a starlet's career in the 1940s. What Michalski delivered was attention – of the right kind for a start-up – that of the venture capitalists, bankers, and movers who make the high-tech industry in the US sing.

So, if he were still the editor, how could you be blessed with Michalski's attention? He saw hundreds of companies each year. "If there's something you have that's really great, I want to meet you," said Michalski. An audience with him was brief. "If they can't explain it in 5 to 10 minutes," he said, "then they haven't got anything that the user is going to understand, let alone buy." Getting tagged as "hot" by Michalski was a key to success, but getting tagged as "Jerry should see this" by his secretary was a vital first step.

Being noticed is important, but being noticed *for* some special quality or aspect of ourselves is the key to getting ahead and staying there. Attention is a scarce resource. The total amount available per capita is truly limited. Don't believe us? Well, where is your attention right now? Sure, some of it is one the manifold problems you are not paying mind to while reading this chapter, but the rest of your attention is focused right here, on these very words. The notions of emergence we have stressed in prior chapters do not apply to the total quantity of attention available. In this instance, we are all facing a zero-sum game. The attention you get, I can't and vice versa.

The old common sense separated people with signs. Some erected them. Some labeled them. Some read them. Many wanted them torn down. The next common sense is about recognizing these tensions and developing a balance among them. The tensions between the desires to post signs, to read them, to tear them down, and perhaps to rewrite them cannot be avoided. But, like muscle tension, the good parts can be capitalized on, and the remaining bits eased.

As in any competition in a zero-sum game, emotions can run high when there is much at stake. How to get credit for things you do or have done – achieving "credit assignment" – is important to most of us at some point in our lives. We want our work and our projects to be tagged with our names. Once such a label enters the realm of ordinary conversation, our piece of the future is assured (for good or bad – ask Michael Milken or Ivan Boesky). So, the task is how to generate such labels for others to use. These are the road signs that this chapter will address.

The chapter is about the importance of posting road signs to guide your way and to give credit where credit is due. It is also about the dark side of road signs, which too often goes unexplored. To label with a sign or tag is to give credit – so far so good – and to limit the manner in which some idea, project, or task is perceived. Our mental models are all too happy to incorporate tags; indeed, it is easier to manipulate a label than a work team, or a division, or a building. But by grasping for labels as the abstract items for such manipulations, we limit ourselves to the identity we have associated with the label itself – related but tangential items may go by the wayside, and with them the next innovation, next year's profits, and perhaps in two years your job.

Taking and giving credit

In corporations, the tagging question presents itself as a partial answer to the question: "How do I create a performance ethic in large numbers of people?" For the sales staff – where measurement is easy – the tagging issue is often limited to resolving infighting over whose sale it was and how much of this year's revenue were due to last year's outing on the golf course. There are more than enough management books about how to reward sales teams or stockbrokers, and this will not be another. Our focus, instead, is on the fact that today, people depend on their knowledge, rather than their hands, for making a living and succeeding.

Rewarding people for knowledge, learning, and the development and sharing of the same can only happen when those engaged in such activities are noticed. In practice, this is a issue about how you credit and reward knowledge development in organizations. Strong emotions of fear, rage, and envy emerge when people don't get the credit they feel they deserve (think of the reaction you had when Michael Eisner paid himself $500 million and at the same time cut the Disney development budget by 20 percent. Think of the reaction the guys in development had…).

Assignment of "credit" for knowledge-based activities is an increasingly important managerial issue in all companies. The practice of tagging ideas, or parts of ideas, may be a mechanism that helps managers do this better. But posting road signs has its pluses and minuses. While tagging can help the individual with getting noticed and being recognized (Eisner owes some of that $500 million to Barry Diller who "tagged" his work as "Eisner's"), it may work to constrain further knowledge development by the organization and its network or web. The constraints occur because the very existence of the signs can interfere with the concept of breaking ideas into building blocks and or with recombining those building blocks into new knowledge.

When to post a particular sign or not can have powerful effects on how ideas are generated and dissipated throughout an organization. Innovation and creativity will be affected. In short, the notions of credit assignment – tagging, naming, recognizing, posting signs – all are critical to how ideas get formed and to how knowledge accumulates. Not talking explicitly about the tagging process and its intra-company norms is to risk an important asset – the innovations necessary to compete tomorrow.

Where is the risk? One risk is found in the boundaries that are drawn around an idea when it is labelled – boundaries can mean "do not alter, do not innovate." So signs can also mean "this is mine, do not touch." A second risk lies in the emotional reaction people have to feeling that either their work is ignored or that credit has been "stolen" by someone else. Let's look at that second risk first.

Consider this posting from one of our friends on the Internet's Complex-M list:

> I'd like to throw my two cents in on credit assignment. While I have no problem with anyone using the ideas I've generated, I think it's helpful for those people to know they came from me and to attribute them, where possible. Two reasons for this position: 1) If you like one of my ideas and use it to good effect, it is to your benefit to know it came from me – in case you want to pursue it further without reinventing that particular wheel. 2) I'd rather not go into a presentation one day and have someone say, "That's old hat. I heard it six months ago from another writer." I have no problem with people using my ideas. But, I don't want to be in a position where I have to defend my use of ideas that I generated.

The issue presents itself as one of "justice" and "fairness." After all, if you are the one who came up with an idea, shouldn't you be the one who is given credit for it? Nice as that concept sounds, it is a difficult one to put into practice. Scott Adams has much to say (or draw) on this.

If an idea isn't yours, what risks do you take by insisting on a tagging or credit that is not deserved? We could argue about whether there is such a thing as a wholly original idea, but such an argument is probably not very fruitful. What matters much more is the idea that the recognition involved in tagging can be both an incentive and a constraint.

The idea of passing along credit – of "assigning some value" – is another form of labeling. This form, though, is concerned with incentives and evaluations and making sure that "good" things prosper while "bad" things wither. It makes use of attribute tags – what is an attribute of something and whether that attribute is good or bad. You can't claim ignorance of these tags: we are certain your spouse or parent uses them in referring to you all the time. (At least ours do, both good and bad, and sometimes both at the same time.)

"What, if anything, constrains an idea?" is the key starter question, possibly to be followed by: "What are existing idea-constraint systems costing us?" and "What sort of model(s) will be emerging in the near future?" Our goal should be generating useful ideas that people frequently apply in their work, whether that work is management practice or generating more ideas.

Building a knowledge base with credit assignment requires proper tags, which identify good idea sources and avoid repetition and circularity. When people retag existing ideas, we can lose the threads to earlier sources. But, and this is the killer, an idea is generally a synthesis of other ideas … possibly ideas of yours contain elements of other people's ideas … so how can you claim them as your own? Are you going to give recognition to all those people, and what about the unknown people whose ideas you have subconsciously picked up when talking to them?

As we all know, claims of "this is mine" do get made. They can infuriate those who think that they were the true "prior" source and in organizational settings can "chill" the ability of an idea to attract resources and still further ideas. So what can we do?

Managing signs

Posting signs can be looked on as one of three separate functions. Each involves very different types of signs or tags that get associated with ideas. First, there is the "name" tag – we need something to identify the idea by, some word. Second, there is the "whose this is", the originator tag, the "ownership sign" – words that tells us whose idea it is, or who originated it, or in what division it belongs. And finally, there is the "value judgment sign" – words that tell us about aspects of something and allow evaluations of good or bad, like those brown signs on the highway that suggest you want to stop for a "scenic view" or a "historic place" (which in the industrial heartland of America might be an abandoned strip mine once vital to the ghost town you are passing through). All three of these functions come into play. Indeed, all three are critical to the success of Michelin and Gault-Millau guides.

Posting a sign (of any of the three varieties) affects how you think and what you do. For example, the success of the Japanese watchmakers in the 1980s was due primarily to their ability to overcome constraints formed by combinations of all three types of signage. To the Swiss watchmakers (whose quartz movement technology the Japanese were using), a watch motor was a watch motor. That was the label and that was how they regarded the idea or the thing. The name tag was watch motor. The originator tag was the watch motor group. And the value judgment tags all related to the watch motor as a unified whole. But to the Japanese, the watch motor had three building blocks (e.g. a rotor) that could be thought of quite separately. They optimized the production of each of the building blocks and then put them back together. This proved to be both cheaper and more efficient than the Swiss method of making a united item – the watch motor. The Swiss were constrained by their label – their minds saw only a non-decomposable whole, watch motors. Further, the Swiss watch makers were invested in the concept that a "watch motor department" made watch motors – i.e. the name evoked a sense of territory. There was even a nice sign out front labeled "motors."

In organizations, such constraints can often be found in the practice of labeling projects and ideas by department, function or division. IBM did not see the personal computer as a computer for a long time (and perhaps not until the spreadsheet got invented, but that is another tale). In many technologically oriented companies, the control of personal computers shifted from the "engineers" (when the PC was seen as a sophisticated calculator), to the "accountants" and "secretaries" (when the PC was a "tool" for spreadsheets and word-processing), and finally to the "computer network people" (only in the PC's latest incarnation) as the perception of the PC as a "serious" computing device changed. The number of corporate horror stories regarding "network implementation" which are the result of this labeling and perception process is beyond count. Similar stories can be told about projects that started as "Tom's" and once so labeled could not get resources from Dick or Harry, to the detriment of the company as a whole.

Picking a tag, posting a sign, assigning a word is viewed by almost all of us as an act of "naming." This type of word choice is important to how we think and act toward the named item. Naming directs actions toward the object or experience you have named because of the related attributions of meaning carried by the very words used to make up the "name." To change the name connotes changing your relationship with the experience. Naming implies anticipations, expectations, and evaluations toward the named. Finally, to name something is also to classify it or to put it in a category.

Conflated purposes and meanings

The main problem with the whole concept of tagging is that the separate ideas of naming, describing attributes for evaluatory purposes, and identifying originators are intermingled or **conflated**.

All three notions of a tag are important. We must have some way of talking about things – they must have a name. And we must have some way of knowing that this idea is good and should be rewarded (encouraged, developed) and that this other idea is worse – attributes must be recognized, tagged, and evaluated if we are to have change. By labeling parts with a tag, we have an increased ability to recognize that the part is "a part" – a decomposable fragment of the whole – and to imagine ways of recombining those parts to make new wholes. Finally, the "whose this is" tag is important if we are to

Conflate – *to bring together,*
to collect, to consolidate, to mix
different elements.

optimize our search functions – who do we turn to for what kinds of information? Tensions arise from the frequent fact that these three functions become conflated.

One of our Complex-M friends likes to say:

> *Ideas, like technologies, grow combinatorially. There are lots of*
> *unique combinations of known and tested components. Many*
> *are useless, some are real breakthroughs. When you put*
> *together an original breakthrough combination, you deserve a*
> *good deal of credit for it, and you pass some of that credit back*
> *to the people who supplied the needed components.*

An organization's ability to adapt to change is greatly enhanced by the ability to recognize parts and to imagine how they might be recombined. The danger of posting signs lies in our tendency to associate ideas with persons – to label not only with a word (tags of the value judgment or naming kind) but also a person's or group's name (tags of the originator kind). The conflation of the signs allows for the creation of ideational territories – spaces of ideas that are identified as belonging to someone or to some group. And to this, the mixture of originator, value judgment, and naming tags adds a large amount of excess informational baggage – excess data to be considered when contemplating an idea. (Picture running for an airplane carrying all the many labels and tags with you – it is so convenient bringing the entire *Encyclopedia Britannica* with you for a little light reading. You get the idea.)

This conflating is an old and honored practice. In the Hebrew Talmud, the command is that "one should only speak of things in the name of he who said it." Indeed, the Talmud is a series of 38 books of quotes and quotes about the quotes. And it illustrates the inherent risk of mixing together the "originator tag" and the "value judgment tag" – ease of applicability and accessibility disappear. As more names of originators, and of attributes, and of originators of attributes get piled together and required to travel as a group, a lack of adaptability is created – at least in what we would consider to be a timely manner.

It currently takes more than seven years to go through the Talmud, and a "quick" pace is considered to be a page each day. Our secular society maintains a similar tradition by the way in which we teach the common law – court case by painful court case, for three years of law school.

Max Boisot, in his book *Information Space*, writes extensively of the differences between the "coded" ideas of individuals that are situational and heavily annotated by those who are doing the coding, and socially codified ideas that are much more general and allowed to be used in more simple application. There is a time and a place for each of these approaches. John Seely Brown has written of the Xerox repairmen who gather round the lunch room and trade heavily annotated stories about how to fix machines. In their culture this is the equivalent of the Talmudic explanation, and the tags assigned to these stories will bear the name of the client or the storyteller. Xerox also has a repair manual. There you will find codified knowledge – knowledge that has been made general and with a simple description. As an initial place to turn for advice, the manual works fine; but for detail, one needs the technicians' stories. Each has its place.

Dealing with the issues

The first thing a manager who wants to deal with the issues of posting signs, tagging and credit assignment must do is recognize the tension that is inherent in the very ideas. We need to find the "right amount" of tagging – that which allows adaptability and innovation, allows originators to be rewarded, yet which also does not inhibit the process of taking ideas apart and recombining the pieces. Individuals need signs both to convey searching information and to get "credit" in incentive systems. Collective entities need signs to minimize resource expenditure (searches should cost as little as possible) and to get the most out of the troops (incentives again). The tension arises as the needs of the individuals and the collective entity conflict.

Word choices, especially names, are a form of what cognitive scientists call frames. Frames, as we saw in Chapter 4, are patterns of organized information by which people make sense of the world. These patterns, schemas, or frames form part of the "discursive universe" in which people interact with each other. People learn frames as they learn to use a language fluently and as they learn the narrative structures and ideologies present in the cultures which use that language. When people encounter new information or a new experience, they make sense of that information or experience by fitting it into an existing frame. As people share framed information, they need not refer to all aspects of a frame directly. Instead, they need only to make reference to one dimension of a pattern to enable hearers or readers of their text to recall the whole frame.

Names are thus a means for summoning the picture or concept of a whole frame from a piece – the label, name, or tag. The helpful part of this is the referential aspect: with a name you don't need the whole description. The two unhelpful parts of this are (1) that the name may cause that picture to be perceived as one integral, not decomposable whole; and (2) that the name may conjure up territorial issues to be dealt with by both speaker and listener.

The second thing a manager must do is make room for – create the space for – the members of their network to see the building blocks within things despite their tags and labels. Recall the discussion in Chapter 5. Developing ideas requires, among other things, the ability to discern the "component-ness" of items so as to be able to break them into building blocks or components and then to recombine those components into something new. The component-ness of items – the fact that things have parts that are themselves separable (including ideas) – is not obvious. The tags, signs, and names that we use for things influence our perceptions. Our mental schemas, like those of the Swiss watchmakers, can easily interfere with our ability to recognize the decomposability of an item – its ability to be separated into building blocks.

Reify – to consider an abstract concept to be real or concrete.

In Western society and similar environments, there is a tendency to **"reify"** ideas, to assert concreteness to something that has been given a name. That which is tagged is now prescribed to be "a" thing. The notion of "a" thing is different from the notion of a composite (a composite is made up of several things). Thus, the very act of naming introduces an obstacle to the ability to recognize the component-ness of ideas and things. Overcoming that obstacle requires effort. That effort may force attention away from such "recognition of building block" activities towards others which do not involve that effort.

As a result of this process, it is less likely that tagged items will be recognized as building blocks for new things. Recall the story of the inkjet. Excited by its obvious commercial potential, its discoverer, John Vaught, showed the device to anyone who would take the time to look at it. Unfortunately, neither his manager nor any of the other people who saw it shared his enthusiasm. Because its inner workings were not understood, even a number of the people who actually saw the device operating told him that his approach could not work. Vaught's reply was: "But it is working." The resolution to this curious impasse would have to wait until the underlying phenomenon had been explained. Other than Vaught, those who saw or heard about the device only knew that heat and ink produced either a coagulated solid or ugly blots. They held to those preconceived labels even when shown a working device.

This story illustrates the idea that the building blocks which make up tagged items are less likely be used in the creation of new composites – i.e. new knowledge. Instead, they may only have incremental work done on them, work accepts the pre-existing labeling rather than challenging it. Signs help point the way, but they also get in the way.

Resolving the tension? No. Striking a balance? Yes.

Some people argue that if we were not competing for attention, then knowledge development – the exchange of ideas – would clearly flourish best (where they define best as the maximum production of new ideas) in an untagged environment, one without road signs. Such a utopia would allow for the maximal amount of decomposition and recombination. Yet in the real world evaluatory schemes and other methods for attracting and allocating attention predominate. Such evaluations will be in the mode of the pre-existing labeling scheme, such as organizational titles, divisional frames, organization chart items, and the like. The signs thus created will enhance an individual's opportunities for recognition and advancement, but, at the same time, will work to dissipate the organization's ability to maximize the recombinations that lead to new knowledge.

The flip side of this argument is that it is easier to build on prior work than to reinvent it. Furthermore, you're only tagging a particular combination, and not the individual components or building blocks. Most innovators like to see extensions of their work. Tagging with a source helps extenders identify the earlier sources of the combined components more easily. Not only that, but in an environment with many potential building blocks to choose from, road signs help you determine which ones to choose.

These two goals – maximal knowledge development and evaluation – have different demands. Both activities will go on, but they should not be confused or conflated with each other. Posting signs allows for evaluation and reward. But posting signs interferes with further combining and recombining just as it assists with incrementalism. By tagging, you restrict the search process to a defined local neighborhood. By allowing free-form search through the whole range of possibilities, you promote the creativity and free association of ideas necessary for innovation. Both activities are important, but they interfere with one another. We are back to the choice of explore or exploit.

The explore or exploit choice is a spatial metaphor. It refers to landscapes – competitive ones. Should a company exploit its present position by attempting to eke out incremental improvements (or in the case of the old Boston Consulting Group model, milk a cash cow), or should it take advantage of the entire landscape and explore for a new spot from which to compete in the future? It is unusual for managers to think about tags and labels as causing shifts in physical space, but that is precisely the thinking required to deal with the explore/exploit questions raised. For example, the "who gets credit for this" type of label acts to promote the identification of an idea with a territory. That identification, in turn, triggers both acquisitive desires (for more territory) and defenses.

By thinking about the tradeoffs in terms of physical space rather than in terms of labels and "who gets credit," a manager can see the way to the balance point more readily.

Guidelines for posting road signs

Using the next common sense is a matter of recognizing individual contributions and allowing others to leverage them, while combating the tendency of individuals to stake out territory and post "no trespassing" signs. In a world of interactions, knowledge of opportunities is key to realizing them, and awareness of fences is an awareness of opportunities missed.

❖ Post only a few signs in your landscape. Tags are more than just "giving credit." They have consequences and create tensions as they get applied.

❖ Recognize that assigning credit for ideas is to create a tension between the name of the originator and everyone else. That tension is good if it spurs the whole team to explore its possibility. It is bad if it allows fiefdoms to develop and walls off ideational territories among the fiefs.

❖ To minimize the negative tension, seek to split up the signing and tagging function. Ideas need names, but those names need not be associated with specific groups or people. Do not follow the Talmudic injunction of speaking through the name of he who said it. Instead, assign non-fief-causing names. Use metaphorical language that can be related to in storytelling.

❖ Reward active participation in the process of idea exploration at both individual and team levels. Minimize the extent to which value judgment tagging is associated with individuals rather than teams or larger work units.

❖ Exploit competitors' road signs. Take advantage of the times when they have posted too many signs. When the number of visible signs is large, blockages to recognizing and using building blocks abound. Their mistake can be your competitive edge.

Management principles

	Next common sense	Old common sense
The world	Complex	Complicated
Management	Guiding interactions	Leading entities
Simple principles	Adopting a global viewpoint, allowing interactions to happen	Dealing with local situations and trying to "sort things out"
Mental models	Recognizing that my model does not need to be yours, and things can still work	Giving lip service to difference, while giving incentives to conformity
Landscape images	Thinking about ecosystems	Thinking about a car race or a football game
Combine and recombine	Asking about how parts can be combined into new and better wholes	Segregating parts to be treated as their own self-sufficient wholes
Multiple roles	Allowing people to be themselves	Insisting that the company come first

Canyons not canals	Guiding viewpoints not controlling actions	Controlling actions in an attempt to control outcomes
Tell stories	Providing meaningful context and allowing employees to draw their own conclusions	Providing bullet lists of conclusions and demanding that employees fill in the necessary details
Scouting parties	Asking what can be learned from the environment and, on finding a good idea, using it	Asserting that we know best and that all good ideas are invented here
Road signs	Recognizing individual contributions and promoting leverage	Staking out territories and allowing individuals to post "no trespassing" signs

Fuel Coherence with Aligned Words

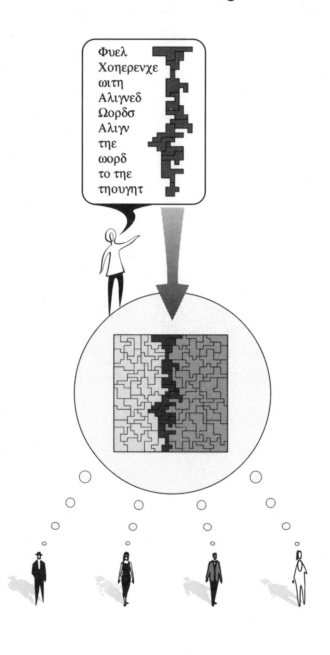

11

USE ALIGNED WORDS TO FUEL COHERENCE

D o you eat tomatoes? Red tomatoes? Home-grown tomatoes? Those not so tasty – but conveniently packaged – six
to a plastic container tomatoes? Spaghetti sauce?

Do you eat bread? Homemade bread?

Do the words "genetically engineered" endear you to a food item or frighten you away? And the words "mutant gene?"

We are sure you have heard the story of Watson and Crick's discovery of the DNA double helix. We suspect you know the story of the computer's journey from the ENIAC to the PC. But have you considered how these two stories have evolved together and been intertwined?

When we think of DNA, an image which comes nearly instantly to mind is that of the "genetic code." DNA is the stuff our bodies and cells use to program their way through life. DNA is what makes our cells "tick."

When we think of making a computer run, we also use the word program. A computer program, its instruction set, is what gets the computer through a given task. Windows, for all of the hoopla surrounding Bill Gates, is just a program. Programs are what make computers "tick."

DNA research caught the public's eye in the 1950s and has been making headlines ever since. The same is true of computer research. These two phenomena have been intertwined in the public's understanding and imagination for nearly 50 years.

So what? Well, let's go back to the tomatoes and the bread.

In a computer, when a program has a small error – when there is a mutation – the machine has a nasty habit of crashing. It won't do what we want it to and it may cause more than a little ancillary damage in the process.

In life, when a cell or its genes have a small error – when there is a mutation – this is the source of new variety and adaptation. Indeed, mutations and "errors" are the very stuff from which evolution is made. The mutation may mean that the living thing is not quite like the others before it, but such differences overall are how species adapt and survive.

Thus the concepts of "error" and "mutation" are different between biology and computer science. The biologists understand this, but the general public? Well…

Are you happy with the idea of genetically engineered tomatoes? Square tomatoes pack easily. Orange tomatoes add color to a salad. Thin-skinned tomatoes have more juice for sauces. Thick-skinned tomatoes allow chefs to do those fancy carvings. All were genetically engineered from mutants. The same is true of the bread you eat, but the process of engineering grain took a bit longer. Our ancestors of thousands of years ago could only cross-pollinate by hand and without the benefits of the chemical knives of DNA research.

When we hear terms such as "mutant gene" and "genetically engineered," for most of us it is the computer programming images that immediately get called to mind. In this mental model error is bad, mutation is horrible, engineering is exact, and the very idea of deliberately engineering mutation is distasteful at best and unethically disturbing at worst.

The debate has moved on from tomatoes and wheat to children, drugs, and food supplies. Public policy is shaped by the public's reaction, yet we react not from the "informed" stance of biology (mutation is variety, is good) but from the "obvious" stance of the computer programmer (mutation is error, is crash).

Somehow, the concepts of programming and DNA have become aligned. The coherent response to mutation is "yuck."

So the grocer does not display a sign that says "genetically altered" tomatoes. The "wholewheat" lover in your family does not speak of the "untoward acts" which were necessary to produce that Vitamin E enhanced, "all-natural" wheat. The Europeans hesitate to approve American "engineered" corn and soya beans, ignoring 5000 years of botany and agronomic science. Funny, most of those same delegates have definitive opinions on wines. How do they think the grapes got that way?

Given the old common sense, word choice did not matter. Each word had defined meanings or at least defined meanings in obvious situations. Quality improvement meant the types of materials purchased and error rates in the manufacturing process. Human resources meant salaries and vacation policies and some hiring and firing. Why would anyone want to conflate the two? If we perceive mutations to be "bad," this is because they are.

Given the next common sense, interrelations and interweavings mean that words only have meaning in usage. So mutations can be good or bad depending on context. The HR people may indeed have a lot to say regarding your quality improvement program (and your quality engineers may have even more to say regarding HR).

When words take on meanings through use, they have the power to affect mindsets and thus actions. The story of the mutant gene is just one example.

This chapter is about using aligned words to fuel the sense of coherence in your organization or team. Word choice matters. Words affect mindsets and mental models. So aligning words with each other, with underlying values, and with actions can be a potent self-enhancing force.

The right words at the right time

The very words that organizational members use to describe and communicate the changes they experience help shape that experience. Experience shapes the lenslike, cognitive structures through which managers see the world. The rules for using words greatly depend on the institutional setting in which the usage occurs, such as in an organization. The setting provides the appropriate vocabulary for saying something meaningful – for understanding and establishing rules, as well as finding, creating and using terms. In effect, the words are part and parcel of defining the environment. Nystrom and Starbuck put it:

> *What people see, predict, understand depends on their ... logically interrelated and mutually reinforcing systems of values and beliefs ... [which] manifest themselves in perceptual frameworks, expectations, world views, plans, goals, ... myths, rituals, symbols, ... and jargon.*

Let us illustrate with the example of Tripod, Inc., an Internet content provider and web community. When Tripod was begun, its founders, two college students and a professor, were focused on the idea that ready access to information regarding "life tasks" (money, health, travel) was unavailable to college students. As the company evolved, that focus became both a self-identity and a catch-all slogan – "Tripod: Tools for Life." The slogan appeared throughout the Tripod web site, in print, and all over the company's office. More importantly, it was actively referred to as the "guiding idea" behind virtually all of Tripod's activities by all members of staff, and, as revealed through interviews, by most of Tripod's members. The Tools for Life idea was illustrated by images of hammers and wrenches and was embodied by web content on such items as "how to rent an apartment," "getting insurance," and "ask the doctor."

As Tripod grew more successful and attracted outside investors, the basic mission – we are tools for life – remained unchanged. Yet the

Internet and the perceived marketplace were changing. Following the third round of venture capital, the Tripod staff were confronted by their advertising team: "This tools idea is too limiting. We think it only means students to advertisers. Our base is really GenX and we need to sound like GenX if we are to convince advertisers that we are GenX." Three months of all-inclusive debate followed. Every member of Tripod's staff was involved in the process of coining a new slogan and what was hoped to be a new sense of identity. Finally, by a two-thirds vote of the staff the new slogan was established: "LiveSmart, WorkSmart, StreetSmart."

Adoption of the slogan was easy. Nearly every Tripodian was involved both in the decision of what the slogan would be and in how it should be implemented. But not two months following the adoption, trouble was evident. When one of the authors interviewed staff to ask about comfort with the new slogan, he was surprised to hear time and again: "What new slogan?" As the next few months unfolded, staff's use of the new slogan took a dramatic plunge. The content editors found themselves forced to spend hours each week manually inserting the slogan somewhere in each page (a task never needed with the previous slogan, which seemed to be incorporated into the content automatically). Staff made more and more reference to the old slogan and it began reappearing in web content. Finally, six months after the "LiveSmart, WorkSmart, StreetSmart" slogan was adopted, it was dead. "Tools for Life" reappeared and was reasserted as the Tripod identity.

What had happened? This was not a top-down decision, and no Tripod staff member identified "management" or "power" as even a relevant issue regarding what was wrong with the slogan, either during the six months or in post-event interviews. Similarly, a leadership analysis sheds little light. The Tripod staff gathered frequently, worked in close proximity to one another and felt considerable influences from one another. Yet the leadership was continually attempting to attract the staff to "LiveSmart, WorkSmart, StreetSmart" without success. And even the leaders would fail to use or find relevance in the slogan other than when exhorting others to do so. Everyone agreed it was important; few and ultimately none "bought in" to its concept. An organizational culture analysis produces only confusion. The process by which the "LiveSmart" slogan as artifact was created was fitted well with the prevailing Tripod culture, yet the artifact produced was not.

More light can be shed by considering the words themselves and the images, frames, and mindset they evoked among their users. "Tools for Life" was coherent with the self-image the Tripodians had of themselves and their role in the lives of their members. By contrast, it was hard for the typical Tripodian to reconcile the hip, urban "StreetSmart" with the realities of Williamstown (Tripod's location in a rural corner of Massachusetts), a town of 8000 people with one main street and no crime. Further, the realities of Tripodians' day-to-day tasks better matched the old tools than the new Smarts. Staff were engaged in writing about money, housing, healthcare, travel, jobs, and computers. These were the practical and the mundane. Perhaps mastery of the mundane rendered one Smart, but to the writers and providers of the content the task was never finished, each day opened with new information to be learned and disseminated, and thus mastery seemed quite elusive. Reasserting the potency of Tools was reasserting the identity they already and continually felt.

To us, the Tripod slogan misadventure illustrates the power of word choice, i.e. **the right words uttered at the right time can be very effective**.

Words shape thinking and actions

Herb Kelleher uses the word *family* as an aligning force. Steve Case uses the word *welcome* (said by that ubiquitous voice each time you log in). In fact, when Microsoft launched MSN (the Microsoft Network), AOL flew a plane above Microsoft's big party in Redmond. The plane had a banner with a single word: welcome.

Not just any word will do the trick. Somehow we don't think that if the Southwest Airlines motto were "pumpkins" that much would be conveyed to either employees or customers, beyond an uncanny sense of an overbearing presence of orange. The words that have the potential to shape thinking and actions are words which:

❖ align with existing values and impressions
❖ recur frequently
❖ resonate with the situation and the context
❖ create meaning.

Richard Dawkins calls words which fit these criteria "memes." He treats the universe which speaks of a given meme as larger than the work teams, organizations, and family units which are our focus here, but his use of the meme concept and our use of "aligned words" is much the same.

How is a word or phrase (for nothing says this only applies to single words) **aligned**? As the surfers at Intense Moments would tell us, an aligned word helps one catch a wave, a misaligned word leads to a watery crash, and an unaligned word leads only to becalmed surfers or the sand-hugging crowd, for both of which the wave has passed by. The wave is the ongoing force of existing values as we, or our unit, or our team continually attempt to make sense out of the current situation. These values – which are already present – help to frame the situation, bringing certain aspects to the forefront and leading others to become background. Similarly, the awareness of a situation – its current impression on you, your unit or team – is composed of both foreground and background, the sorting variables which evoke the existing value set.

It matters not whether you are aware of the values first and then sort the situation (make sense out of it) or have the impression first (which then triggers the values) – either way, the values are present and exerting a force. In the first case (aware then sort) the force is alignment. In the second case (sorted situation evokes) it is resonance. But the force itself is the same. Aligned words go along with that force. Not as simple yes men, for respectful reshaping is possible, but still in a manner of continuing not fighting.

Misaligned words attempt to assert an immediate new direction. Like the distracted surfer, all that happens is the wave comes crashing in on top. Remember "new" Coke? Or perhaps the diet supplement "Ayds"? Maybe you were one of the 100-odd people who bought a videophone in 1965 to "get connected." The words themselves are just symptoms of the misaligned push. Their meaning is what is misaligned, but what we sense (see, hear, read) is the word. As the Bible put it, "In the beginning was the word." When meanings are aligned, the emotion is comfort. When they are misaligned, discomfort results.

Words may also be simply **unaligned** (like the surfers waiting adrift or the crowd on shore) – surely pumpkins at Southwest would be, except at Halloween. There are many famous unaligned statements: "512k is more than enough memory for anyone" (Bill Gates). "The world market for computers is perhaps five or six machines" (James Watson of IBM). "This will be the mother of all battles" (Saddam Hussein). "I didn't inhale" (Bill Clinton). How many AOL diskettes do you use as drink coasters?

Repetition and recurrence are critical to the effectiveness of words. The AOL diskette example we just used only has meaning because of the hundreds of millions of free diskettes AOL has mailed to everyone (over and over again). If you had received only one or two, we would not have been able to make our point. Similarly, the "mother" word Saddam is so fond of has lost all of its meaning. When everything is the mother of everything, how does one take any particular usage seriously? (We all have taught our children about the boy who cries wolf.)

With aligned words, recurrence is reinforcement of the alignment. With misaligned words, it is reinforcement of the "miss." With unaligned words, it is reinforcement of the *lack* of relevance. The more an aligned word is repeated and used, the stronger the alignment becomes.

Aligned words resonate. They summon a comfortable emotional reaction which may not be separately articulated in words. The act of alignment is essentially an act of articulation – we can say how something is aligned. Resonance, by contrast, is more of a tacit feeling. Things resonate, but we can never be quite exact in saying how. Resonance carries over into action. Our words and actions can resonate, whereas our words and only our descriptions of actions can be aligned.

Aligned words are different from resonating words. Words that resonate are uttered first and happen to resonate. Aligned words are thought about first with the goal of alignment. When resonance works its effects are the same as alignment, but resonance is not purposive. It works when it happens to work. Alignment, by contrast, is conscious, purposeful, and conceived from an intent. When you find language that resonates, remember it. It can be used as aligning language.

Aligned words work well when they help to create meaning. Words which focus us in on previously recognized aspects of situations and merely serve to narrow our scope are much less effective than words which act to open up new possibilities and expand our range of either autonomy or action. Thus, when using words it works well to tell a story, thereby adding to the meaning implicit in the word.

We all know these lessons; we just seldom practice them. Yet each of us, when learning a new word or when helping a child do so, knows all too well the phrase "now use it in a sentence three times." Why? Using it is aligning it. The three sentences are both recurrence and the creation of meaning (since it does not count to use the same sentence twice). Getting the child to say the sentences aloud and act them out is a means of evoking resonance. We have much better understanding of and feel more deeply something that we have experienced compared to something that we have merely articulated.

At the extreme lies **imprinting**. Certain words, if repeated enough and in sufficiently important situations, get imprinted on our brain. The little duckling imprints the first thing it sees

Imprinting – to fix indelibly or permanently in the mind or memory.

as mother. We each have imprinted "welcome" (in that certain tone) as AOL. Highly successful brands have imprinted on many of us. Do you use a Band-aid or a bandage, a Kleenex or a facial tissue, ketchup or sweetened tomato sauce, Xerox or dry printing technology copies, FedEx or an overnight courier service? The purpose of taking a name is to have it imprinted as your symbol for something. But when the name goes wrong or the imprint fails, problems ensue. When was the last time you used Western Union? Or the Pony Express?

The danger lies in imprinting something that is no longer aligned. If Johan's son August were seen as a duckling's mother, there may be a food problem (ducklings don't like to eat LEGO). It was Bill Gates who said the Internet was just a toy. And it was Netscape which was a browser company. Or Intel a memory company. And Woolworth's the five and ten. It is hard to go upscale once you have imprinted a brand as "downmarket," as many a fashion designer has learned to its dismay. Park Avenue ladies do not shop for clothes at JC Penny, except, perhaps, for their garden.

Coherence can be fueled by aligned words

The fuel of coherence is more coherence. In complexity science terms, such fueling is known as an "attractor." Attractors pull. Think of a drainage ditch at the bottom of a steep driveway – the ditch seems to pull the rain water to it. Think of those who are labeled as a "charismatic personality" – they will draw people in, be it to a conversation, an entertainment event, or the grand opening of some new store. Picture Leonardo DiCaprio arriving at a crowded restaurant or Frank Sinatra in his heyday.

Pull and fuel are energy words. Energy is what attractors are all about. Like gravity, we move toward an attractor when we are in its neighborhood. Tom Petzinger (of *Wall Street Journal* fame) writes:

> *Clearly, organizations do have attractors in the sense that physical systems do. At precisely 6 a.m. 200 people along an assembly line simultaneously begin work; for them 6 a.m. is an attractor. The rules, policies, and procedures of the organization are in a sense pure attractors. And perhaps the informal side may harbor attractors as well, such as when some event rallies or demotivates a workforce.*

You could say that *Star Trek, Seinfeld,* and the soccer World Cup are attractors in the popular culture. Millions of people alter the rhythms of their lives to spend an hour with these shows. The fact that they are attractors is what draws millions of dollars of advertising revenues.

Like a magnet, we can be confused or suspended if caught between adjoining basins of attraction. Attractors can be overcome, but it takes a lot of outside force. Netscape and the Internet were, for a time, an unbeatable attractor, but Bill Gates was not to be denied. Given sufficient force, sufficient energy, and enough time and resources, Microsoft has demonstrated clearly that even the strongest attractor can be overcome. Coherence, however, is found in "catching the wave" of an attractor – going with the flow, becoming one with its nature. Fighting attractors is not coherent unless you are using one to do battle with another.

A good storyteller implicitly makes use of the power of attractors. They will hunt for just the right words to make the connection between the story being told and the audience's current context. If the audience can "buy in" to what is being told, then the emotional power of the story is that much greater.

Management gurus do this naturally. The stories they tell – stick to your knitting, the value chain, reengineering, total quality management, and economic value added – would be cut and dried if the guru did not find a way to relate the lesson(s) to the audience. They pitch their "message" to the attractor already present in the room – to the context of the audience. Academic management experts have not quite learned this lesson. They tend to present the "right message," which does not vary from audience to audience and perhaps even from year to year. If you want the audience to buy in to your message, you must first catch their wave. You can't pull them unless you have respected their pull toward you.

The power of simple rules stems from their attractive force. When a simple rule works, it can draw in an audience and the power of the draw fuels additional power. Consider the pricing conflict between AT&T, MCI, and Sprint for long-distance phone service in the US. Price cuts are worthwhile if met with sufficient increased volume. So MCI proposes a simple rule – the calling circle, give us the names of your friends and family and we will give each of you a discount for calling the others. The rule draws in customers. Sprint counters with a simpler rule: every call on the weekend is 10 cents a minute. The simpler rule draws in more customers. AT&T offers the simplest rule in response – nine cents, all the time, as long as you spend more than some minimum each month. All the time is simpler than 10 cents on weekends and x during the week, and does not require that you recruit your acquaintances. The simplest rule tends to have the most drawing power. MCI and Sprint ultimately match the offer and then offer cash to get a customer to switch. Again, attractors can be overcome by sufficient force, but in general the attractor wins.

The right words also have an attractive force. When Herb Kelleher says "family," that is an attractor. So too is "copier" for Xerox. They align with both the underlying values of the audience (Herb's employees and Xerox's customers) and the existing impression the audience has of the company and the many situations where company and audience intersect. Southwest Airlines seems comfortable with the attractive pull of "family," but Xerox has begun to feel constrained by the pull of "copier." Whether the "document company" can work to become an attractor remains to be seen.

Kodak tried printers and copiers, but remains stuck with the attractors of "camera, film, and photography." In fact, these attractors were so powerful that Kodak retrenched from its moves to become a "document company" and went on to be "the image company." Image is a word more closely aligned with the old attractors of camera, film, and photography. Kodak is trying to broaden the basin of its attractor with "image" – it is building a canyon and fighting the tendency of Fuji and others to restrict it to a side canal.

By picking aligned words, you can add energy to an existing attractor. This will broaden the basin of its pull. The larger the basin of attraction, the greater the possibilities for coherent action (the possibility space gets bigger). By contrast, the use of the wrong words will subtract energy and narrow the basin of attraction. When Psion and three mobile phone companies announced an alliance in 1998 focused on "communicating" and "making it easy," they were mutually broadening their basin. "Communicate" has more resonance than "net access" or "Windows." There is more pull to an attractor focused on communicating – pull that seems likely to leave Windows CE off on a side canal. Such is the power of words.

Which words to pick

Remember, it is not just any words. It is **aligned** words. So how do you choose which words to use?

You pick those words which give you the most leverage in trying to get across your meaning. By most leverage we mean the greatest on-target response for the least expenditure of energy. Notice that it keeps coming back to energy – words are a means of communicating and each of the acts of communicating, of making sense, of remembering, of storing for future recall, of retrieving, and of further communicating demand energy to accomplish.

This type of leverage is Max Boisot's "least action principle" once again. Ideas will go to the place where the least action is required to get them there. Boisot claims (and we agree) that information flows are governed by the least action concept. Even standing still (the physics idea of inertia) requires energy. Inertia demands energy for the purpose of storing an idea and making it available for recall and for use. With information, ideas, concepts, mental models, and so on there is a constant energy demand. Least action suggests that like water flowing downhill, we attempt to minimize the energy which needs to be expended to "deal" with the information. "Deal" may mean use, store, communicate, reinterpret, or forget – no matter what our choice, some expenditure of energy will be required.

Boisot's theory distinguishes among concepts which get coded (restated in some truncated form), abstracted (reclassified as part of some larger idea of which they constitute but a part), and diffused (spread around or communicated). Others looking at this notion have further distinguished among the actions about which concepts speak – these may be decomposable (separable into parts, remember Chapter 5), and themselves diffused or distributed. Each of these categories exists as a scale ranging from strong to weak. The scales form a multidimensional space in which each concept and the communication flows among people about those concepts can be located. By locating these aspects of an idea or concept in space and being able to describe how ideas move among people, it is possible to discuss the energy requirements of the information/communication situation. So as words get used, we can chart the energy requirements of that use.

These energy requirements and their accompanying mathematics follow the leverage principle we articulated above. We would need a computer to calculate what course of communication would use the lowest possible energy, but we can say generally that words that reflect the energy and emotion of a given situation have a lower energy "requirement" than those that seek to change the emotions of the audience. Words that summon up pre-existing images, concepts or mental models can take advantage of the effort that has gone before them. Words that are familiar or simple require less effort to interpret or make sense out of than do new words or new usages for old words. Words that are reflective of a situation – that don't try to add some new twist – require less energy to be accepted than do words that seem "force fitted." Our normal example of the latter is a bad excuse.

Aligned words are words that require the least energy to be meaningful. Since energy is a constant, the less energy required to extract meaning, the more energy is available for actions. If your purpose is action, aligned words give both managers and team members the most leverage. So aligned words tend to:

❖ be reflective of the situation
❖ be reflective of the emotions of the audience
❖ make use of pre-existing ideas or concepts
❖ tap into pre-existing mental models
❖ be familiar
❖ be simple.

Most importantly, aligned words are "easily" used – that is, they evoke meaning in both speaker and listener.

The very act of writing this book is an effort to put into practice the advice we are preaching. The arguments we make could have been presented in some form of pseudo-scientific technobabble. Indeed, some of our closest friends have adopted such words for their day-to-day speech patterns. But, while such talk may resonate with some readers, it is unlikely to align with most of you. Instead, we have aimed to use language that is familiar, as simple as we can make it, and well illustrated with management and life stories, not physics or metaphysics.

Hopefully, we have not gone overboard in the other direction and given you too much academic babble from the world of "organization studies." Such language often has defined meanings to the professors in the field but other meanings to practitioners. The words may be the same (and the familiarity leads to resonance), but the contrast in meaning ultimately leads only to expressions of frustration, arrogance or both. Perhaps Einstein phrased it best: "Everything should be made as simple as possible, but not simpler." When that balance point is reached, it is easy to sense which words are aligned. The further we get from that balance point, the more effort alignment takes.

Guidelines for aligning words

It was never true that words had only one meaning, but many managers operating from the old common sense sure acted as if they did – the boss's meaning. Reflection on the next common sense reveals an essential truth: the words we use can help to enact the context for our actions. Words that are aligned with values and purpose can assist intended acts; words that are not aligned can act instead to obstruct. Word choice matters.

❖ Words can fuel coherence, if they are aligned.
❖ Use words or phrases that align with people's basic values.
❖ When you find language that resonates, remember it. It can be used as aligning language.
❖ Aligned words have an attraction force. Like a magnet, they can make you alter the way you think and act.
❖ If you understand the current situation, including the emotions involved, picking aligned words is easy. What seems to be "common sense" is a good benchmark.

Management principles

	Next common sense	Old common sense
The world	Complex	Complicated
Management	Guiding interactions	Leading entities
Simple principles	Adopting a global viewpoint, allowing interactions to happen	Dealing with local situations and trying to "sort things out"
Mental models	Recognizing that my model does not need to be yours, and things can still work	Giving lip service to difference, while giving incentives to conformity
Landscape images	Thinking about ecosystems	Thinking about a car race or a football game
Combine and recombine	Asking about how parts can be combined into new and better wholes	Segregating parts to be treated as their own self-sufficient wholes
Multiple roles	Allowing people to be themselves	Insisting that the company come first

Canyons not canals	Guiding viewpoints not controlling actions	Controlling actions in an attempt to control outcomes
Tell stories	Providing meaningful context and allowing employees to draw their own conclusions	Providing bullet lists of conclusions and demanding that employees fill in the necessary details
Scouting parties	Asking what can be learned from the environment and, on finding a good idea, using it	Asserting that we know best and that all good ideas are invented here
Road signs	Recognizing individual contributions and promoting leverage	Staking out territories and allowing individuals to post "no trespassing" signs
Align words	Using words to create meaningful context	Assuming that words all have one global meaning – the boss's meaning

12
THE FIVE STEPS

In this book we have distinguished between the old and the next common sense. The old common sense is for those of you who still believe that the world is complicated and for whom management as a practice boils down to leading SBUs, organizations, functions, work teams, or other entities.

As a manager, your job is to try to deal with local situations as they arise and to attempt to sort things out. Difficulties should not rise to head office level. You are used to giving lip service to "difference," but in reality you create large incentives for conformance and disincentives for its opposite. You are most comfortable when thinking about your business as a competitive sport (football to your friends, a car race to your spouse who doesn't, and never will, understand football) and enjoy using those 2 × 2 matrices to plot strategy and portfolio allocation. It is important to you and to the company to make full use of a "divide and conquer" strategy. Thus, strategic business units are to be broken out and managed separately, lest the subordinate manager dare to suggest corporate-wide initiatives. Similarly, you stress the idea that the company comes first – productive subordinates who have a family life are preventing you from gaining even greater profits.

You never provide a detailed illustration or story when a nice bullet list will do. Your employees are more than capable of understanding what you mean. If this implies that some of them have staked out individual territories, well, internal competition is a good thing. After all, good ideas originate here – how else can you get credit for them? And this new-fangled notion about being careful with your words – that's all poppycock. You speak more than clearly and everyone knows what you mean; if they don't, they should be looking for another job.

The **next common sense** is for those of you who shudder, laugh, or get angry when reading the above paragraphs. To you, the world is a complex place. Interactions mean more than entities. Not that the SBUs and the like are not there, but how they relate to and with each other is what counts. Thus your job as a manager is to step back, adopt a global viewpoint and allow the interactions to happen. This requires you to recognize that your model does not need to be everyone else's model. In the long run, things will work just fine despite this divergence in views.

To you, the consultant's 2 × 2 matrices are expensive nonsense. The world cannot be adequately captured in pictures that are less rich than the ecosystem they try to model – business is lived on a changing landscape and not tossed around like a football. You are continually searching for new ways to combine existing things and people – to make new work teams, new projects, and perhaps new products. Old divisions or labels for parts of the firm are just temporary, since the best things emerge when new combinations are allowed to flourish. There is too much to be done and you can neither do it yourself nor demand that others do it your way as your proxy. Your role is to provide guidance and plenty of running room. You trust people to be themselves and in so doing to help meet corporate goals. Thus, you see yourself as a guider of viewpoints and not as a controller of actions.

In this role you often tell stories – by providing context to your illustrations, you enable each employee to extract conclusions relevant to their task and their situation. Similarly, you encourage your staff to explore the landscape. Great ideas are out there for the taking, or at least for the being improved on. If you don't look, how can you find? As these ideas are found or developed, you publicly recognize the employees involved. This both inspires others and allows enough knowledge for leveraging. By contrast, you hate it if an employee says "this is mine" and actively fight the notion of territory. Through all your activities you are very mindful of the words and symbols you use. The words create both context and filters and the next set of actions may depend on them. Your task is to be ever vigilant in promoting alignment and coherence.

Coherence must be *made* and it requires active maintenance. This way of being can't be found and isn't a possession. In the world of managed entities, coherence was often merely asserted or, worse, insisted on by those above. Such arrogance, it seems, was an unfortunate facet of management in the complicated world. But coherence – a unified sense of purpose, self, identity, and values – must be created, woven together from the many interrelationships that characterize the complex world of today.

This final chapter is about creating coherence. More importantly, it is about helping you to create a context that makes coherent action most likely.

Chapters 2–11 have given you building blocks for both making sense of things and developing a coherent point of view. Now these building blocks need to be used to construct an action plan. This chapter is about using what you have learned. Five steps are key to realizing the next common sense in any organization:

* Identify yourself and your goals.
* Use the right language.
* Create the right context.
* Turn people loose and then get out of the way.
* Use communication that works.

It is critical to realize that the five steps are a package. The parts can be decomposed and recombined into something new, but our observation is that you need at least something from each of the steps. For instance, leaving out the final, communication, step is an invitation for an initially coherent program to dissolve due to centrifugal force. The very people you turned loose in the fourth step may well have very different destinations in mind and, without communication among them, will go in different ways. Equally, leaving out the context step may turn your goals into an exercise in philosophy. Lots of words will be spouted by frustrated people turned loose to act, but encountering the wrong context in which to do so.

Dee Hock (the Visa founder, mentioned in Chapter 1) argues that the critical qualities for management are integrity, motivation, capacity, understanding, knowledge, and experience, in that order. We agree with these observations from him (in *Fast Company*):

> *Without integrity, motivation is dangerous; without motivation, capacity is impotent; without capacity, understanding is limited; without understanding, knowledge is meaningless; and without knowledge, experience is blind. Experience is quickly put to use by people with all the other qualities ... It is essential to employ, trust, and reward those whose perspective, ability, and judgment are radically different from yours. It is also rare, for it requires uncommon humility, tolerance, and wisdom ... Substance is enduring, form is ephemeral ... Preserve substance, modify form; know the difference.*

The question, however, is not merely to describe these essentials, but to help *you* realize them in practice. To do so, this chapter will walk you through our suggested approach to creating coherence. When we lead companies through these exercises, it takes about a week. As a reader, you have the luxury of shortening or extending the timeframe as you wish. But remember that if you leave out any one of the steps, trouble will be around the next bend.

When we work with senior management teams, we begin by putting coherence on their strategic agenda. If you have come this far in the book – without skipping ahead – not only will coherence already be on your agenda, but you will be familiar with the arguments we use to get it on the agendas of others. If, by chance, you have skipped ahead to be reading this, we suggest you turn back to Chapter 1. This framing exercise is important. Scientific research has shown that conscious perception will not happen without attention, and attention requires choice – we want managers to be able to distinguish between coherence and incoherence from their own perspectives.

Challenged to sort the coherent, incoherent, and decoherent pieces of their world, experienced managers often come up with a wide multitude of stories, from the amusing to the depressing. The frequent flier who was accused of stealing when he asked for accommodation as recompense for a canceled flight is one type of depressing story. The female executive who was fired for going to be with her child in an emergency room is certainly another. These are offset by the story of the European alliance partner who enthusiastically thanked his American counterpart in English while cursing him in German, only to discover, much to his chagrin, that his colleague was the token bilingual American in the group. And by the executives who hear our Herb Kelleher stories and ask how large Herb's dining room is at home: "After all, how can they be family if they don't eat together?" Perhaps most common is the American management mantra: "long-term thinking, and quarterly results."

From our experience, the stories of coherence are few and far between. That is why we wrote this book. But then again, perhaps that is why we get to speak with senior executives. The coherent ones are with their families, not spending time with us.

Step 1: Identify yourself and your goals

The next common sense is about creating a coherent viewpoint for coherent actions. If you know who you are and if your organization knows what it is – truly knows – then coherence will guide you through the maze of complexity. Knowing yourself (or your organization knowing itself) requires having a firm sense of identity and purpose, as well as the ability to recognize which aspects of a situation or context are aligned with that sense of self.

In effect, what coherence does is allow you to shape an aligned context all your own out of the swirling ambiguities about you. In an aligned context, coherent actions are those that require the least energy and that have the greatest rewards. To create such a context, you must help the necessary others, i.e. everyone you interact with, with the process of finding meaning. Another label for this process is "making sense."

If coherence is so important, why are well-cohered business stories so hard to find? Coherent action is hard to achieve, because a coherent viewpoint is hard to arrive at. Promoting and maintaining coherence requires effort. Too often, as management puts its day-to-day energies into improving what is measurable and easier to do, little attention is paid to the ingredients necessary for creating coherence. Further, many companies are able to function with seemingly incoherent or, worse, decoherent viewpoints. Even in a decoherent environment, most employees will show up for work, know they are supposed to be helpful, and deliver decent products or services. Coherent actions add to higher levels of performance and can make the company a more long-lasting concern, but they are not necessary for day-to-day activity.

Alignment

Collins and Porras in *Built to Last* refer to one ingredient of coherence, alignment. They say:

> *Alignment is elusive. It is hard to discern without a holistic and total view of a company. Strong alignment requires three things:*
>
> ❖ *Clarity about what the key goals of the organization are.*
> ❖ *Commitment to initiatives that promote the key goals.*
> ❖ *Accountability for actions that affect the key goals.*
>
> *Companies can function with relatively poor alignment, but they cannot be consistently creative unless they are strongly aligned. Alignment is often overlooked – it is intangible and elusive, and as far as corporate creativity is concerned, its effects are readily visible only when a company is either extraordinarily well aligned or misaligned.*

What Jim and Jerry call alignment we call the first step in the action plan: identify yourself and your goals. Ask yourself a few questions. **Why** are you doing what you are doing? Identifying your **purpose** – as an individual or team or company – your reason for being or doing, is an important step in knowing where you are on the landscape. "**Who** am I?" is the next question, to be followed immediately by, "Who are we?". In the evolving, moving intersection of the inner and outer forces that make each of us who we are we find an **identity** – the words or symbols we use to answer the previous two questions.

Both purpose and identity are rooted in ethical and esthetic values ("right versus wrong, good versus bad, and beautiful versus ugly") and filtered through a set of guiding principles ("reward cooperation"). These filters are not grand missions nor high ideals nor instructions, but simple checks and balances that what is expressed as purpose or identity matches the values from which it is drawn.

The key point is that **when purpose and identity are aligned with basic values, they evoke the possibility of a coherent viewpoint**. Such a viewpoint, in turn, is what enables actions to be coherent. Those actions, in their turn, promote the further development of the coherent point of view. The goal is to get on to this self-reinforcing, virtuous circle. But you cannot do so without having a good understanding of who you are and what you want.

Teams and groups

Remember, too, that these questions are not just about you as an individual, but also about the teams or groups of which you are a part. Given that groups and members have different beliefs, values, and histories, developing a set of shared meanings usually requires a resolution of the tension between wishing to follow one's beliefs on the one hand and building consensus by including other points of view on the other. Thus, you must talk with other people to develop a coherent view of who you – collectively – are and what you – collectively – want. A coherent viewpoint on these issues is more likely to emerge when:

❖ Participants in the dialogue have had adequate opportunity to explain their own points of view and to influence the discussion of plausible interpretations of what is being said.

❖ Those participants understand the logic behind the selection of the shared interpretation and how it can further the group's previously articulated goals.

❖ Participants recognize that the shared interpretation (the now articulated coherent viewpoint regarding identity and purpose) can be revised or even replaced when warranted by new events or a perceived need for more dialogue.

❖ The dialogue itself is conducted in a non-threatening and non-intimidating way. Yes, the boss can frighten everyone into a temporarily coherent viewpoint – but it will survive only for so long as he or she stays in the room. If having "safe" dialogue is difficult for your group, involve a facilitator. Having a safe context for dialogue on issues of identity and purpose is the only way to cut the Gordian knot of incoherence.

Using landscape images

In earlier chapters we discussed the importance of landscape images and words. Take advantage of our natural propensity to think in landscape terms. Landscape images align with today's world – just look at the ascendancy of the landscape motif in numerous book titles, articles, conferences, and media events. Landscapes provide context. They work much more easily than jargon.

Ask yourself and your organization landscape image questions: Does your landscape hold together? Does it have a sense of integrity and coherence? Fragmented, disconnected landscapes are difficult places to traverse and to use as a base. Examine your landscape for integrity. Poke around to discover what is missing about missing pieces. Treat every hill as a potential volcano.

Remember that viewing landscapes is an act of framing. Like the artist of old or the photographer of today, the business manager must choose which items, situations, or events will be captured within the frame. Integrity is also a function of the frame.

What rules are you using for framing? Do they fit the landscape

or do they feel forced? Is there a natural coherence to the values you
are applying or do you have to force fit the jigsaw puzzle piece? Do
your rules encourage examination of the landscape and of adjacent
landscapes, or have you retreated to a village and exiled the world?

Articulating your goals

Consulting clients of ours have stumbled mightily over this. It is hard
to know what to consult them on when they can't identify a goal for
themselves.

Imagine our shock at being summoned to a meeting where the
manager said: "We don't know our task. We were sent to meet with
you, but our bosses are meeting next week to figure out what we want
to do." Our clients had been given a title – the global strategy group
– and a vague task – increase the bottom line – with no resources, no
authority, and no parameters concerning what was and was not within
their purview. We suggested that the bosses meet with us after their
meeting and offered not to charge for the waste of time. Would it surprise you to learn that both offers were declined? It took four months
to get an answer to the question: "What is the goal?"

When we run an executive education course on mastering complexity, we ask our participants the following:

1 Consider a major challenge your organization is facing that con-
   cerns you. Articulate this challenge in your own words (please
   write what you think, not what your corporate literature provides).
2 What is your individual goal in connection with the challenge you
   described in Question 1?
3 What part of your personal goal (from Question 2) is your individual responsibility?
4 What part is the responsibility of colleagues at work?
5 What elements are already in place to enable you to meet your
   personal goal?
6 What elements are missing which would otherwise enable you to
   meet your personal goal?

You may want to ask the same of yourself.

Having identified self and goals, you are almost ready for Step Two. In order to make this as simple as possible, pick one area where you will try to create coherence. The exercise can be repeated, but start with one topic, or one problem that you perceive as particularly urgent. There is no need to complicate a complex process. Work on one weaving at a time.

Step 2: Use the right language

Throughout the book we have illustrated "good" words and "bad" words, "good" phrases and "bad." The task for you is to identify those categories of language for yourself and the problem area you are addressing. Remember that no word in and of itself is either good or bad. The question is one of usage, and more particularly usage with respect to the context created by the problem area.

An example from Terry Winograd, a leader in artificial intelligence research, may best illustrate this point. Winograd draws our attention to a pair of sentences. They differ in only one word. The sentences are:

❖ The committee denied the group a parade permit because they advocated violence.
❖ The committee denied the group a parade permit because they feared violence.

The difference is just in the verb: "advocated" or "feared." As Winograd points out, the pronoun "they" in each sentence is ambiguous. It is possible to imagine a world in which government committees in charge of parade permits advocate violence in the streets and, for some strange reason, use this as their pretext for denying a parade permit. But the natural, reasonable, intelligent reading of the first sentence is that it's the group that advocated violence, and of the second that it's the committee that feared violence.

Mere rules of grammar or vocabulary will not fix the right reading. What does determine the right reading for us is knowledge about the world, about politics, social circumstances, committees and their attitudes, groups that want to parade, how they tend to behave, and the like. One must know about the world, about the context of the problem area, to make sense of the words being used.

In this step of the process, you need to make lists of words and phrases. Good words are those that seem to add to coherence. Bad words are those that diminish it. Having listed the words, you must practice using them. It is only in their use (or lack of use in the case of the bad words) that they acquire value.

Consider the questions we ask of our executive education participants:

1   What words would you use to describe your corporate challenge to yourself and/or your spouse and/or your mother?
2   What words do you use to describe the challenge to your boss?
3   What words do you use to describe the challenge to your most important client?
4   What words differ in your answers to questions 1, 2, and 3?
5   What words are similar in your answers to questions 1, 2, and 3?
6   Using the words you wrote in your response to the last question describe your own role in attaining your personal goal as you identified it earlier.
7   What words do you use with your work team members to discuss the corporate challenges and/or your individual goals?
8   What words would you not use with each other?
9   So, who would you use these words with?
10 What makes those words work in describing the challenge to others and not among yourselves?

In one instance, a group of SBU managers had been assigned the task of suggesting new ways to make the corporation "indispensable" to its customers. The word indispensable was used by corporate top management to describe the relationship they thought appropriate with customers. When the SBU team began their assignment, they undertook our coherence program. Within hours, a new realization had dawned: the very heart of their assignment – the word indispensable –

was also the source of the problem. The word implied a superiority and manipulativeness to the relationship that was the exact opposite of what potential customers may desire. Worse still, top corporate management had both coined the "indispensable" goal and dictated a new atmosphere of "deep trust" that was supposed to pervade the corporate culture.

In this dictated environment of trust, the old common sense prevailed. The SBU managers were scared of bring up the notion that the word indispensable was best dispensed with. In the complicated climate they operated in, there was a perception that the word was indispensable rather than the SBU team. It would take months of work to guide management through the complex interactions necessary to arrive at "beyond substitution." While less baggage may be found with the latter phrase, at least in the customer's eyes, it conjured up heavy baggage indeed for our exhausted and scared SBU team.

Finding the right words

We have offered several guidelines in this book for finding and using the right words and phrases:

- ❖ Use words or phrases that align with people's basic values. Words can fuel coherence, if they are so aligned.
- ❖ When you find language that resonates, remember it. It can be used as aligning language.
- ❖ Aligned words have an attraction force. Like a magnet, they can make you alter the way you think and act.
- ❖ If you understand the current situation, including the emotions involved, picking aligned words is easy. What seems to be "common sense" is a good benchmark.

We have also noted that most stories involve landscapes and that all landscapes have meaning. The word "meaning" has yet another spatial dimension that ties it to the use of landscape images. From *medianus* – one of meaning's Latin roots – derives the word "medial," which not only means the middle but also a medium: "Any intervening substance through which a force acts on objects at a distance or through which impressions are conveyed to the senses." In this era of the Internet, cellular phones, email, video conferencing, and the sky pager, mediums of all types affect our perceptions of both the language and the landscapes we encounter.

Seek to frame landscapes of space, time and meaning. Then talk around these images. Make use of mediums and try to see them. Travel on landscapes and transformation of landscapes both require mediums, tools, or vehicles. Speaking of members of one's network in this way conveys a sense of how important each member is and of what actions each member can take. It is important to realize that we often see through mediums (indeed, that is why they are mediums) but that they play vital roles on the landscape.

Senior management of our SBU friends pictured a hill with only one road and where they controlled the bulldozers. This made them "indispensable" and able to extract tolls from those seeking to traverse the road. It also made them blind to the idea of tunnel-digging equipment, blasting machinery and telecommunications. The SBU team knew that the answer to indispensability lay in making the journey as attractive as possible so that the customer would seek no substitute. This was a very different attitude from that of the toll keepers at the top of the mountain. The higher they raised the tolls, the more attractive both tunnel digging and teleconferencing seemed. The landscape imagery played a crucial role in convincing senior management of the arrogance implicit in its point of view.

How do your employees see the landscape? How do they see where they and you fit in? Do you talk about it? Do they?

Step 3: Create the right context

The next step is to create a context in which people can thrive. In our executive education programs we ask:

1 What elements are already in place to enable you to fulfill your corporate challenge?
2 What elements are missing that would otherwise enable you to fulfill that challenge?

3 Review the list you prepared of "how" to "fix" the missing elements. What words will you use to communicate these steps to colleagues?
4 What are some simple rules of thumb or other heuristics, which you believe will underlie the accomplishment of the corporate challenge?
5 What parts of your individual goals will these guidelines help you address?
6 How can you use these guidelines in communicating about your work on the challenge?

Context ultimately depends on perception. Philosophers of education (recently Donald Oliver and Edmund Wilson, more notably at the turn of the twentieth century John Dewey and Alfred North Whitehead) have, at times, made much of the notion that coherence is an ability to deal with "wholeness." When dealing with wholes as wholes, these educators say, analysis is not what matters. Appreciation of, empathy for, and acceptance of context dependence are what matters instead. John Dewey made the classic comments on the words "context" and " situation" – comments which highlight that situations are conceptual first and foremost, not descriptions, objects, or data:

> *What is designated by the word situation is not a single object or event or set of objects and events. For we never experience nor form judgments about objects and events in isolation, but only in connection with a contextual whole ... An experience is always what it is because of a transaction taking place between an individual and what, at the time, constitutes his environment, whether the latter consists of persons with whom he is talking about some topic or event, the subject talked about being also a part of the situation; or the toys with which he is playing; the book he is reading (in which his environing conditions at the time may be England or ancient Greece or an imaginary region); or the materials of an experiment he is performing. The environment, in other words, is whatever conditions interact with personal needs, desires, purposes, and capacities to create the experience which is had. Even when a person builds a*

castle in the air he is interacting with the objects which he constructs in his fancy.

Guiding principles

In this way, our contexts are created. In so creating them, guiding principles are key. Remember, these are the filters to your identification of purpose and values that allow you to identify and create a coherent point of view:

* Always ground your guiding principles in values.
* Ensure that these guiding principles are aligned with the purpose, identity, and values of individuals and those of the organization as a whole. Don't just cite guiding principles or hang them in a nice wooden frame. The guiding principles must encourage people to act in a certain way as a means to the end of achieving what is important to them. As people find that the new behavior is valuable in its own right, and aligned with their values, these principles will be internalized in day-to-day actions.
* Seek to find guiding principles that are allowed to interact, like these two: "management sets the goal, workers fulfill it," and "reward teamwork." Underspecified guiding principles, like "work hard," are useless. Overspecification, like "if... then...," make guiding principles equally useless.

Jack Welch makes extensive use of the concept of guiding principles in articulating his view of the "boundaryless" corporation he wants the General Electric of the twenty-first century to become. Welch described his notion of "boundarylessness" in a letter to shareholders:

> *We cleared out stifling bureaucracy, along with the strategic planning apparatus, corporate staff empires, rituals, endless studies and briefings, and all the classic machinery that makes big-company operations smooth and predictable – but often glacially slow. As the underbrush of bureaucracy was cleared away, we began to see and talk to each other more clearly and more directly ... Freed from bureaucratic tentacles, and*

*charged to act independently [the businesses have done] so, with
great success. Corporate management got off their backs, and
instead lined up behind them with resources and support.*

In a hallmark speech to several hundred GE managers in 1994, Welch
explained the concept of boundarylessness using a simple analogy:

*In this company, if you can picture the house, the house got
taller and taller and taller. As we grew in size, we added floors.
The house got wider and wider and wider. As we got more complex, we built walls functionally. The objective of all of us in
this place is to blow up the internal walls – the floors vertically
and the horizontal ones. That's the game we're at, that's what
we are fundamentally after.*

He went on, changing metaphors, to explain that:

*[the] layers are insulators. They're like sweaters. When you go
outside and you wear four sweaters, you don't know that it's
cold out. You haven't faced reality. You're not getting the
straight scoop on the temperature. You're all covered up. As you
peel each sweater off, you learn more about the temperature.
That's the same thing about layers.*

Welch's boundarylessness is a context that is totally dependent on values and guiding principles. If his people do not share the same set of
values and guiding principles, then quite literally they will be "off the
reservation." There is little to distinguish the absence of boundaries
within the new GE from the lack of boundaries between that GE and
the outside world. Indeed, the notion of boundaries now needs to be
internal to the mental model of the GE employee. At the core of a
boundaryless company, Welch claims, are people who act without
regard for status or functional loyalty and who look for ideas from
anywhere – including from inside the company, from customers, or
from suppliers.

Creating canyons

When we hear this we think that boundaryless is not the right concept. Welch still wants his employees to have a sense of what is GE and what is not, of what is the GE way and of what is not. Instead of no boundaries, what we think Jack really means is that he wants to alter the GE culture from one of having many little canals (not really Amsterdam, more like an agglomeration of 200 Bruges) to one Grand Canyon (or perhaps a few). The context Jack wants to create is the free roaming one of a canyon, not the unfenced, undifferentiated one of the Anatolian steppes.

Think of the values you express and enact as forming a canyon in which ideas and action, just like a river, are free to seek out the most appropriate route. Remember that your canyon needs to be wide and deep, as do your values. Narrow allows too little freedom of movement. Shallow is too easily overrun. So don't fall into the trap of overspecifying actions or values.

Making sense

Welch's boundaryless canyon depends on the mental models of the GE employees. In creating contexts, it is critical to realize that you can only influence mental models, you cannot create them (something we are not always sure that Welch understands).

Remember that you can only force interpretations on others – causing temporarily cohered, but never coherent, actions – at a cost. **To have truly coherent actions, you must allow people to make sense for themselves.** An organizational context for coherent actions is recognized by the respect it allows for the necessary others and for their own individual points of view. In the absence of time, don't fall in the trap of assuming that coercion has successfully revamped people's mental models. It hasn't, and it won't. The need for context and stage setting will merely lie dormant, waiting for the next crisis to strike.

It is these interpretations (or sense making) that make people act. How much information we need for making sense is up to us. We have the power to decide if it is too little or too much. Beware the overgeneralizations that result from choosing to take in too little information. Beware the escape from reality that can result from taking in too much.

Seek to change mental models and priorities as the situations you encounter change. In our modeling, the abstractions we bring out must be open enough to allow for the context. In our priority setting, that openness requires a flexibility to allow for the next idea and for the interesting stuff out on the periphery. Mistakes are essential to developing new mental models and to coherent action. Learn from the daily slogan of the IDEO Design Lab: "Fail often to succeed sooner." The question is how to get enough practice at making mistakes and learning from them without having an adverse effect on the organization of which you are a part.

Help people develop new mental models by creating experiences that broaden their ability to apply their common sense to new circumstances. By putting people into one situation and then another and talking about their behavior and the reaction of the others involved, they can learn. Through stories, people learn to create new mental models and, more importantly, to help others create them too.

New mental models and new ideas are the ultimate acts of imagination, attention, and perception. The context you create will be better if it encourages the evocation of new ideas. Command and control can't encourage such evoking. And in their failure, some management gurus are quite stumped.

> "Microsoft's only factory asset is the human imagination," observed the *New York Times Magazine* writer Fred Moody ... After exposing an audience to the Microsoft quote, I ask a telling question: "Does anyone here know what it means to 'manage' the human imagination?" So far, not a single hand has gone up, including mine. I don't know what it means to manage the human imagination either but I do know that imagination is the main source of value in the economy. And I know we better figure out the answer to my question – quick. (Tom Peters)

One of the potential answers to how to manage and evoke imagination lies in our discussion of parts and wholes in Chapter 5:

❖ Treat ideas as if they were LEGO building blocks. Recognizing parts that can be used as building blocks is the first step to creating a context for new actions. Combining the parts is the second step. Stories are a tool for helping yourself and others to recognize what is a part, what is a whole, what is salient, what is not, and what kinds of combinations make sense.

❖ Always ensure there is potential for recombinations. LEGO and its competitors have appeal precisely because they encourage combinations and recombinations in a limitless fashion. They cohere around the idea of "see parts – combine – make wholes – bust into parts – recombine – make new wholes." Herbert Simon, Nobel laureate, wrote about the power of decomposition. To make new things first we have to recognize that existing ones are made up of separable parts. Then we recombine. In computer science this is known as object-oriented programming. In the home it is known as gourmet cooking.

❖ Recognize functionality as an important component and separate it as a new building block. This is a key to innovation and to ongoing corporate success. Swatch recognized style as a functionality and markets hundreds of different watches each year Much like fashion designers recognize the value in separating their names and their designs, it is critical to learn to see how something is used as separate and distinct from the thing being used.

❖ Ensure that combinations and recombinations are aligned with the two components of coherence, purpose and identity. If not, it is inevitable that you will lose your best people – to the coherent place next door, around the block, or a URL away.

In this last guideline we stress the importance of viewing all five steps as a package. Creating the right context is critical and if you don't, someone else will.

Step 4: Turn people loose and then get out of the way

Once identity has been asserted, the right context put in place, and the right language prepared for use, it is time to get out of the way. Let's take a hint from Dee Hock (from his *Fast Company* interview):

> Here is the very heart and soul of the matter. Invest 40% of your time managing yourself – your ethics, character, principles, purpose, motivation, and conduct. Invest at least 30% managing those with authority over you, and 15% managing your peers. Use the remainder to induce those you "work for" to understand and practice the theory. I use the terms "work for" advisedly, for if you don't understand that you should be working for your mislabeled "subordinates," you haven't understood anything. Lead yourself, lead your superiors, lead your peers and free your people to do the same.

What you need to avoid is an ancient Roman error repeated *ad infinitum* throughout the corporate landscape. Consider General Petronius's description of the reaction to rapid change in the Roman Empire:

> *We trained hard to meet our challenges but it seemed as if every time we were beginning to form into teams we would be reorganized. I was to learn later in life that we tend to meet any new situation by reorganizing; and a wonderful method it can be for creating the illusion of progress while producing confusion, ineffectiveness and demoralization.*

When we meet with executives and have reached this stage, the following types of questions are usually appropriate. You may wish to ask them of yourself:

1   Have you reorganized your company, work unit, or team in order to address your corporate challenge? If yes, how? How many times?

2   If more than once, why?

3   If more than once, what went wrong with the last one?

4   How have you formalized the last reorganization?

5   Why have you formalized them?

6   What informal arrangements exist for meeting the challenge?

7   How many times have they been rearranged?

8   Why have these informal arrangements been rearranged?

9   In the present formal arrangement, what is the relevant unit's defined mission?

10   What is the formal arrangement's access to new resources?

11   In the present informal arrangement, is there access to new resources?

12   Does the financial office know of the existence of the informal arrangement?

13   Does the CEO?

14   Does the informal arrangement have the authority to meet the challenge?

15   If not, why not?

The very stuffiness of these questions belies their purpose. It is not enough to think of an organization as it may get drawn on paper. This formal view of the environment is rooted in the concept of entities. There is the research department and there is sales. John reports to Harry and is not supposed to meet with Sue.

The interactive view of an organization is very different. When you examine the relationships that actually get things done, there is much less focus on entities and much more on the very processes that work. Too seldom do corporate organizations reflect their actual working arrangements when attempting to organize or reorganize to meet a challenge. Instead, they opt for the bureaucratic forms of the old complicated world. The questions above are supposed to get our participants thinking about the contrast between that world and the very challenge they face.

Prepare the landscape

The goal is to avoid obstacles and to create what is in effect a free-flowing river. If the setting has been properly prepared, i.e. the appropriate canyon created, then the river can run free and its full energies be exploited. This is as true for your company and the people you work with as it is for a river. And the same cautions apply. If the river bed is too shallow, the river may wander away. If the river hits too many obstacles, a local area may flood. If the river is overly regulated (on rivers this means dams, locks, and canals – with people it means organization charts, budgets, job descriptions, and other formal arrangements) it will lose much of its energy in fighting that regulation.

Balance exploitation with exploration. Your canyon demands to be exploited and the outside world (beyond the canyon walls) explored, but resources are limited. In the canyon exploit all surprise, outside it explore the truly surprising and the unexpected tangents. Ignore the vast middle.

Reward active participation in the process of idea exploration at both individual and team levels. Minimize the extent to which value judgement tagging is associated with individuals rather than teams or larger work units.

Post only a few signs in your landscape. Tags and labels are more than just "giving credit." They have consequences and create tensions as they get applied.

Exploit competitors' road signs. Take advantage of times when they have posted too many signs. When the number of visible signs is large, blockages to recognizing and using building blocks abound. Their mistake can be your competitive edge.

Visualize your multiple roles. You are not a many-headed Hydra, but there is a different version of you needed for various situations. They are all you, but acknowledge and respect their differences. Whenever possible you want to be multifaceted. After you have visualized this about yourself, try to remember that it applies to everyone else as well.

Be flexible in what is foreground and what is background. The great picture may be the sunset, but your spouse wants to be included. The camera of life is flexible enough to accommodate both within a short timeframe. If you like, think of it as flickering a diamond's many facets so as to catch the light best.

In finding the balance between foreground and aft, between the individual and the group, between the sense of boundary of the canyon and the boundarylessness of Jack Welch lies the potential for the led to be leading. In the complex world of interactions, the leader's role is that of message and influence, not command or control.

Step 5: Use communication that works

When you have made it through the first four steps, the final one is either the most easy or the most difficult. Remember that the leader's role is messages and influence. Another word for this is communication. **Coherent communication is communication that works – it is communication about meaning.**

Meaning is not something that we possess; it is something we make. It is what we are – makers of meaning. Every time we tell our story, we help others make sense of who they are, and then they know how to behave, in contexts with which they are familiar. All the members of the team become behavioral role models in the myriad of contexts in which members of organizations find themselves. The central "message" – the behavior – spreads like a contagious disease.

Tell stories
The guidelines for coherent communication revolve around stories. Words alone have no meaning. Words in usage do. Stories are verbal contexts, the next best thing to actual usage. Leaders tell stories and, more importantly, leaders listen to the stories of others:

❖ Only relate stories that you can tell from your heart. These are the ones you can tell most easily and the ones that will evoke canyons.
❖ Tell stories that reinforce the basic values shared in your organization. These are the ones that lead to coherent action.
❖ Make use of stories that challenge the listener's imagination.

❖ Be open to discussing the stories and their implications.

❖ Always ask your listeners about the images your stories bring to mind for them.

❖ Always be prepared for surprises.

Remember, too, the parting words of Hatim Tyabji, onetime CEO of VeriFone: "The essence of leadership is authenticity." We have had occasional trouble with his products, but not with his sage advice. If your role is to be a guiding force, the guiding must come from an authentic self, a coherent self.

Applying coherence in an e-world

We have not dwelt on the internet and the electronically enabled interconnected world since the introduction more than 200 pages ago. Back then we stressed that what mattered was how to manage, not how to e-manage. Here we are at the final chapter and you, as an e-manager, have a right to ask, "Now what?" If we were merchants of hype we'd tell you to go to our web site, fill out a customer profile, and follow the constantly updated and individualized data with which we would then supply you. But, we aren't merchants (or consultants, or even media folk) and you have paid good money for this book. So we end with some practical advice aimed at helping you apply the next common sense when you get back to work on Monday morning.

Management is hard work. It involves strategy and drudgery, fame and fear of exposure. As many an HR chieftain has said, much of it is less than glamorous. Managers have to deal with people, and people are much more difficult to understand and deal with than machines (though many management theories attempt to model people simply as machines). Managers will fail as well as succeed. Before the interdependent, cell-phoned, interneted, networked world, change happened more slowly. A manager not only had a simpler system to deal with, but also generally had more time to make decisions, and also more time to realize whether the decision was correct or not, and then still more time to put things right if they were wrong. In a simpler world, the gap between what theory prescribed and what managers experienced was less apparent, and far less important.

The ability to connect to the rest of the world allows an organization to influence and to be influenced by a greater network of organizations, societies, etc. Connectivity has grown exponentially. This combination of reduced time and increased complexity means that the gap between management theory and experience has grown and become more apparent than ever before.

Identifying a gap is one thing. Acting on it is something else, And it is this that interests you. So what can you do?

You need to know which are the old, the new, and the virtual parts of your firm and its business landscape. Begin by asking: What is your task? Why are you in that particular team? Who are your customers? Your suppliers? Your competitors? Your neighbors?

Do any of your answers to the above depend on the internet? If you are in the internet application business you will say yes. And if you are in the road paving business you might say no. But in both cases we would suggest you reconsider. The reality is that parts of your business are in the old economy, parts in the new, and parts in that virtual space the media calls the "e." This is true for AOL, now with a media company, a production studio, a fiber network, a cable network, a telephone business, and more than 20 million internet chatters. It is true for Delta Airlines, now a transport company, a repair shop, a travel agent, and a large investor in Priceline.com. It is true for Columbia University, which has a 200-year history, an overcrowded urban campus, and an e-learning division called Fathom.com.

Task 1: Map the varying parts of your organization to these environments, each of which calls for its own rules.
In other words, separate the components of your organizational environment. This does not mean identify each SBU. It does mean determine which areas fall into old industrial labels, which fall into new economy interconnected labels, and which are purely virtual. For example, when Boo.com was still an internet darling it was heralded for its ability to wow the Gen-X consumer with 3D graphics, deliver

its catalog in multiple languages, and have shipping and delivery nearly worldwide. At least that was the hype. When Boo.com went bankrupt, the vaunted 3D graphics became "its dependence on high-speed broadband," the delivery system was revealed to have been outsourced, and only the multilanguage catalog was deemed to have asset value. At a stroke, $135 million was transformed into $350,000. Now the delivery system was old economy, the catalog new economy and the 3D graphics purely virtual. Perhaps if the managers of Boo had recognized that the rules differed across these sectors, they would not have treated all three as a "marketing venture."

To act consistently (one size fits all, one rule fits everyone) across the organization would *not* be coherent; indeed, it would be the very opposite. Acting coherently is acting with respect for—not in disregard of—the environment in which one is acting. The rules are different for each part of the enterprise. The environments are different. Each part makes its own contribution to the whole. There is a common identity, and perhaps a common overarching purpose, but within that identity and purpose lie vastly different challenges and vastly different resources.

It is likely that in your organization you will find a similar pattern. The old economy is not dead, it just is not glamorous or intellectually challenging. **Parts of your company will find coherence in the old common sense and that is OK.** For those parts, the very rules that we have tinged with irony and sarcasm need to be looked at as the enablers of efficiency, economy, and profits. In general, relationships with the rest of the firm will take the form of information requirements regarding these old economy areas and not be involved with the actual tasks those areas accomplish. **For other parts of the firm, where the relationships are what matters most, different guiding principles apply.** In the new economy parts of the firm, relationships are what matter. People count more than things. Still other parts of the firm will be purely virtual. Marketing, image, graphics come to mind. In each of these parts, the language used will be different, the notion of what is important will be different, and the required management techniques will be very different. The key is to recognize not only that the parts have different rules, but that the main source of internal company tension is likely to be their intersections.

By identifying the intersection points between old and new economy components of your firm and of its economic environment, you can identify the places for management leverage. Try to identify the goals you have for each component and the rules that make sense for that component to achieve the identified goals. Then (and this is the critical part), clearly identify what teams and who on them has responsibility for managing the intersections. Make sure that everyone within the organization knows that these people are bridges across two worlds and that they have been assigned to manage the differences.

Perkins-Elmer Applied Bio-Systems, manufacturers of customized equipment for genome decoding and PCR replicating, has specifically identified people whose formal task is to shield the creative scientists from the accountants. In *The Innovator's Dilemma*, Clay Christiansen cites numerous examples of clashes between old and new worlds—clashes that could be avoided if the concept of human bridges were employed. Leverage comes from managing the bridges and they need to be managed in a special way. It is here that our adage "turn people loose" is most important.

What this public identification does is allow the old economy components to function more or less on their own (and in accord with old rules) and yet it keeps the interfaces between these components subject to the new rules. The interfaces (those people charged with duties regarding the intersections) will have their own identities as bridges. To act coherently as bridges they will give the old economy units just enough room for self-sufficiency while tying the informational requirements of those units back to everyone else. Only the human bridges will know enough about what is happening within the black box of the old economy unit and about the needs of those to whom it relates to master the interrelations between the two. If you, the manager, attempt to micro-manage here, only disaster can result. You will either not have enough information and perspective to make informed decisions, or you will be so overwhelmed by the data you need to gather that you lose your grip on the rest of the firm.

Interfaces are, of course, an important concept in the e-world. Innumerable hours of debate have gone into construction of the user interfaces between us and the guts of the software we make use of every day. When an interface works, the user does not feel a need to penetrate into how a task is performed. The same test can be applied to the human interfaces between the old, new, and virtual parts of your firm. If you manage the bridges so that they work, you will not feel a need to ask how tasks get accomplished. By contrast, if you do feel that need the bridges are failing you.

Task 2: creating a context in which a common coherence can be enabled across the firm as a whole
While the first task is to identify, distinguish, and mentally separate the various components of the organization by their respective contexts and rules, the second task is to provide a context for bringing them together into a common coherent force. This context will include a set of constraints that reinforce the notion of boundary: this is part of the firm and that is not. Coherence depends on a sense of shared identity and it is all too easy in the e-world to forget both where one is and who one is.

Such a context will take many forms: the physical environment, the language used within and outside the firm, and the perceived space that employees, customers, and vendors feel they occupy with respect to the firm. Good contexts are hard to create and nuture. If they were easy, we would not have a paucity of master architects and city planners the world over. Instead, we have a healthy supply of master gardeners. Plants cannot easily express their individual wants, desires, needs, and frustrations—people can and do. This difference gives the lie to much of the hyperbole in the e-world about organic and biological metaphors. The business environment can indeed be viewed as if it were a landscape, but it *never* should be treated like one. The landscape metaphor that we talked about in Chapter 4 is a tool for mental thought, not a prescription for how to treat people.

Creating a context for coherence across the firm requires that the individuals who make up the firm's business environment be respected as both individuals and as members of that environment. They need to be addressed using language they will recognize as appropriate. The table at the end of Chapter 11 provides examples of the kinds of variables that the appropriate rhetoric will need to encompass. When creating contexts, remember that language matters and that you as a manager are one bridge among the other bridges. Your language has the potential for significant ripple effects (especially at just the wrong times and in just the wrong ways). Nina Brink thought the word "disposed" had an obvious meaning with regard to her shares in World Online, yet when the investment community discerned that she meant "sold," the ensuing outcry cost her the chairmanship of the company and its shareholders billions of dollars. Michael Sayler discovered much the same when he acknowledged the need for MicroStrategy to reclassify income from 1997 and 1998 to 1999 and 2000. It was not as if the money had disappeared (it was merely moved on the accounting books), but more than $10 billion of shareholder value disappeared overnight.

Bill Gates is perhaps the epitome of both good and bad language use. His 1996 memo summoning Microsoft to face up to the internet and its challenges was a superb means of pulling the many disparate parts of that empire together. His continued use of violent imagery in internal emails and his obfuscatory words in court testimony helped to shape the initial outcomes of Microsoft's antitrust battle in 2000.

Context is more than just language use. It is also the boundaries of behavior that are set for the members of the firm and its business environment. Some firms tolerate bribery; others do not. Some firms participate actively in their communities; others do not. Cummins Engine was almost single-handedly responsible for the physical environment of Columbus, Indiana (a collection of award-winning architectural monuments), just as many incubators are responsible for the revival of high-tech jobs in communities across the western world. Employees of public participatory companies often are encouraged to put time into the community of which they are a part. By contrast, many of the companies in the Silicon Valley and Alley areas pride themselves on having 20-hour days for employees and untold sacrifices of family life. To hold an employee's family in utter disregard is unlikely to create a context of respect and trust, both of which are prerequisites of coherence.

Context also demands that the various pieces of the business environment be respected as worthy in their own right. Internet companies are wont to ignore this at their own peril. Consider the following tale of woe.

For years, Toys 'R' Us has struggled against giant discounters like Wal-Mart and Target. But the 1998 holiday season brought into focus an even more formidable threat: a tiny online retailer called eToys. The net startup's $30 million in sales in 1998 equaled that of maybe two—out of 1,486—Toys 'R' Us stores. But when it came to ringing up the online register at Christmas, eToys left toysrus.com in the dust. Even worse, eToys scored a market cap of $7.8 billion on its first trading day, in May 1999, dwarfing the $5.6 billion of Toys 'R' Us.

With visions of an Amazon.com-type rival emerging in his own backyard, Toys 'R' Us CEO Robert C. Nakasone went into overdrive. But rather than attempting to refine his online operation in-house, he tried to set it up as a separate unit. He formed a partnership with Silicon Valley venture capitalists Benchmark Capital, funded it with $80 million from his own coffers, and moved the budding online business from the company's New Jersey headquarters to Northern California. "Over time, we could have gotten it right," Nakasone told the *Financial Times*. "But we don't have the time." Nor had they established their own coherence. The agreement with Benchmark Capital to help expand the web site was abruptly canceled in August of 1999. Faced with this turmoil, Nakasone resigned.

Things only got worse, however. The Toys 'R' Us web site was jammed in November 1999, apparently because of overwhelming demand as the holidays approached. "We're sorry, an unexpected error has occurred...You can return to our home page to retry your request by clicking here," stated a message, which included a link back to the homepage so shoppers could conveniently continue to test their patience. "Or, if clicking the link above does not correct the situation and you are continuing to see this message, you may try to begin a new shopping session by clicking here." Visitors were also greeted with a brief posting that read: "Due to the overwhelming popularity of the BIG BOOK of savings, we have had to limit the number of guests to our web site...Please accept our sincere apologies

and try again later." Toys 'R' Us had mailed out a special catalog promoting holiday discounts, capping several days of national advertising
in print and on television to kick off the shopping season. This may
have been the cause of the spike in demand. Scores of users drawn to
the site by a marketing blitz were blocked from entering the site, a situation that continued for over a week. Company officials said that
traffic reached 10 times the site's previous peak levels, and despite
quadrupling the number of servers prior to the ad blitz, the site was
still overwhelmed.

What worked for bricks and mortar failed online. And Toys 'R'
Us is not alone. Even virtual merchants need real people in real ware-
houses to get products into customers' hands.

So how do you avoid this happening to you? By remembering
that the key to mastering complexity is to step back and gain a perspective you wouldn't get otherwise. Analysis works in the complicated case (*plic* means folds, if you remember). But, the interweavings
(*plex*) of the complex do not yield to reductionist analysis or to a con-
centration on details. One needs an overview to gain a handle on
complexity. Remember that half of the perspective is you. It is you
that looks and it is you that interprets. Thus, a large part of enabling
a coherent context begins with you.

*Task 3: evoke coherence in the stories and narratives that you and
those around you tell*
It is the stories and narratives that provide the basis for interpreting
what goes on day by day. Half of context is interpretation and half
of interpretation is prior context. This interplay of nested context
and narrative is reminiscent of the e-world itself. After all, the e-
world can be viewed as a series of nested networks. Within these
networks, every node has a respected identity and purpose, but
relies on interconnection for its being, becoming, and belonging.
Those interconnections can be static—without growth—or
enabling. Only with the latter are new possibilities and new relationships possible. Enabling interactions take the form of dialogue,
a way of encountering and understanding oneself and one's world
that opens up possibilities of grasping the fundamental meanings of

life, individually and corporately, and its various dimensions. This in turn transforms the way we deal with ourselves, others, and the world in which we live. To create and foster such dialogue, we need new protocols and conversations.

Thus the stories we tell shape the language we use. Together, the stories and the language affect the way in which we interpret the context. And the context helps to shape the way we act. This in turn affects the stories we tell—and so on. The interweaving continues. Day in and day out.

As a manager, your job is to recognize the processes that produce these interweavings and to identify leverage points along the way. You cannot control the narrative. You cannot command the stories that others tell. But you can—through the exercise of self-reflectiveness and perspective—affect the language you use, the stories you tell, the tolerance you show, and the respect you ascribe to others. By acting in a coherent manner and asking others to do likewise, you become the master teacher to the many willing students around you, the master craftsman to the willing apprentices. Mastering complexity is a process and a journey. How you tell it and how you live it will shape the stories and actions of others.

Complexity is too vast and too interwoven to be understood via analysis and falsification. Time is too short and the required experiments too many. If it is to be mastered, complexity must be accepted for what it is: the environment in which you find yourself. So be yourself in that environment. As for you, so too with your team, your organization, and even your community. It was coherence that led Alexander to slice through Gordian's knot. The alignment between his sense of self and his actions provided the context needed to build an empire. Your tasks are not so mighty, but the process is still the same.

If this book gives you no message other than this final one, let it be this: Step back and take perspective. Look into your inner sense of who you are and what you are about. Act in a manner that reinforces your sense of self—at that moment, for it is only that moment that matters. Be coherent yourself. Inspire coherence around you. Enable coherence in others.

Acting in a coherent manner is the next common sense—and the only sense for an e-manager in the e-world.

E-men.

INDEX

3M 108, 158, 165

ABB 59
abstractions 56–7, 61, 221
action plan 204—28
alignment 6, 17, 19, 22, 38, 49–50, 52–3, 99, 128–30, 186–203, 206, 208–11, 215, 218, 222; *see also* misalignment, unalignment, word choice
Allegis Corp. 114
ambiguity 8, 9, 48, 51, 58–9, 96, 145–6, 218, 213; *see also* uncertainty
America OnLine (AOL) 3–5, 25, 45, 47, 159, 192, 194–5
Andersen Worldwide 115
Apple 65, 67–70, 74–5, 116
AT&T 69, 197
attractors 50, 52, 54–5, 196–8, 201, 215

background 13, 21–2, 107–8, 119–20, 124, 132–3, 144, 193, 225–6; *see also* foreground
Barksdale, Jim 47
Bauman, Robert 43–5, 53, 147
boids 30–34, 37
Boisot, Max 123, 129, 179, 199; *see also* least action principle
Bond, Jon 100
boundaries xiii, 7, 21, 64, 66, 86, 129, 173, 218–20, 226
Branson, Richard 116–19, 136; *see also* Virgin

Bricklin, Dan 69
bridges 71–2; *see also* gaps
building blocks xiii–xiv17, 44–5, 86–92, 95–8, 101, 150, 172, 180–82, 206, 222, 225; *see also* combining and recombining
Burnett, Leo 123

canyons xiii, 17, 19, 21, 22–41, 150, 153, 155, 158–61, 163, 166–7, 169, 185, 198, 203, 220, 225–6
Case, Steve 25, 47
chaos xiv, 42
Clark, Jim 47
coherence xiii–xiv, 1–19, 22, 25, 29, 32, 38, 44, 52, 61, 77, 81–2, 97, 99, 102, 106–7, 116, 127–8, 131, 137–8, 147, 153, 186–203, 206–9, 211–15, 217, 220, 222, 226–8
coherent viewpoint 14, 16, 61, 138, 144, 146, 151, 206, 208–11, 218, 228
Collins, Jim 125, 130, 209
combining 17–18, 84–103, 121, 140, 154, 169, 178, 184, 202, 205, 222; *see also* recombining
common sense *see* next common sense, old common sense
communication 206–7, 226–7
Complex-M list 50, 53, 173, 178
complex systems 11–12, 42, 57
complexity xiii, 1–19, 29, 32–3, 39, 42, 63–4, 83, 97, 101, 103, 107, 112, 121,

complexity (*cont.*) 124, 127, 132, 140, 144, 147, 154, 165, 168, 184, 202, 205–6, 208, 213, 215, 227
complexity, mastering 5, 9–10, 212, 227
complexity science xiv, 9–14, 16, 42, 67, 196
complication 1–2, 13–14, 17–18, 25, 39, 63–4, 83, 97, 101, 103, 107, 112, 121, 124, 127, 140, 154, 168, 184, 202, 204, 206, 213, 215, 224
conflation 177, 182, 189
constraints 128–9, 174, 198
context 6, 9, 19, 21, 32, 37–8, 42, 45–6, 50, 53–4, 56–8, 60–61, 76, 81, 90–96, 99, 101, 108, 111, 124–6, 129, 132, 148, 150, 153, 155, 169, 185, 189, 193, 201, 203, 205–7, 211, 214, 216–23, 227–8
credit assignment 172–5, 179, 182–3, 205–6, 225
culture 6, 192

dams 124, 136–7, 139, 225
Dawkins, Richard 30, 193
DEC 67, 69–70
decoherence 6, 208–9; *see also* coherence, incoherence
Dennett, Daniel 153
Dentsu 94
Dervin, Brenda 71
Dewey, John 217

Edvinsson, Leif 162, 165
Einstein, Albert xiii, 201
emergence 10–11, 25, 32, 45, 53, 90, 172, 174
energy 197–200, 208
entities 3–4, 7–8, 18, 37, 39, 63, 83, 101, 103, 106, 121, 139–40, 154, 168, 184, 202, 204–5, 224, 227
Epstein, Richard 32
exploitation 158–60, 166–7, 182, 225
exploration 158, 160–63, 166–7, 182–3, 205, 225

Federal Express 6, 35, 47–9, 55–7, 67, 76

foreground xiii, 13, 21–2, 107, 118–20, 124, 132–3, 144, 193, 225–6; *see also* background
framing 66, 75, 82, 86, 179–80, 207, 211, 216
functionality 97–9, 101, 222

gaps 71–2; *see also* bridges
Gates, Bill 45, 47, 49, 56, 70, 75, 93, 159, 194, 196–7; *see also* Microsoft
GE 25, 77–9, 130, 218–20; *see also* Jack Welch
GM 3, 59, 91–3, 99, 158
goals 206, 208–14, 225
Gordian knot 2, 146, 211
Grove, Andy 75, 119
guiding principles 2, 6, 11, 13–14, 16–18, 24–39, 63, 83, 93–4, 103, 121, 140, 154, 168, 184, 202, 210, 218–19; *see also* simple rules

Hall, John 125
Hallmark 125
Hatsopoulos, George 13, 108, 120; *see also* Thermo Electron
Heisenberg, Walter xiii
Hock, Dee 15–16, 207, 223
holism 17
holons 110–11, 114, 116, 118, 120
Honda 59
Hughes, David 112

IBM 65, 67–70, 89–91, 95, 162, 176
ideational territories 178, 183
identity 5–6, 14, 38, 44, 99, 102, 206, 208, 210–11, 218, 222–3, 228
IDEO Design Lab 62, 221
IKEA xiv, 97
images 64–83, 89, 149–51, 200, 216; *see also* landscape images, metaphors
imprinting 195
incoherence 6, 9, 208–9, 211; *see also* coherence, decoherence
Intel 65, 70, 75, 114, 159–60, 196, 227
Intense Moments 126–7, 136, 193

interaction 3–4, 6, 10–11, 17–18, 25,
    27–8, 32–9, 43, 61, 63, 83, 101, 103,
    121, 138, 140, 145, 149, 154, 167–8,
    180, 183–4, 202, 205, 209, 217–18,
    224, 226–7
interface 64, 74
interpretation 47–50, 52–3, 61, 71, 96,
    144–6, 150, 211, 220; see also making
    sense
interrelationships 1, 3, 75, 127, 189,
    206, 227
interweavings 13, 97, 124, 127, 138,
    144, 189, 227

Jobs, Steve 67, 69, 74–5, 116, 119–20;
    see also Apple
Jones, Patricia 125
JR East 88–91, 94

Kahaner, Larry 125
Kaiser Permanente 43, 48
Karan, Donna 98
Kelleher, Herb 17, 28–9, 150, 192, 198,
    208; see also Southwest Airlines
Kiam, Victor 99
Kirby, Philip 112
Klein, Gary 148, 151, 165
Knight, Phil 76
Kodak 198
Koestler, Arthur 8, 110–11
Kuhn, Thomas xiii

labels 22, 150, 172, 176–8, 180, 182–3,
    225, 227; see also tagging
landscape images 103, 121, 140, 154,
    168, 184, 202, 211; see also images,
    metaphors
landscapes xiii–xiv, 17–18, 64–83, 129,
    158, 161, 163, 182, 205, 212, 215–16,
    225
Lawrence, David 43–4, 48, 52–3, 147
leadership 14, 16, 22, 52–3, 60, 79–80,
    162, 226–7
least action principle 123–4, 129, 199
LEGO 85–6, 90, 101, 149, 222

leverage 19, 94–5, 183, 185, 199–200,
    203, 206, 228
Lippman, Walter 9
Lucent Technologies 35–7

making sense 5–8, 16, 47–8, 60–61, 66,
    71, 143–6, 193, 199, 206, 209, 214,
    220, 226; see also interpretation
mastering complexity 5, 9–10, 212, 227
McDonald's 76
MCI 197–8
mediums 82, 216
memes 193
mental models xiii, 4–5, 16–18, 40–63,
    65, 67, 69–70, 73, 75–6, 83, 103, 121,
    140, 144, 150, 154, 166, 168, 184,
    188–9, 199–200, 202, 219–21
metaphors xiii–xiv, 17–18, 46, 64–5, 67,
    71, 74, 77–9, 90, 93, 96, 148, 153,
    182, 219; see also images, landscape
    images
Michalski, Jerry 171
Microsoft 45, 47, 49, 57, 65, 70, 74–5,
    116, 159–60, 192, 197; see also Bill Gates
misalignment 193–4, 209; see also
    alignment, unalignment
mission statements 36, 43, 50, 99,
    125–9, 131–2, 136–7, 143
multiple roles xiii, 17–18, 21, 104–21,
    140, 144, 154, 168, 184, 202, 225
myths 143, 190

naming 177–8, 180–1, 183
Netscape 45, 47, 56, 160, 196–7
next common sense xiii, xv, 1–2, 13, 16,
    18, 23, 25, 27, 38–9, 42, 47, 61, 63–4,
    81, 83, 86, 94, 101, 103, 107–8, 118,
    120–21, 124, 127–8, 138, 140, 153–4,
    157–8, 167–8, 172, 183–4, 189,
    201–2, 204–6, 208, 228
Nike 76, 131, 147, 157

old common sense 1, 13, 18, 38–9, 42,
    47, 63, 81, 83, 93, 101, 103, 107–8,
    121, 123, 127, 138, 140, 154–4, 157,

old common sense (*cont.*) 167–8, 172, 184, 189, 201–2, 204, 215
open book management 92–3

parts 18, 72, 86, 95, 101, 103, 107, 111, 121, 140, 154, 168, 177–8, 184, 199, 202, 221–2; *see also* wholes
patterns xiii, 10, 12, 55, 59, 65, 72–3, 86–7, 95–6, 179–80
Petzinger, Thomas xii–xv, 35–6, 196
Porras, Jerry 125, 130, 209
purpose 5–7, 14, 38, 43–4, 99, 102, 128, 177, 201, 206, 208, 210–11, 218, 222, 228

Reason, Peter 48
recombining 17–18, 84–103, 121, 133, 140, 150, 154, 168, 172, 177–82, 184, 202, 206, 222; *see also* combining
reflective practice 13
reifying 137, 180
remote sensing 161, 163
resonance 194–5, 200–1, 215
Reynolds, Craig 29–33, 37
rituals 143, 190
road signs 17, 19, 22, 170–85, 203, 225
Roos, August 85, 91, 149, 195
rules, bad 26–7
rules, simple 29, 31, 34–8, 43, 54, 57, 59–60, 82; *see also* guiding principles

sagacity 67, 133–5; *see also* serendipity
Sainsbury's 118, 136
Schon, Donald 13
Scott-Morgan, Peter 34
scouting parties 17, 19, 21, 138, 156–69, 185, 203
Seely Brown, John 179
sense making 5–8, 16, 47–8, 60–61, 66, 71, 143–6, 193, 199, 206, 209, 214, 220, 226; *see also* interpretation
serendipity 67, 88, 133–5, 167; *see also* sagacity
Sharp Corp. 131–2
Shaw, Gordon 165

Siemens Nixdorf Information Systems 164, 166
Simon, Herbert 222
simplicity 10–11, 13, 16–18, 24–39, 63, 83, 103, 112, 121, 130, 133, 140, 154, 168, 184, 201–2
simplification 41, 165
simulations 147–9
situatedness 37, 57, 59–60
Skandia 162, 166
SmithKline Beecham 43–4, 52
Sony 97
Southwest Airlines xiv, 17, 22–3, 28–9, 49, 52, 150, 192, 198
Sprint 197–8
steps, five 2, 204–28
storytelling xiv, 17, 19, 21–2, 60, 74, 79–80, 97, 101, 142–55, 157, 160, 165–7, 169, 179, 183, 185, 197, 203, 205, 208–9, 215, 221, 226
Swatch 97, 222
symbols 143, 190
synthesis 110, 112, 114, 116, 118, 174

tagging 22, 172–83, 225; *see also* labels
Thermo Electron 13, 108–9, 115, 158
Thomas, Corey 100
Tichy, Noel 77, 79–80
Tripod 72, 132, 190–92
Tyabji, Hatim 227

unalignment 193–4; *see also* alignment, misalignment
uncertainty 8–9, 48, 52, 57–8, 146; *see also* ambiguity
United Airlines 2

values 6, 8, 14, 16–17, 29, 38, 43, 50, 55, 59–60, 124, 127–8, 130–3, 135, 138–9, 143, 149–51, 153, 159, 189–90, 193, 201, 206, 210, 212, 215, 218–20, 226
Vaught, John 135, 181
Virgin 117–18
Visa 14–16, 207
vision 8, 50, 125, 127, 162

Vogel, Steven 11–12
von Moltke, Graf 59–60

Watson, Tom 89, 94, 99
Weick, Karl 78, 146
Welch, Jack 25, 93, 130–32, 218–20,
 226; *see also* GE
Whole Foods 108, 115
wholes 18, 72–3, 86, 95, 101, 103, 107,
 111–12, 121, 140, 154, 168, 177, 180,
 184, 202, 217, 221–2; *see also* parts
Winnicott, Donald 160
Winograd, Terry 213
word choice 186–203, 206, 213–16, 223,
 226; see also alignment
Wozniak, Steve 67; see also Apple

Xerox 67, 69–70, 179, 198